Advance praise for

CHILDREN OF THE BROKEN TREATY

"In reading this historic chronicle of the painful poverty among the Cree in James Bay, Ontario, Canada, I keep thinking how incredible it is that a member of parliament could care so much about his constituency and devote so much of his time to helping the beautiful people of the land of the Cree and Ojibway in sub-Arctic country."—ALANIS OBOMSAWIN, FILMMAKER

"Shannen Koostachin knew First Nations students were dropping out of her school in Attawapiskat because 'It is hard to think you will grow up someone important when you don't have resources like libraries and science labs ... we are not going to give up and we want our younger brothers and sisters to go to school thinking school is a time for hopes and dreams of the future—every kid deserves this.'

"As a child inspired by Shannen said, 'Childhood does not wait around for politicians to do the right thing,' and so thousands of children joined together to write letters to the government demanding a proper education for all First Nations students. The Prime Minister's mailbox began filling up with letters made with crayons and sparkles, and the largest child-led rights campaign in Canadian history was born.

"In this must-read book, Charlie Angus shares Shannen's inspiring journey from a child going to school in run down trailers next to a toxic waste dump to one of 45 children in the world nominated for the International Children's Peace Prize. Shannen did everything in her power to ensure First Nations children would get the proper education they deserve, and after reading this book you will, too."—CINDY BLACKSTOCK, FIRST NATIONS CHILD AND FAMILY CARING SOCIETY OF CANADA

"Charlie Angus's *The Children of the Broken Treaty* is an incredibly important book. Gripping. Disturbing. Maddening. At its core, though, this call for justice doesn't only promise hope, it shines bright light toward a real road of redemption. The legacy of Shannen Koostachin will live on for many generations. And the resilience of not just her Cree people but of all First Nations in this country is beautifully and concisely documented. Here's a strong lesson that demands to be read."—JOSEPH BOYDEN, AUTHOR OF *Three Day Road, Through Black Spruce*, AND *The Orenda*

"This book, along with Edmund Metatawabin's *Up Ghost River*, tells the story of sustained evil done by our government to indigenous peoples, who have the right to the rights of Canadian citizens. This is discomforting reading, but essential."—JOHN RALSTON SAUL, AUTHOR OF *The Comeback*

"If you think Canada provides equal treatment to all of its citizens and that our injustices to indigenous people were in the past, think again. Angus sheds light on one of the ugliest features of our nation, that we deny First Nations children the chance at a proper education, that we have written them off and that the legacy of unequal education that began with residential schools continues to the present."—JAMES DASCHUK, AUTHOR OF *Clearing the Plains*

CHILDREN OF THE

CANADA'S LOST PROMISE AND ONE GIRL'S DREAM

BROKEN TREATY

CHARLIE ANGUS

 **University of Regina Press**

Printed and bound in Canada at Friesens.

COVER AND TEXT DESIGN: Duncan Campbell, University of Regina Press
COPY EDITOR: Dallas Harrison
PROOFREADERS: Courtney Bates-Hardy, Anne James
COVER PHOTO: Shannen Koostachin at her first high school powwow when she was in grade nine. Courtesy of the author.

Library and Archives Canada Cataloguing in Publication

Angus, Charlie, 1962-, author
    Children of the broken treaty : Canada's lost promise and one girl's dream / Charlie Angus.

Includes bibliographical references.
Issued in print and electronic formats.
ISBN 978-0-88977-401-8 (paperback).—ISBN 978-0-88977-404-9 (html).—
ISBN 978-0-88977-402-5 (pdf)

1. Native children—Education—Ontario—Attawapiskat Indian Reserve No. 91A. 2. Children's rights—Ontario—Attawapiskat Indian Reserve No. 91A. 3. Native students—Ontario—Attawapiskat Indian Reserve No. 91A. 4. Native children—Government policy—Canada. 5. Koostachin, Shannen, 1994-2010. 6. Youth protest movements—Canada. 7. Attawapiskat Indian Reserve No. 91A (Ont.). I. Title.

E96.65.O58A54 2015   371.829'970713   C2015-904219-4   C2015-904220-8

10 9 8 7 6 5 4 3 2 1

University of Regina Press, University of Regina
Regina, Saskatchewan, Canada, S4S 0A2
TEL: (306) 585-4758 FAX: (306) 585-4699
WEB: www.uofrpress.ca

U OF R PRESS

We acknowledge the support of the Canada Council for the Arts for our publishing program. We acknowledge the financial support of the Government of Canada. / Nous reconnaissons l'appui financier du gouvernement du Canada. This publication was made possible through Creative Saskatchewan's Creative Industries Production Grant Program.

Canada Council for the Arts   Conseil des Arts du Canada   Canadä   creative SASKATCHEWAN

To my dear friend Grand Chief Stan Louttit,
who worked for the betterment
of the Mushkegowuk Cree
with such determination and vision.
It was an honour to work alongside you.
Go to the angels, Stan.
Shannen will be there to greet you.

Perhaps you have heard the story of how Rosa Parks helped start the civil rights movement. Well, we are the children who have been sitting at the back of the school bus our whole lives. And we don't want to stay there anymore.

—FOURTEEN-YEAR-OLD CHELSEA EDWARDS,
ATTAWAPISKAT FIRST NATION

CONTENTS

ACKNOWLEDGEMENTS .... **XI**

INTRODUCTION .... **XIII**

PART I: THE SHADOW OF ST. ANNE'S

Duncan Campbell Scott Comes to James Bay **5**
The Mission School **13**
Three Little Boys **25**
The '60s' Solution **29**
The Chrétien Letter **36**
One Little Boy **43**
The Dark Legacy **47**
James Bay Education after St. Anne's **54**

PART II: FIRE AND WATER, 2004–06

James Bay Journey **67**
The Water Crisis **71**
Fire and Flood **85**

PART III: ATTAWAPISKAT SCHOOL CAMPAIGN, 2007–09

The Third Generation **95**
Students Helping Students **101**
Containing the Damage **107**
The Spark **116**
Shannen Meets Chuck **119**
The Disappearing School **130**
The Fight Goes International **140**
Education Is a Human Right **147**
Grade Nine **151**
Six Boys, One Girl **155**
The Year of Emergencies **160**
The Darkest Part of the Night **165**
People in Tents **173**
Labour Joins the Fight **179**
Attawapiskat Wins **184**

PART IV: SHANNEN'S DREAM, 2010

Tragedy.....191

A Litter of Puppies.....196

The Dream Is Launched.....208

PART V: CANADA'S KATRINA MOMENT, 2011–12

The 2011 Housing Crisis.....219

Rise of the Trolls.....231

Christmas in Attawapiskat.....241

From Hawaii to Idle No More.....248

PART VI: THE FUTURE IS NOW, 2012–15

The United Nations.....259

The Rogue Chiefs.....269

Shannen's Team.....278

CONCLUSION.....284

NOTES.....291

SELECTED BIBLIOGRAPHY.....319

ACKNOWLEDGEMENTS

Thanks to Andrew Koostachin, Jenny Nakogee, Serena Koostachin, and their family for their faithfulness to an incredible young woman. Thanks to the Hunter family, Chelsea Edwards, Rose Koostachin, John B. Nakogee, Bill Blake, Alvin Fiddler, Leo Friday, and all those from Treaty 9 territory who have taught me lessons in life.

Thanks to Edmund Metatawabin, James Daschuk, Catherine Morten-Stoehr, Cindy Blackstock, Karihwakeron (Tim Thompson) for their careful reading of the manuscript and wise suggestions.

Thanks to the Timmins-James Bay team that have always been there for me: Gilles Bisson, my great friend; David Schecter, Sue Cardinal, Lise Beaulne, Felicia Scott, Dale Tonelli, and especially Janet Doherty for her work in helping coordinate and document the Shannen's Dream campaign. Thanks to my colleagues Jack Layton, Thomas Mulcair, Pat Martin, Jean Crowder, Romeo Saganash, and Nikki Ashton.

Thanks to Christine Guyotte, Jeremy Huws, and Emilie Grenier for assistance with Access to Information and government files. Thanks to Fay Brunning and Katherine Hensel for the legal documents.

Thanks to Bruce Walsh and the team at University of Regina Press: my editor David McLennan, and Duncan Campbell, Karen Clark, Donna Grant, Nickita Longman, Diane Perrick, and Morgan Tunzelmann. This whole thing got started because Bruce mailed me a copy of James Daschuk's *Clearing the Plains*. The book hit me like a thunderbolt and launched me on the path of this work.

Thanks most of all to Brit, my best friend in life, and our daughters—Mariah, Siobhan, Lola. They not only put up with the chaos of political life but serve as an extraordinarily creative editorial department. The family team did yeoman duty in pulling narrative out of a jumble of data. Mariah was relentless in her attempt to clean up her old man's source notes. Thank you. Love you more than you know.

INTRODUCTION

If Shannen Koostachin were alive, she would
tell you this story herself. . . . She feared nothing,
that girl. Not strangers, not defeat.
—LINDA GOYETTE[1]

Ten-year-old Hasna is telling the story in front of 600 students at Boxwood Public School in Markham, Ontario. She is nervous and fiddles with her PowerPoint presentation. A first-generation Muslim Canadian, Hasna has never done anything like this before. She isn't the type of girl who is comfortable standing out in a crowd, but the issue is important, and she wants to do it justice. So she pulls herself together and tells the story the way that it should be told. The way that Shannen would tell the story. This is how it goes.

Shannen Koostachin was a girl from the Cree First Nation who lived in a very poor community called Attawapiskat in the far north. She had never seen a real school. The children were being educated in broken-down portables on a toxic site. Some of them were getting sick and losing hope. For years, they had waited for the government to follow through on its promise to build a proper school. But nothing ever changed. And then one day a government minister told the children that they weren't getting a school at all.

The children were heartbroken but not Shannen. She said that what was happening to them was wrong. She told her classmates that education is a human right. "School is a time for hopes and dreams of the future," Shannen said. "Every kid deserves this."[2]

Shannen and her friends went to Ottawa to challenge the government. They reached out to students across Canada for help. The students formed clubs. They wrote letters to the prime minister. They held rallies. The fight for a school in Attawapiskat became the largest youth-driven rights movement in Canadian history.

Shannen had to leave home when she was thirteen in order to get the kind of education that wasn't available on her reserve. She was homesick having to leave her family and culture, but she dreamed of becoming a lawyer to help her people. Unfortunately, she died in a car accident while living far from home. But the story doesn't end there. Other students came together to carry on her work. Thus was born the Shannen's Dream campaign to fight for equal education rights for every Indigenous child in Canada.

Hasna looks up. The students are spellbound. Like her, most of them are first-generation Canadians. Their notion of Canada is a country built on fairness. This confidence in the national character of inclusion is manifest in their school, a bright and open building where the children are encouraged to become whatever they dream. Shannen would call this a "comfy" school.

But now that they have heard the story, they learn that there is another Canada—where children are being denied basic rights. These students don't know much about the treaty signed by the government and Shannen's people, but they do understand the meaning of a broken promise.

The story teaches them that there are children of the broken promise who are just like them—students with names such as Chelsea, Chris, Serena, and Shannen. And this is the transformative part: Shannen said that, if the young people stood together, they could make a difference. They could make Canada a fairer place. This is why Hasna is so excited and has worked up the nerve to bring the story to a gymnasium full of youngsters.

"We can be part of the change," she tells the students.

• • •

The story of the young Cree leader who fought for education rights in Canada has been told in a video, a novel, textbooks, and a full-length documentary film that premiered at the Toronto International Film Festival.[3] A made-for-TV movie is also in the works.

DC Comics used the story of Shannen Koostachin as an inspiration for the latest member of the Justice League.[4] In the comic, a young James Bay student draws on the traditional strengths of her people to be transformed into the hero Equinox, taking her place alongside iconic figures such as Superman, the Green Lantern, and Wonder Woman.

In 2012, on the 600th anniversary of the birth of Joan of Arc, CBC host George Stroumboulopoulos placed Shannen Koostachin at the top of a list of five teenage girls who kicked ass in history. She was named alongside Joan of Arc, Mary Shelley, Anne Frank, and Buffy the Vampire Slayer. The newly opened Canadian Museum for Human Rights in Winnipeg has featured Shannen and her campaign for education rights.

In 2012, the House of Commons unanimously passed the Shannen's Dream parliamentary motion, calling on the government of Canada to close the funding gap faced by First Nations students and to establish quality First Nations education. The motion has become a historic benchmark in the fight for Indigenous child equity in Canada.

This ongoing fascination with a girl from an impoverished reserve is even more striking because her public career was a scant two years, stretching from when Shannen challenged a minister of the crown at the age of thirteen to her death in a highway accident before her sixteenth birthday. All in all, quite an impact for a girl who just wanted what every other child in Canada takes for granted—the chance to go to school.

And this is where the story of Shannen Koostachin takes on larger political significance. The story of the inequities faced by students in Attawapiskat provides a window into a world that most Canadians never knew existed. It has opened a political and social conversation about how a country as rich and inclusive as Canada can deliberately marginalize children based on their race or, more accurately, marginalize them based on their treaty rights.

What Shannen's story shows us is that, though the conditions in Attawapiskat might have been extreme, they were by no means an anomaly. All over Canada, First Nations youth have significantly fewer resources for education, health, and community services than those available to non-Indigenous youth. Certainly, there are many reserves with proper school facilities. But other communities make do with substandard schools or condemned schools or, in some cases, no school at all. It is the arbitrary nature of the delivery of education that speaks to its inequity. What all these communities have in common is systemic underfunding for education by the Department of Indian Affairs[5] compared with communities with students in the provincial school systems.

So it is possible that a youth leader such as Shannen could have come from any of the reserves spread across Canada. But I believe that it is significant that she came from Attawapiskat in the territory of Treaty 9. The lands of Treaty 9 cover a vast region of northern Ontario. Duncan Campbell Scott secured control of this land in a treaty negotiated in 1905–06. The promise of education for children was a fundamental commitment in enticing the people of the region to sign the treaty.

With the treaty in hand, Ottawa and Ontario assumed control of some of the richest mineral, hydro, and timber resources in the world. Within a few short years, exploitation of Treaty 9 resources transformed Ontario from an economic backwater to an economic powerhouse. Meanwhile, the treaty partners were reduced to living in internal displacement camps known as reserves. The government of Canada leveraged the power of the Indian Act to assume control over every aspect of Indigenous life—economic, spiritual, and social. But the worst impacts resulted from the legislative powers used to break apart family structures by separating generations of children from their families and placing them in distant residential schools designed to eradicate their culture and language.

To understand the crisis facing children in Attawapiskat, it is essential to understand the historical context. Thus, this book begins with a history of the treaty and the subsequent imposition of the residential school system. In the case of the James Bay Cree, generations of children were sent to Bishop Horden Residential School in Moose Factory or the notorious St. Anne's Residential School in Fort Albany. The warning signs of criminal abuse at St. Anne's exist in the department files, reports, and letters. But government officials didn't intervene because the federal government has never acknowledged the legal and moral obligation to protect Indigenous children under its watch.

Thus, the criminal culture at St. Anne's flourished in the moral vacuum created by the policies of the federal government. The government's prime objective was not to educate children but to off-load fiduciary responsibilities while ensuring that minimum resources were spent on their educational and health needs. In adhering to this policy, the Department of Indian Affairs consistently turned a blind eye to a brutal institution that failed to meet the most basic needs of children.

It would be comforting to think that such failings simply reflected the myopia of the era. However, though the language of such policies might have changed in the century since Duncan Campbell Scott, the objective—eradication of the "Indian Question"—remains intact. In terms of delivering programs to Indigenous people, there is a clear pattern of systemic negligence rooted in a long-standing pattern of obstructing treaty obligations under the guise of saving money for the government. The result has been a continual crisis in underfunded housing, health care, child welfare, and education.

●●●

I have been the elected Member of Parliament for the eastern part of Treaty 9 since 2004. Through my time in Parliament, the James Bay region of Ontario has been ground zero for some of the definitive social conflicts between First Nations and the federal government: the Kashechewan water crisis of 2005, the Attawapiskat school fight, the Mushkegowuk suicide crisis of 2009, the Attawapiskat housing crisis of 2011, and the hunger strike of Chief Theresa Spence in 2012.

It isn't possible to fully appreciate the campaign for education rights without understanding the immense pressures faced by the communities of James Bay in dealing with the ongoing crises in housing, infrastructure, and unsafe water. This book attempts to connect these political flashpoints to the larger fight for child equity and treaty recognition. In telling this story, I recognize that I bring my own political perspective. I have limited wherever possible my personal anecdotes or undocumented exchanges with officials, opting for sources that are documented and verifiable by a reader who might wish to undertake more research. Nonetheless, I cannot tell this story without drawing on my own role as a political actor. Readers will make of this what they will.

This book is about two places: James Bay and Ottawa. It is about the people who stood up to inequity and paved the way for a young leader such as Shannen Koostachin. But it is also the story of those who were empowered to make a difference but chose not to. Among them were a comparatively small number of powerful people who showed a criminal disregard for the welfare of their citizens and failed their responsibilities to safeguard the Canadian people's treaties. These key players were aided and abetted by many people working in bureaucracies, agencies, and church orders who opted to serve the narrow interests of their organizations above their obligations to do what was right.

This isn't to say that there haven't been well-meaning people in these positions of responsibility. Over the decades, officials have commissioned countless reports on the state of education, child health, clean water, and so on. The various government departments dealing with Indigenous issues have been subject to oversight by parliamentary hearings and investigations by the auditor general. The best bureaucratic minds were questioned and asked for explanations. But the unwillingness of these empowered persons to take responsibility has left too many children in needless deprivation.

This is why the story of Shannen Koostachin has such power. She cut through this bureaucratic fog. She spoke with the directness and urgency of a child. She called on the government to stop hiding behind department missives and policy prevarications and start being accountable as adults and parents. She asked them to explain why they had failed to protect the children.

Which brings me back to Boxwood Public School. As I step up to speak to the gymnasium of youngsters, a student puts up her hand and asks, "Did you really know Shannen?"

Yes, I knew Shannen. Not a day goes by that I don't think of her. My thoughts of her remain a muddle of emotions and regret. What I remember most is a young girl with a big heart who had a helluva lot of moxie.

But the answer that I give is simple and affirmative. "Shannen was just like you. She would be so proud to see that you are standing up to make change."

These students don't know all the ins and outs of what has gone wrong with Canada's relationship with Indigenous people. They just know that the children deserve better. This is perhaps the real power of the story. It offers us a resolution: just do what is right by the children. If I were to sum up the purpose of this book or explain its political agenda, it would be to underline the urgency of this imperative. (Put simply, Canada can't afford to squander the potential of another generation of First Nations children.)

PART I
THE SHADOW OF ST. ANNE'S

To understand the issues of education and life on the Ontario side of the immense waters of James Bay, one needs to know about the treaty. So this book will begin where the Mushkegowuk Cree say the issue began—with the signing of Treaty 9.

This section explores the legacy of Duncan Campbell Scott and the promise made to provide education for the children of the James Bay Cree. The result was imposition of the residential school system, which included schools such as the notorious St. Anne's. The abuse at St. Anne's existed under the oversight of the federal government and within the context of government policy.

St. Anne's Residential School was finally closed in the mid-1970s, but its legacy continues to haunt generations of James Bay Cree. The government not only turned a blind eye to the abuse that these people suffered but also compromised their attempts to receive justice.

Following the residential schools, children were moved into underfunded day schools operated by the Department of Indian Affairs. In the case of Attawapiskat, negligent construction of a fuel line at the school resulted in catastrophic contamination.

DUNCAN CAMPBELL SCOTT COMES TO JAMES BAY

Further, His Majesty agrees to pay such salaries
of teachers to instruct the children of said Indians, and also to provide such school buildings
and educational equipment as may seem advisable to His Majesty's government of Canada.
—DUNCAN CAMPBELL SCOTT[1]

D uncan Campbell Scott made the promise to provide
education to Cree children at Fort Albany on the
western shore of James Bay on August 3, 1905. The
promise was contained in the text of Treaty 9. It was,
he assured them, a solemn commitment of goodwill.
The promise was repeated in the hall of the Hudson's Bay Company (HBC) post in Moose Factory three days later. Scott had been
given the mandate to secure legal control of the vast region of
northern Ontario above the height of land (where the waters of
Ontario flowed north to the Arctic). In his view, there was little
to negotiate. Either the Indians signed Treaty 9 or the federal and
provincial governments would simply bypass them and do what
they liked. The prospect of education was one of the few benefits
that Scott and the commissioners of Treaty 9 put on the table in
order to reassure the Cree of the good faith of the government. It
was a promise, he told them, that would last "so long as the grass
grows and the water runs."[2]

In exchange for education for their children and annual treaty
payments of four dollars, the Cree, Oji-Cree, and Ojibwe of "new"
Ontario were expected to legally "surrender" their stake in the

land on which they had always lived. What this surrender meant in practice was shrouded in legal language, nuance, and a call to trust the goodwill of the crown.

The treaty commissioners were impressed with the James Bay Cree. They noted in their report to Ottawa that the Cree were not only well dressed but also "remarkably intelligent and deeply interested in the subject to be discussed."[3] In fact, in an article written a year after the negotiations, Scott described the Cree of Moose Factory and Albany as "very brilliant at a theological argument." He noted how they mixed discussions on religion while negotiating business in what he likened to "savage and debased 'tea-meetings.'"[4]

Scott shouldn't have been surprised at the debating skills that the Cree brought to discussions with the crown. Moose Factory, founded in 1673, was the oldest English-speaking settlement in Ontario. The Cree of James Bay had been trading with the British crown for 200 years before Canada was even named a country.

But by the time that Scott arrived, the once mighty fur trade was in decline. The HBC was facing competition from all manner of white interlopers, from trappers to lumbermen. In some areas, beavers had been almost trapped to extinction—bringing famine and insecurity to the families dependent on this trade. Thus, the people gathered in that hall knew that their traditional way of life was under stress. They knew that the long-standing relationship with the whites, which in the previous 250 years had been based on trade, was now facing a dramatic change.

The discussion about education reassured the Cree that the government had their best interests at heart. The treaty commissioners noted in their official report that the promise of schools helped to seal the deal:

> Frederick Mark, who in the afternoon was elected chief, said the Indians were all delighted that a treaty was about to be made with them; they had been looking forward to it for a long time, and were glad that they were to have their hopes realized and that there was now a prospect of law and order being established among them. John Dick remarked that one great advantage the Indians hoped to

derive from the treaty was the establishment of schools wherein their children might receive an education.[5]

But Duncan Campbell Scott, poet, musician, and hard-nosed bureaucrat, hadn't come all this way because he was interested in academic opportunities for Cree children. He was there to ensure the legal surrender of this immense tract of land in the north. Between 1871 and 1921, the federal government set about to obtain legal control over Indigenous lands through a series of numbered post-Confederation treaties (1–11). The treaties were designed to give Ottawa certainty in its control over the lands while bringing the Indigenous people under the "care" of the federal government.

In northern Ontario, a number of bands[6] had been calling on the government for years to sign a treaty. The Indigenous people of the region believed that a legal agreement with the crown would provide some protection from encroachment on their territory. The building of the Canadian Pacific Railway through the regions north of Lake Superior in the 1880s had a huge impact on previously isolated bands. The railway brought an influx of prospectors, trappers, timber crews, and traders. The whites were stripping the land of fur, and with them came the spread of alcohol, tuberculosis (TB), measles, and pneumonia.

Indian people wrote letters to the government protesting these illegal incursions into their territory. In 1872, Chief Blackstone expelled gold prospectors from the Jackfish Lake region near present-day Atikokan, telling them that they had no right to be on Indian land.[7] He said that the miners would not be allowed back into the territory until a treaty had been signed.

In the early 1900s, this pressure began to mount exponentially with the building of the National Transcontinental Railway across the northwest and the Temiskaming and Northern Ontario Railway north toward James Bay.[8]

As mining exploration opened up near Osnaburgh, the Ojibwe objected to the government that these incursions constituted a "trespass" on their land.[9] In 1903, a team from the Geological Survey of Canada was ordered to leave the territory of the Crane Band. Their chief stated that the government had no right to explore there without the express consent of First Nations.[10]

Chief Moonias waiting for the treaty-signing ceremony, Fort Hope, July 19, 1905. *Archives of Ontario, I0010653, Duncan Campbell Scott fonds. Black-and-white print, photographer unknown. Reference Code: C 275-1-0-6 (S 7528).*

Having taken such stands, it is hard to imagine that, within two short years, the bands would suddenly agree to extinguish all rights to their lands in exchange for a small annual payment from the government. Yet, throughout 1905 and 1906, Treaty Commissioners Scott, Samuel Stewart, and Daniel McMartin made their way across the great rivers of northern Ontario to affix signatures to a treaty stating that "the said Indians do hereby cede, release, surrender and yield up to the government of the Dominion of Canada, for His Majesty the King and His successors for ever, all their rights, titles and privileges whatsoever, to ... the said land containing an area of ninety thousand square miles, more or less."[11]

The treaty was a written legal agreement, but the people who signed it were an oral-based culture. When the treaty was explained to them, emphasis was placed on the goodwill of the crown to ensure that their way of life would carry on unimpeded. The treaty report confirmed that the commissioners promised the people that their way of life would not be affected:

Missabay, the recognized chief of the band, then spoke, expressing the fears of the Indians that, if they signed the treaty, they would be compelled to reside upon the reserve to be set apart for them, and would be deprived of the fishing and hunting privileges which they now enjoy. On being informed that their fears in regard to both these matters were groundless, as their present manner of making their livelihood would in no way be interfered with, the Indians talked the matter over among themselves. . . . [After considering, they said that] they were prepared to sign, as they believed that nothing but good was intended.[12]

At Fort Hope, Chief Moonias openly questioned the deal, asking why they were being paid money if there would be no impacts on their lives:

Moonias, one of the most influential chiefs, asked a number of questions. He said that ever since he was able to earn anything, and that was from the time he was very young, he had never been given something for nothing; that he always had to pay for everything that he got. . . . "Now," he said, "you gentlemen come to us from the King offering to give us benefits for which we can make no return. How is this?"[13]

The First Nations people of the region knew that they weren't negotiating from a position of strength. Scott was clear: if they didn't sign it, then the government would simply impose its will on Indian land. To be fair to Scott, he didn't have much to sweeten the deal. The Ontario government had told Ottawa that, treaty or no treaty, it would allow expansion into Indian territory by issuing mining and timber licences. "If the incursion of whites was the gun pointed at the head of the Indian people, Ontario's finger was on the trigger," wrote historian James Morrison.[14]

So education became the one tangible benefit that the people of Treaty 9 could look to as reassurance that the crown would deal fairly with them in the future.

• • •

Duncan Campbell Scott in a freighter canoe on Abitibi River during Treaty 9 negotiations, 1905. *Archives of Ontario, I0010557, Duncan Campbell Scott fonds. Black-and-white print, photographer unknown. Reference Code: C 275-2-0-2 (S 7569).*

Duncan Campbell Scott's Treaty 9 journey across the north cemented his reputation not only as an Ottawa mandarin but also as a poet. Scott returned from the treaty negotiations to assume control of Indian education for the Department of Indian Affairs, eventually taking full control of the department. But he liked to consider himself a "sometime bureaucrat," preferring to be known as a "poet and short story writer."[15] Thus, Scott used the treaty voyage as a backdrop for his growing reputation as one of the premier colonial poets of the age. The photograph of him in the long freighter canoe as it cut along the Abitibi River captured the image of the white explorer subduing the dark lands of the "Natives." It could have been taken in the James Bay lowlands or in Rhodesia. Scott played on this image as the frontier man subjugating a dangerous threat: "The Indian nature . . . was ready to break out at any moment in savage dances, in wild and desperate orgies in which ancient superstitions . . . were intensified by cunning imaginations inflamed with rum."[16]

Scott's poems have been studied for decades in Canadian poetry courses. But his poems on the First Nations people of the north are striking not for what they tell but for what they leave out. For example, his famous "Powassan's Drum" doesn't give the reader any hint of Scott's real-life encounter with the drummer Powassan. In the poem, Scott conjures up the image of a primitive other world:

> He crouches in his dwarf wigwam
> Wizened with fasting
> Fierce with thirst
> Making great medicine
> In memory of hated dead things
> Or in menace of hated things to come
> And the universe listens
> To the throb—throb—throb—throb—
> Throbbing of Powassan's drum.[17]

In reality, Scott overheard a drumming ceremony on the other side of Lac Seul during the treaty negotiations of 1905. He stormed across the lake accompanied by two policemen and threatened the celebrants with arrest if they did not stop.[18] Indian cultural practices had been made illegal by Ottawa. Scott demanded that the drummer identify himself. The man told him that his name was "Powasang." In his notes, Scott referred to Powassan as a "cunning old devil."[19] Cunning indeed, for his real name was Neotanaqueb, but when pressed by Scott he invoked the name of a powerful chief from the Lake of the Woods area. Scott took this drummer to be the real Powassan and created a poem that titillated his readers with images of primitive hatreds. But the poem doesn't give readers any sense of Scott's desire to crush the cultural life of the people of the Treaty 9 region.

Scott believed that the eradication of Indian cultural practices was one of his fundamental bureaucratic responsibilities. In 1921, he issued orders to outlaw all dancing celebrations and limit the movement of Indian people:

> It is observed with alarm that the holding of dances by the
> Indians on their reserves is on the increase. . . . You should

suppress any dances which cause waste of time, interfere
with the occupations of the Indians, ... or encourage them
in sloth and idleness. You should also dissuade, and, if
possible, prevent them from leaving their reserves for the
purpose of attending fairs, exhibitions, etc.[20]

Nowhere did the text of Treaty 9 state that the cultural, spiritual, social, and familial structures of the James Bay Cree would
come under control of a man who held them in such disregard. Yet
the laws prohibiting Indian cultural and religious practices were
enforced by local Indian agents on reserves across the country. In
the James Bay region, John Metatawabin was one who suffered
under these laws. He was arrested by the RCMP for engaging in
"Indian cultural activities" and taken to prison, and his family
never heard from him again.[21]

Presumably, Scott's order to eradicate the cultural celebrations
of Indians was written in his large office in Ottawa, where Scott
kept a piano for practising. He also used his house in the capital
as a venue for celebrations of music and poetry. He told his artistic
friends that he enjoyed being the head of Indian Affairs because it
wasn't an overly busy department, thus giving him time to pursue
his favourite passions: playing the piano and writing poetry. His
attitude toward work was described by biographer E. K. Brown:
"The centre of his life was not in his office, where he seldom came
early, and never stayed late."[22]

Norm Wesley's grandfather Patrick Stephen signed the treaty.
Wesley says that the communities took Scott at his word: "Elders
have held steadfast to the words of Duncan Campbell Scott, holding them in the same high esteem as they did the Union Jack and
the king whose promise was to see to our well-being."[23]

Yet, within a few years of signing the treaty, the James Bay Cree
found that they had become social and political hostages of the
Department of Indian Affairs. None of this had been mentioned
when Scott had sat down in the hall of the HBC post at Moose Factory to assure them of the goodwill of the crown.

THE MISSION SCHOOL

Ｉn 1905, Duncan Campbell Scott promised the people of James Bay that the government would build schools and send teachers north. But he soon undermined this promise. Scott had enclosed the language required to break the promise on education in the legal nuance of the treaty—that the government would provide education "as may seem advisable." What was advisable to Scott was education delivered as rudimentarily as possible and with as little cost to the federal government as possible. The directive for education of the James Bay children was laid out in his 1907 government report: "The Indians [of James Bay] do not require an advanced education on ordinary subjects. They require an elimentary [sic] training and instruction in cleanly modes of life both in the preparation of food and personal surroundings, as well as the most important hygienic rules."[24] Scott's obsession with "hygiene" and "cleanly modes of life" is odd since just two years before his party had been impressed by the well-nourished and comfortably dressed parents who had participated in "intelligent" discussions with the commissioners. But now back in his office in Ottawa, Scott was reneging on the promise that he had made to those well-attired negotiators.

Delivery of education to the children was downloaded to the churches as part of a much larger national strategy of having them attend "residential" schools. Scott defined the terms of Indian education at James Bay in a manner fit more for serfs than for citizens. He told government officials that the fundamental objective of the Department of Indian Affairs was clear: "I want to get rid of the Indian problem.... That is my whole point. Our objective is to continue until there is not a single Indian in Canada that has not been absorbed into the body politic and there is no Indian question, and no Indian Department."[25]

The residential school system had been in place long before Scott assumed his position at Indian Affairs. But he worked to institutionalize the mission school as a means of eradicating the language, culture, and community structures of Indian people. The phrase "to kill the Indian in the child" has often been attributed to Scott, and though he never uttered the phrase his policies were in line with the sentiment. The "Kill the Indian" policy was to be accomplished by utilizing two key policy tools.

The first tool was giving the Department of Indian Affairs legal power to remove children from their communities. These children could then be placed in distant residential schools. The second tool was the accounting ledger. The department was obsessive in limiting government spending on health, social development, and education. In handing the responsibility for education over to churches, the department set the transfer payments for students so low that it institutionalized the abuse and deprivation that followed.

This system was formalized in 1892 when the government introduced a per capita funding formula for paying for Indian education. The order in council was for a "forced system of economy" to "relieve the pressure of present expenditure."[26] According to Jerry Paquette and Gérald Fallon, "per capita funding was deliberately set substantially below actual cost to force churches to practice more 'economical management.' From its inception and throughout its existence, residential education of First Nations children existed under a regime of debilitating fiscal restraint."[27] This policy of underfunding basic education requirements led to the overcrowding and third-rate facilities that contributed to the sickness and death of many children.

This race to the bottom for payment was in place when the Anglicans and the Catholics submitted bids for running schools at James Bay. Looking over the bids, Scott found that the Catholic Oblate missionaries were more willing to meet the department's financial objectives. The Oblate Missionaries of Mary Immaculate had first arrived in Montreal from France in 1841. Within a few years, their missionaries were working across the vast frontier of Canada from the Red River (1845), to the Columbia River

(1847), and into the James Bay basin (1850).[28] The Oblates were a militant band of priests and brothers intent on pushing back the long-standing presence of Anglicans and other Protestants in Indian territory.

The Oblates set up a mission at Fort Albany, where Father Fafard established a large boarding school run by the Grey Nuns.[29] As residential schools were being institutionalized under the federal government, the Oblates underbid the Anglicans for access to Cree children.

In a report to the government, Scott explained that the Anglicans were asking too much money for educating children: "Therefore, that so far as the practical needs of education are concerned a grant of $1,200.00 to the Church of England [for establishment of James Bay mission school] ... cannot be productive of any very great results."[30]

Whereas the Anglicans were offering to educate the children for eighty dollars per capita, along with the retrofitting of a building for a boarding school (to be paid for by the government), the Oblates were offering to do the job for sixty dollars a student, with a building already supplied by the missionaries. "All the assistance the Roman Catholic Church has received for education is a grant of $300.00, nominally for the salary of the day school teacher but which really goes to meet the expenses of the boarding school at Albany. This boarding school ... is a commodious building, part of a small group of buildings which constitute the settlement at Fort Albany."[31]

Duncan Campbell Scott didn't ask for commitments from the priests on how they would supply this education. The Department of Indian Affairs was not concerned that money designated for a qualified teacher could be diverted by the mission for whatever costs it deemed appropriate. To seal the deal, the department threw in another $900 to get the school project moving, and the Albany mission school (St. Anne's Residential School) was now institutionalized under the federal government.

In order to keep the peace between the two competing denominations at James Bay, Scott offered to meet the higher fees of the Anglicans for a residential school being set up at Moose Factory: "As it will be necessary to deal justly with both denominations ...

the recommendation is made with due consideration for economy and is by no means an extravagant one."[32]

The cost of keeping the Anglican mission happy was an agreement to spend $500 to convert the Anglican bishop's house in Moose Factory into Bishop Horden Residential School. The government offered a further $1,500 for equipment and an annual per capita payout of eighty dollars per student. Thus, the Anglicans settled for per pupil funding 25 per cent higher than that offered for the children at Fort Albany.

• • •

In the world of 1907, it might have seemed reasonable to establish a series of boarding schools to serve the children whose families were still living in small groups on traplines across the vast territory of James Bay. Boarding schools were a common form of education, particularly for the upper class. These institutions had a long history of heavy discipline.[33]

But there was a world of difference between the traditional boarding school and the residential schools. In 1907, the year that Scott was negotiating with the churches for residential schools at James Bay, an internal report showed that residential schools were a horrific failure. Peter Henderson Bryce, senior health inspector for the Department of Indian Affairs, had begun documenting the death rates of children in church-run residential schools in the west. He released his findings in a report entitled *On the Indian Schools of Manitoba and the Northwest Territories.*[34]

Bryce produced evidence that children in mission schools in western Canada were dying at a staggering rate. He found that 24 per cent of students who had entered the residential school system died either in the schools or shortly after leaving them. However, in some institutions, such as the File Hills Boarding School (the only school to provide full statistics), the death rate was actually 69 per cent.[35]

To Bryce, it was not simply a case of negligent local school officials but also a systemic failure of the federal government to ensure adequately funded education and health for Indian children. The government's policy of deliberate underfunding had led to overcrowded dormitories, poor ventilation, and a number of

Child being taken to St. Anne's Residential School, Fort Albany, date unknown. *Edmund Metatawabin collection, 2012-001-001-001, Shingwauk Residential Schools Centre, Algoma University. Courtesy of Edmund Metatawabin.*

institutions that didn't even bother to provide soap or clean water for the children. Dean Neu and Richard Therrien, in *Accounting for Genocide: Canada's Bureaucratic Assault on Aboriginal People*, connect the high death rates to government policies of institutional negligence: "This intersection of an inadequate funding mechanism, the lack of enforcement of departmental rules and the substandard facilities resulted in mortality rates of around 40 per cent for Aboriginal youth sent to such institutions."[36]

As a result of Bryce's report, the Department of Indian Affairs was forced to make some changes to how residential schools were overseen. Nonetheless, Scott did his best to limit Bryce's research, which showed the inescapable connection between government policy and numerous child deaths. Scott had come up through the department when the issues of Indian sickness and death were understood as a collateral factor in the process of subjugation.

That was how it had been since John A. Macdonald had taken over the department as both prime minister and Indian Affairs minister.

Since Confederation, the Department of Indian Affairs had imposed a bureaucratic culture of deliberate marginalization and neglect. The results were widespread death of and loss of independence for Indigenous people. This history has been documented recently by James Daschuk in his award-winning book *Clearing the Plains: Disease, Politics of Starvation, and the Loss of Aboriginal Life.*[37]

Two Cree students at St. Anne's Residential School, year unknown. *Fort Albany and Albany River photo album, Shingwauk Project collection (residential school photo album series), 2011-019-001, Shingwauk Residential Schools Centre, Algoma University.*

In fact, the template for Scott's relationship with Bryce closely parallels the relationship between two other department bureaucrats three decades earlier: Dr. Daniel Hagarty and Edgar Dewdney. Hagarty was on the front lines of the famine and illness hitting the western prairies between 1877 and 1880. His work as a dedicated public servant resulted in the eradication of smallpox among First Nations people on the southwestern prairies. Dewdney was a senior civil servant denounced in the House of Commons for ignoring four official requests to send aid during the long winter of 1882–83 for "over two thousand Indians here almost naked and on the verge of starvation."[38] When finally pressed to send food supplies five months after the initial request, Dewdney stated that it was government policy to use famine to force Indians onto reserves. He went on to an illustrious public service career and was promoted by Macdonald to both Indian commissioner and lieutenant governor of the western region (known as the North-West Territories). Hagarty, on the other hand, was fired on the pretext that the cost of his medical interventions, which had saved so many lives, was money that the department could have better spent elsewhere. As Daschuk writes, "Hagarty's dismissal reflects the cynicism of Indian administration while Macdonald served as both prime minister and minister of Indian Affairs.... The abandonment of a successful medical policy precisely when the Indian population ... was most in need because of the famine stands as a testament to dominion indifference."[39]

In a five-year period (1891–96), the First Nations population across Canada dropped a staggering 17 per cent, with tuberculosis accounting for the majority of deaths. Megan Sproule-Jones points out that department officials and politicians such as Clifford Sifton viewed the death rate on the prairies as "an opportunity to reduce expenditure on services like education and medical attention."[40] Indeed, throughout the 1890s and the first decade of the twentieth century, the federal government cut spending on First Nations communities by 60 per cent.[41]

Ronald Haycock describes the role of the federal government in addressing Indian issues as a form of "Darwinistic paternalism." Indian policy was seen through the principle of survival of the fittest—the white population versus the ever-weakened Indian population. Thus, as whites became ascendant across the continent, Indians were "unable to survive in competitive evolution," and whites tried "to make the death struggle of the primative [sic] as soft as possible."[42]

But there was nothing "soft" about "the death struggle" facing First Nations communities. The deaths were the inevitable result of a government policy that withheld badly needed funds, food, and medical support. The Department of Indian Affairs ignored clear evidence that preventive programs were stemming the devastating advance of tuberculosis in non-Native communities. The adoption of such programs would have spared untold lives on the reserves.

Bryce pointed out that Indian Affairs had allocated a mere $10,000 to control tuberculosis for 300 bands across Canada (about 105,000 people). In comparison, the city of Ottawa (with about the same population) had a medical budget of $342,000, of which it spent over $33,000 in 1919 to fight the spread of the disease.[43] Such efforts had dropped TB rates in some urban areas by 40 per cent. Meanwhile, the refusal of the federal government to initiate similar measures among a population that had already been weakened by hunger and poverty resulted in skyrocketing death rates.

As the chief medical officer for the department, Bryce insisted that all officials under his watch begin tracking the monthly rates of illness in First Nations communities. The numbers obtained gave him the evidence that he believed was needed to push for fundamental policy changes within the department.

But these recommendations ran counter to departmental objectives. For example, Bryce recommended that churches be removed from Indian education and that the federal government initiate an overhaul of education responsibilities with adequate financial support.

He wasn't the only one speaking out. An ally was church-man Samuel H. Blake of the Missionary Society of the Church of England in Canada (MSCC). Blake was also appalled by the failure of the churches to protect the children under their watch. In a letter to Archdeacon Tims, who ran an Indian industrial school in Calgary, Blake wrote that he did not know "how in the world you can be satisfied with statistics which show that out of from 900 to 1,000 children which pass through our Indian schools 300 of them pass out of our hands to the grave within ten or twelve years. I cannot conceive except upon the hypothesis that we grow callous amidst such a frightful death rate."[44]

Blake soon found himself marginalized by church leaders for his advocacy. Bryce was also running into roadblocks set up by Duncan Campbell Scott. Bryce's report, presented to the Department of Indian Affairs in the spring of 1907, was leaked to the press on November 15, 1907.[45] *Saturday Night* magazine said that the report should "startle the country.... Indian boys and girls are dying like flies in these institutions.... [This is] a situation disgraceful to the country."[46] This wave of media attention to the conditions uncovered by Bryce made him a marked man in the department. As far as the government was concerned, any media coverage of Indian issues was bad press. Bryce's crusading work had become a problem.

Scott prevented Bryce from presenting his findings at a national conference on TB prevention.[47] In 1913, Scott was appointed the overall director of the department, and he suspended funding for

Gathering at the graveyard in Fort Albany with the bishop, date unknown. *Fort Albany and Albany River photo album, Shingwauk Project collection (residential school photo album series), 2011-019-001, Shingwauk Residential Schools Centre, Algoma University.*

Bryce's research work. As with the firing of Hagarty three decades earlier, Scott claimed that the cost of keeping track of deaths in residential schools far outweighed the "benefit" of the research. Bryce's position as chief medical officer became redundant during the year of the Spanish flu, when over 4,000 Indian people died.[48]

Bryce quit the federal service in disgust. With his professional career in tatters, he called out both Duncan Campbell Scott and the federal government in a publication entitled *The Story of a National Crime: Being an Appeal for Justice to the Indians of Canada.* He accused them of "criminal disregard" of their treaty obligations.[49]

Scott went on to be celebrated for his years of "public service." He was named a fellow of the Royal Society of Canada and received honorary doctorates from Queen's University and the University of Toronto. He was made a companion of the Order of St. Michael and St. George. He still has many defenders in the poetry world who see in Scott a poetic voice of a sepia-tinged era in Canada's colonial existence. They remember his poetry more so than his "part-time" job overseeing Indian education. For such supporters, the issue is balancing the legacy of "Scott the sensitive writer and Scott the pragmatic administrator."[50]

But as the impacts of the residential schools have become more widely known, the image of Scott the heartless bureaucrat has begun to replace the image of Scott the sensitive poet. Scott triumphed over Bryce in their lifetime, but the evidence supplied by Bryce dogs the legacy of Scott. Simply put, why did he fail to address the appalling death rates among children under his watch? With survival rates a mere 30 per cent in some institutions, they were veritable death camps for children.[51]

For much of the past century, the idea that Canada had institutionalized systems that knowingly caused the deaths of so many First Nations children just wasn't a concept that people were willing to entertain. Yet an obscure report prepared for the Ontario government in 1967 raised the question of whether or not Canada's Indian policy had been led by a homegrown Eichmann. The report was written by rural sociologist R. Alex Sim on the need to develop Indian-based education. He looked at the historical record of Indian-government relations in the century since the treaties had been signed and asked whether or not there was a similarity between the architect of twentieth-century Indian policy and the architect of "the final solution":

> The condition of the Indian in Ontario, if measured by the commonly accepted yardsticks of progress and well-being, is so poor that it is almost impossible to believe that he could have arrived by accident at such low levels of income, health, and educational attainment. Yet to say that their deprivations were deliberately engineered by the high-minded agencies who have assumed custodial responsibilities leads to implications that are difficult to face. . . . They bring forth the ambivalences that were evoked by the trial of Eichmann. For then Everyman was in the bullet-proof docket.[52]

When Sim was writing, Duncan Campbell Scott was still revered as a Canadian man of letters, so perhaps it is not surprising that Sim did not mention the famous poet by name. But his quotation from George Steiner on the Eichmann trial is chilling:

> We know now that a man can read Goethe or Rilke in the evening, that he can play Bach or Schubert, and go to his day's work at Auschwitz in the morning. To say that he has read them without understanding or that his ear is gross, is cant. . . . Moreover, it is not only the case that the established media of civilization—the universities, the arts, the book world—failed to offer adequate resistance to political bestiality; they often rose to welcome it and to give it ceremony and apologia.[53]

To be fair, the invocation of Eichmann in Sim's report was based on the 1960s understanding of Eichmann that came from Hannah Arendt's work. Her study of the banality of evil presented Eichmann as a diligent bureaucrat who simply didn't take personal responsibility for the evil that he wrought. Newer research on Eichmann has questioned Arendt's interpretation of him as a mere cog in the bureaucratic machine. This research portrays a much deeper level of depravity and culpability in his involvement in the Holocaust.[54] So is it fair to compare Scott with the Arendt image of Eichmann when the word *genocide* did not even exist at the time of the Bryce report?

In deciding whether Sim's allusion is fair, we might consider an anecdote from John Milloy's book *A National Crime: The Canadian Government and the Residential School System*. Milloy refers to a letter written in 1923 by a boy named Edward B., who attended Onion Lake Residential School in Saskatchewan. The boy wrote home telling his family of the constant hunger and brutality experienced by the children. Scott would not have been surprised by such news. He regularly dealt with reports from parents, visitors, and occasional inspectors who raised cases of hunger, beatings, and sexual assaults in various residential schools. Scott saw his role as smoothing over the concerns and generally sided with school authorities. What made Edward B.'s allegations different was that this letter was obtained by a reporter. The journalist pressed Scott for an explanation: "Scott advised that Edward B.'s letter was libellous and should not be published. The boy was just looking for sympathy; he was not trustworthy. Children were well cared for and, in fact, he concluded, 'ninety-nine per cent of the Indian children at these schools are too fat.'"[55]

What should we make of this poet who had read reports of the abuse of children yet chose to mock their hunger? Scott later stated that "I was never unsympathetic to Aboriginal ideals, but there was the law which I did not originate and which I never tried to amend in the direction of severity."[56]

This is the excuse of the bureaucrat who had the lives of thousands of people in his hands and could have done the right thing but chose otherwise. Had Scott acted on Bryce's recommendations, the harsh history of twentieth-century relations between Native and non-Native Canadians could have been altered. But he chose not to act. And on this he is judged.

THREE LITTLE BOYS

In the residential schools, the secrecy began at dawn: we were beaten from the time we first awoke. Speaking out against the injustice in letters home was also cause for punishment. We coped in whatever way we could, often by imitating our oppressors. At St. Anne's, the stronger boys beat the weaker boys either with their fists or with tamarack branches. Sexual abuse was rampant too, with the staff forcing themselves on the girls and boys, and the students forcing themselves on each other.
—EDMUND METATAWABIN[57]

John Kioke told the boys in the dorm that he was going home. Like the other children, he had been taken from his parents the previous fall. Staying with his family hadn't been an option. If he hadn't been compliant, the police would have been sent to take him away to St. Anne's Residential School in Fort Albany. But Kioke was traumatized by life at the residential school. He wanted to see his mother. He was going to run away to see his parents in Attawapiskat. But their village was 100 kilometres north, located where the Attawapiskat River flows into James Bay. He was only fourteen years old.

Even at his young age, Kioke must have known that crossing the vast expanse of the James Bay lowlands in April was a death-defying experience. He was a child of the Attawapiskat Cree who lived in small groups of family-based hunters. The families lived on the traplines in winter and moved to the coastal settlement following the geese migrations in the late spring.

It was difficult to survive on this land of muskeg and rivers at the best of times. But in April it was especially difficult. As the weather began to warm, the ice along the mighty Albany and Attawa-piskat Rivers fissured and pushed toward James Bay. During the spring breakup, massive chunks of ice were thrust upward by the pressure of the moving water. When these huge chunks jammed together along the river bends, they caused temporary jams, forc-ing the fast-flowing water to back up, resulting in huge flash floods across the flatlands.

What made Kioke so desperate to get away from the mission school and return home to Attawapiskat at this precarious time of the year? We may never know. What we do know is that he wasn't liked by the priests. They had him pegged as a troublemaker. He was neither quiet nor obedient, and he didn't buckle under their attempts to control him.[58] In the brutal world of St. Anne's Resi-dential School, it wasn't healthy to be seen as defiant.

Kioke talked his twelve-year-old friend Michel Matinas from Attawapiskat and eleven-year-old Michel Sutherland from the village of Weenusk (near the coast of Hudson Bay) into joining him in the escape. The boys had a narrow window of opportunity to make their break because the mission dog team was away in Moosonee, so it would be difficult for the mission priests to track them down.

In the days leading up to their escape, they tried to squirrel away a few pieces of bread to feed themselves on their journey. As well, Kioke had ten arrows for his bow in order to hunt birds along the long walk home. They escaped on the night of April 18, 1941, and were never seen again.

• • •

St. Anne's Residential School was a world unto itself. The school was run by French-speaking Oblate priests with the help of the Grey Nuns. The post at Fort Albany had no phone, and few outsid-ers ever visited the school. The roads in Ontario ended at the town of Cochrane. From there, it was a 150-mile train ride to the port of Moosonee. From Moosonee, the only way north was by barge in the summer along James Bay or by dog team in the winter.

In mid-June 1941, Indian Agent Dr. T. J. Orford and RCMP Cor-poral George Dexter stopped in for an annual visit to Fort Albany and learned that the three boys had disappeared. Dexter was concerned that nobody outside the mission had been alerted that the boys were missing. He interviewed the principal, Father Paul Langlois, who explained that steps had been taken to find the boys but said that the search had been unsuccessful. Dexter pressed the priest on whether the boys had been maltreated prior to their running away, but Father Langlois swore that there had been no incidents.

Corporal Dexter then asked why the police had not been informed that they were missing. The priest claimed that he had notified the resident Catholic bishop at Moosonee of the incident, but the bishop had decided not to pass this information on to the police.

The RCMP officer, along with the Indian agent, then went to interview the families of the missing boys. The father of Michel Sutherland in Weenusk was willing to accept the story told by the priests, but the Kioke and Matinas families were far from satisfied. According to them, the boys had been mistreated at the school. Among the allegations that they shared with the RCMP was that staff had ripped up letters from children to their parents if they revealed anything abusive going on at the mission school. They also stated that some of the children had told them that Father Langlois had warned the other students not to tell anyone anything about the boys' disappearance or anything that had gone on at St. Anne's the previous winter. The parents also alleged that the death of another child at the school had gone unreported.[59]

Dexter noted in his report that he and the Indian agent took the side of the priests, telling the families that "it was difficult to believe a child regarding treatment received in school." He noted that this comment wasn't well received by the parents, who declared that they would never allow any more of their children to be taken to St. Anne's. "There is no doubt that the children have perished, either by starvation or by drowning," wrote Corporal Dexter. "The whole affair is very regretable and the parents [sic] indignation regarding the loss of their children is readily understandable."[60]

The other issue of concern was that Bishop Henri Belleau at Moosonee had failed to inform the RCMP when the boys had gone missing. When pressed on this oversight, he wrote to the RCMP to reassure them that his failure to alert the authorities had been a good-natured mistake and in no way a sign of wrongdoing. "I frankly confess that I cannot understand how any accusation of negligence could be substantiated against the Father Principal of the school," the bishop wrote, as he tellingly described the missing boys as a case of "desertion."[61]

By the summer of 1942, the Department of Indian Affairs in Ottawa had learned of the incident. The department wasn't pleased to learn through other channels that three boys had been missing for over a year and that nobody had informed the department. Indian Affairs official Phillip Phelan wrote to Orford demanding an explanation of why the department had been kept in the dark. In the end, an inquiry was ordered, with a three-man committee made up of the Indian agent, the school principal, and RCMP Corporal W. Kerr.

Little came from the inquiry. The Sutherland family from Weenusk attended the hearings, as did one of the families from Attawapiskat. The official report, prepared by Corporal Kerr, stated that the two sets of parents who attended were satisfied with the findings and that "they too believed that everything possible had been done, now that they had heard the different witnesses give evidence."[62]

However, the actual evidence supplied contradicts Kerr's conclusion. In the statement prepared for one of the parents, it was recorded that "I am not sure that sufficient search was made for my son and the other boys."[63] The report noted that the parent then went on to testify that he had been told that the priest had ordered the children not to speak of what had happened regarding the runaways. During this testimony, Father Langlois interrupted the parent and assured the inquiry that "he had given the children a lecture but that he had told them they were to tell only the truth." The parent then continued and said that some of the children had told him that one of the boys had been punished and that this was the reason they had run away.[64]

Nonetheless, the police were satisfied, and the case was closed. It would be over fifty years before they would turn their attention back to the goings-on at St. Anne's Residential School.

THE '60s' SOLUTION

Until now, decisions on the education of Indian
children have been made by anyone and everyone, except Indian parents. This must stop.
—NATIONAL INDIAN BROTHERHOOD/
ASSEMBLY OF FIRST NATIONS[65]

From the 1940s through the 1960s, the Department of
Indian Affairs wrestled with the issue of residential
schools. The department knew that the schools had
been a major failure. However, none of the questions
focused on the substandard education and the widespread deprivation in the church-run institutions. Rather, the
department had come to the conclusion that the isolationist and
sectarian control of church-run schools was interfering with the
updated departmental objective of promoting the assimilation of
Indian people into white society.

In the years following the Second World War, eugenics, social
Darwinism, and language about ascendance of the superior race
had fallen into well-deserved disrepute. However, the new buzz-
word, *enfranchisement* (i.e., assimilation), had become a goal of the
department. Government policy became focused on the extinction of Indian identity through intermarriage so that Indians
"will be completely absorbed into the white race and retain of
their past history the vaguest memory."[66] It was clear that, by iso-
lating Indian children in residential schools, the objective of having Indian people bred out of existence through intermarriage
would not be met.

By the beginning of the 1960s, over 40 per cent of Indian children had been moved into white provincial schools. But a substantial number were still being educated in residential schools. Moving students into provincial schools wasn't an option in isolated regions such as James Bay. On top of this, the Oblates openly opposed the government's objective of assimilation.

While other religious denominations had begun to move away from residential school operations, the Catholic Church had entrenched. It has always been militant in defending its right to offer Catholic education. In regions across Canada, Catholic schools historically have had fewer resources than public schools but still had a reputation for producing high academic achievement and youth leadership. Catholic schools in working-class neighbourhoods were seen as models for civic and academic opportunity. However, this was not the case with residential schools. And, as much as the department and the Oblates argued about objectives, the primary obligations of ensuring quality education and safe learning environments were never on the table.

Relations between the Oblates and Department of Indian Affairs officials deteriorated as the government pushed its policy of assimilation. The government wanted the church out of the education business. But it was reluctant to take up the responsibility itself. The Oblates, for their part, pushed their school system as a means of protecting the separateness of Indian identity. At a 1957 conference in Ottawa, thirty-eight Oblate residential school principals declared that a "realistic program of schooling aimed at acculturating the Indian must be based on respect for his ethnic and cultural background and a desire to meet his special needs."[67]

The struggles over education between the department and Oblates reveal interesting divergences in priorities. In a 1954 report on St. Anne's Residential School, the department's inspector of schools noted the "spotlessly clean dormitories," which were "bright and well painted," which he stated was the norm for Roman Catholic residential schools.[68] In describing the quality of education, however, he referred to overcrowded classrooms in which children from multiple grades were forced to learn together. In one class, children from grade three to grade seven were crammed together, and it was impossible to separate the students for grade-based learning because there was only one

Students at St. Anne's Residential School, circa 1945. *Edmund Metatawabin collection, 2012-001-001-025, Shingwauk Residential Schools Centre, Algoma University. Courtesy of Edmund Metatawabin.*

blackboard. "Consequently, a good deal of the work is done in common and one finds grade threes trying to keep up with grade sevens and vice versa." Yet this was not noted as a problem requiring correction, and the report praised the "excellent work" of the school.[69] What was of concern to government officials, however, was children speaking Cree in school. The department pressed the principal on the importance of maintaining an English-speaking atmosphere.

The government opposed Indigenous language instruction in residential schools because it kept the cultural identities of the students alive. Yet the Oblates had relied on Cree language instruction since the earliest days of the Albany school.[70] During the years of isolation, the government had not paid much attention to the instruction being offered by the Oblates. But as the struggle over the direction of residential schools intensified in the postwar years, the teaching of Cree put the Oblates at loggerheads with the government.

R. F. Davey, head of the department's Central Education Division, wrote that teaching Cree was a "waste of valuable instruction time and may even hinder the language programme."[71] Concerns over children speaking Cree at St. Anne's Residential School had been the subject of a number of government reports, including one by the department's regional supervisor: "I was rather surprised to learn recently that the Cree language and syllabics are being taught ... during regular [school] hours.... Teaching the native language only further retards an already retarded group."[72]

Native language use in residential schools had become an issue for the Department of Indian Affairs for two reasons. The first reason was that it violated the assimilationist objective of stripping away Indigenous identity; the second reason was that the department was concerned about learning rates at the schools, so appallingly low that many students were graduating but could not speak even basic English.[73] Rather than question the quality of education being offered by the churches, the department focused its attention on eliminating First Nations languages in the schools.

However, as much as the Department of Indian Affairs wanted to ensure an English-language environment at the school, it was not about to tell the Oblates how to do their job. "Since these ... schools are church-owned we have little jurisdiction over their curriculum," wrote Davey, the supervisor of education, to his superior.[74] It was suggested that the matter be raised with the principal and that a report be made on his reaction.

• • •

In the mid-1960s, the government commissioned a team of sociologists to look at options for replacing residential schools and dealing with the "Indian Question." The result was the substantive two-part Hawthorn Report on Indian people in Canada. The sociologists had little time for the mission work of the priests. They noted in a chapter entitled "Ideology of the Oblates" that one priest had described the department's overhaul of education as the "work of Satan." The Hawthorn team remarked that "this kind of tirade expresses the savage opposition of an Oblate Father to school integration of Indian children."[75]

The Hawthorn team studied the delivery of education and noted the terrible levels of graduation for reserve students. They found that only 2.1 per cent of the people of Attawapiskat had been educated past grade nine. This abysmal number wasn't an aberration—it was an average. In fact, many other communities scored even lower. Communities such as Pikangikum, The Pas, and Fort St. John had no record of any Indian student ever graduating from grade nine.[76]

Such a finding should have shocked the sociologists and the federal Liberal government of the day. However, the report shrugged off the failure of the schooling with the bland admission that there might have been "certain inadequacies in the primary and secondary levels of schooling."[77] It placed the blame on Indian parents for the failure of their children in federal schools: "They [the parents] appear to impose a certain ceiling of aspirations on the children and teenagers (especially male) of these communities, which in turn affects their attitudes towards, and achievements in, the formal educational system."[78] Yet, when those parents made presentations to the Hawthorn team raising their concerns about the deeply entrenched structures obstructing the development of their children in both the residential and the provincial schools, the sociologists continued to place responsibility for the dismal rate of Indian educational outcomes on the Indigenous parents:

> We feel that, because of the distrust felt by the Indians towards the White man, Indian associations have to show a certain aggressiveness, a certain intransigence.... The fact that several hundreds of the Indian children are not attending the schools available to them cannot be explained simply by over-crowding of the Indian schools. It is more likely that in many cases the Indian parents prefer to lavish on their children an "Indian style" education, out of contempt for the White man's education.[79]

Throughout the Hawthorn Report is a casual disregard for the views of the people who had been pushed to the margins of Canadian society. In one anecdote, the report noted how residents in Kenora were outraged when Indian people urinated on the streets when they came into town. The report noted that Indian people were sometimes forced to urinate in public because they were not allowed in restaurants or to use the washroom facilities in stores where they purchased their supplies. The report didn't question how such Jim Crow conditions could exist in Canada at the same time as the civil rights movement was being waged against similar racist structures in southern US cities such as Birmingham and Selma. Instead, it simply shrugged off this example of entrenched discrimination as merely "ridiculous."[80] The inability of the Hawthorn team to view the issue outside their cultural lens made it impossible for them to adequately comprehend the huge impediments facing Indigenous children being pushed into provincial schools as part of the government's overall assimilationist agenda.

Not everyone shared the Hawthorn Report's assumptions. One critic was R. A. Sim, the rural sociologist in Ontario who, as we have already seen, invoked the spectre of Eichmann when describing the failed policies of Indian Affairs. He prepared a report for the government of Ontario that challenged the assimilationist approach. He pointed out that Indigenous children faced huge problems in institutions marked by an overtly racist culture. He stated that the daily humiliations that they faced were sometimes too much to bear and resulted in the failure of education or high dropout rates. Sim concluded that the government's education policy was really another means by which to eradicate Indian identity: "A plan to integrate Indian children in the schools has an implicit assumption about the status of the Indian groups in Ontario. This is that they should be gradually assimilated into white society. Officials will deny that this is so, but what evidence is there that in the educational enterprises available for examination . . . there are other goals?"[81]

Sim offered a number of recommendations for establishing quality-based Indigenous opportunities for education. But his report was not in sync with the vision of the "just society" being promoted by the new Liberal government under Pierre Elliott Trudeau. The new prime minister was a champion of individual rights and had little patience for the notion of collective rights laid out in treaties. In the "just society," treaty obligations were an impediment to the development of a modern democratic and increasingly multicultural state.

In 1969, Minister of Indian Affairs Jean Chrétien was given the mandate to implement the vision of the Hawthorn Report. The result was the so-called white paper that proposed to end the Indian "Problem" by shutting down the Department of Indian Affairs, terminating the treaties, ending Indian status, and converting all reserve lands into private holdings.[82]

What is striking about the white paper was the audaciousness of a government ready to move against First Nations rights without any consultation with the people affected. The pushback was immediate. The white paper launched a generation of First Nations militancy. One of those who stood up to the Trudeau agenda was a young Alberta Cree leader, Harold Cardinal. He responded to the white paper with his own manifesto: *The Unjust Society: The Tragedy of Canada's Indians.* This so-called red paper denounced the efforts to assimilate Indian people as a form of cultural "genocide."[83]

The white paper simply proposed the absorption of Indian students into provincial school systems. For the Indian leadership, this plan for education was a non-starter. In 1972, the National Indian Brotherhood produced a statement affirming that Indian education must be centred on the needs of Indian children within a cultural, familial, and educational matrix:

> If we are to avoid the conflict of values which in the past has led to withdrawal and failure, Indian parents must have control of education with the responsibility of setting goals. What we want for our children can be summarized very briefly:
>
> - to reinforce their Indian identity
> - to provide the training necessary for making a good living in modern society.
>
> We are the best judges of the kind of school programs which can contribute to these goals without causing damage to the child.
>
> We must, therefore, reclaim our right to direct the education of our children.[84]

Backlash against the Trudeau government's agenda pushed the issue of education back onto the desks of officials in the Department of Indian Affairs. Residential schools were being closed one by one across the country, and resistance against the assimilationist agenda had pushed the education file back onto the government's lap. Indian Affairs was now getting into the business of education on a full-time basis.

THE CHRÉTIEN LETTER

Most of us had little schooling in the past, [and] if we had any, it's about religion. The mission never gave the impression that they want to teach us something very useful and informative.... You'd be surprised to find out how [we, as parents, are] unwanted in the mission property.
—FORT ALBANY PARENTS TO INDIAN AFFAIRS[85]

A s residential schools began to close in the 1960s, St. Anne's Residential School was a stubborn holdout. But even there change was in the air. The days when the Oblates could fill their teaching rosters with obedient nuns or lay workers who couldn't get hired elsewhere had ended. The schools had always been able to deliver cheaper education because they didn't hire qualified teachers. But by the late 1960s, they were forced to look to teachers from the outside.

In 1968, six young teachers signed on with the Department of Indian Affairs education branch for what they thought would be an adventure in teaching. They were hired in Toronto to fill vacant positions at the school in Fort Albany. The appearance of qualified young teachers was big news in the community. Parents were hopeful that the teachers could improve literacy and academic opportunities that had been denied to them when they had attended the school.

There was immediate conflict, however, between the teachers and school administrators. The teachers were appalled by the racist attitude of the staff toward the children and their families.[86] They also felt constantly "provoked" by a school administration

Overcrowded student dormitory at St. Anne's Residential School, February 1967. *Archives of Ontario, I022566. Creator: Mildred Young Hubert. Reference Code: F4369-1-0-1.*

that insisted on complete control of their private time. Three of the teachers attempted to get out from under the thumb of the principal by renting a small cabin in the community. Little more than a month after they arrived, the six teachers were fired. They were informed of their termination by a note posted on their door. They were fired because they were perceived to be too friendly with the local Indians. One teacher explained what had gone wrong: "They [the school administration] seemed to very much dislike our fraternization with the Indians and the fact that Indians visited us in our residence. Several Indians were warned to stay away from our residence. Anyone hired directly by the mission is not allowed to fraternize with any Indians on a personal basis."[87]

A group of local parents wrote to the Department of Indian Affairs to demand that the government intervene to rehire the teachers. The parents demanded better education for their children. They also asked for an investigation into "many incidents" taking place at the school.[88]

One of the fired teachers wrote personally to Minister of Indian Affairs Jean Chrétien urging him to intervene to protect

the children. After all, the situation at the school was his responsibility as minister. "Although we may not have understood the
implications of working for a mission run school, we did think we
were employed by the Department of Indian Affairs," she wrote.
She stated that at least four of the teachers would return to Fort
Albany if the department intervened and dealt with the problems
at the school. However, she noted that an Indian Affairs official
had informed her that, according to the department, "it would be
easier to find six new teachers for January than it would be to make
any changes in the attitudes of the administration." The teacher
found this unacceptable. "It would appear that little concern has
[been] shown for the welfare of the children," she wrote. Were the
teachers to go back to work under the administration at St. Anne's,
it would mean having to give up their "basic beliefs about human
rights and dignity and still face the children who are forced to live
in such a sterile, rigid, unloving atmosphere."[89]

The teacher offered to go to Ottawa to meet Chrétien personally: "I am very adamant in my beliefs that this cannot be allowed
to continue and if there is anything I can do to help the Indian
people make the changes they want and help the children help-
lessly caught in this situation, I will happily do it."[90] It is not known
whether Chrétien took her up on her offer to meet and learn about
what was taking place at St. Anne's.

• • •

The letter from this teacher couldn't have come as a surprise to Indian Affairs. There were many complaints about the treatment of
children at St. Anne's. Just four years before, the department was
informed that children were being sent home in clothing that was
in "appalling condition."[91] One father wanted to know what had
happened to the clothes and shoes that he had sent with his son to
school the previous fall.

"Officials of the school were approached to supply an adequate answer, but the case was not investigated," wrote R. F. Hall,
the Indian Affairs officer in charge of James Bay. He assured his
superiors that "we looked into the matter as far as possible, and
advised the school, but no satisfactory reply has been forthcoming."[92] Case closed.

The state of the children's clothes was just one sign that things were very wrong at St. Anne's Residential School. Had the department's education officials followed through, they might have uncovered the culture of abuse that had become the norm in this secretive institution.

Andrew Wesley, an ordained minister in Toronto, describes the degradation that he suffered as a child:

> My number at the residential school was 56 and I was known by that number for many years. I was not considered to be a human being, just a number.... I remember being in the dining room having a meal. I got sick and threw up on the floor. Sister Mary Immaculate slapped me many times before she made me eat my vomit. So I did, I ate all of it. And then I threw up again.... Sister Mary Immaculate slapped me and told me again to eat my vomit.... I was sick for a few days after that.[93]

One time when Andrew was horsing around with another student, he was grabbed by Sister Mary Immaculate (her real name was Anna Wesley) and beaten with a heavy shoe:

> She hit me about fifty times. I passed out for a while. I was not allowed to report the incident, and I was not allowed to go to the clinic. The beating left a large lump on the back of my neck, at the top of my spine (which has never gone away). For many, many days I had a hard time walking or playing because it hurt. I had a regular, severe nose bleed that kept coming back for months.[94]

But the violence wasn't simply random; it was considered entertainment for staff. When eight-year-old Edmund Metatawabin first stepped through the doors of St. Anne's in 1956, he was thrust into a world of violence and sexual abuse. He documented the impacts of St. Anne's Residential School in his powerful memoir, *Up Ghost River*. In an affidavit given to the Ontario Superior Court in 2013, he describes how school staff set up a homemade electric chair in the basement for the torture of children:

> I was a little boy and I had to climb up into the chair because
> I was still small. My legs did not touch the ground. When
> the current went through me, my legs shot out straight in
> front of me and were shaking.... I cannot describe how
> intense the pain was. I could not scream. At St. Anne's, if
> you were being beaten, you could not scream or cry or the
> punishment would keep up.[95]

Such stories weren't shared with parents or even other students. The culture of fear and abuse ran deep in the community psyche. Children and parents were told that they would go to hell if they shared their stories with the outside world. This culture of silence made them easy targets for sexual predators.

While the principal was following the young teachers around with his flashlight to stop them from fraternizing with the locals, other staff were committing criminal assaults on children at the school. The list of those later charged with physical and sexual assaults included two nuns, two kitchen staff (sexual assaults on young males), a childcare worker (who later escaped conviction of indecent assault against a male because the victim wouldn't testify), and a lay worker who went to work for Indian Affairs but also escaped conviction.[96] But these charges were just the tip of the iceberg of the culture of criminal abuse at the institution.

By 1968, all of the residential schools in Ontario, except St. Anne's, had been shut down or transferred to government control. Negotiations with the Oblates carried on until 1970, when the government purchased the property for $349,000. As part of the transfer of the school to federal authorities, the Department of Indian Affairs requested that the Children's Aid Society be sent in to investigate the families before allowing the children to go home finally.[97] The department never thought of sending in Children's Aid to investigate the care of children at St. Anne's, but now that the children were being sent home to their parents the department wanted full investigations of the home life awaiting them.

This "concern" was actually part of a larger government strategy that utilized Children's Aid to pursue the objective of erasing Indian identity. The department believed that moving children into foster care could eradicate Indian identity more effectively and cheaply than maintaining the residential schools. The process began in various parts of the country during the 1950s as the Indian Act was amended to allow provincial laws of general application, such as child welfare laws, to apply on reserves.

The model of the ideal family in postwar Canada was the nuclear family with two parents; the father worked while the mother tended house, and they lived with their children as a self-contained unit. This simply wasn't a reflection of Indigenous reality, in which aunties, *mooshums* ("grandfathers"), *kookums* ("grandmothers"), and cousins all played roles in providing support to children. This model was negated, however, as provincial child welfare and education laws displaced traditional First Nations customs.

Many children were taken into foster care as soon as they were born, depriving them of knowledge of the extended family units from which they came. The children were raised in completely foreign environments in white neighbourhoods across Canada and the United States.

At the time, there were those who opposed this use of child welfare agencies to undermine family-centred child development. In 1971, Deputy Minister H. Robinson stated that it was better to put funds into supporting families to raise their own children than paying money to put children into institutional care.[98] But the preferred route of the Department of Indian Affairs was to use the provincial foster care system as part of a larger assimilationist agenda. "The Department–Children's Aid Society partnership played a critical role in the campaign to eliminate the residential school system," writes John Milloy.

> Fostering was seen as a most effective method of breaking through the welfare bottleneck and ultimately, in tandem with integration, of closing schools. It had, as did the closing of the schools themselves, the added allure of a financial reward.... Children in foster homes, [R. F.] Davey [director of education at Indian Affairs] believed, could "be cared for less expensively since the maintenance costs are on average less than for residential school placement, but in addition the tremendous capital cost of these large institutions is avoided."[99]

The huge number of children taken from their parents under this agenda has been named the "Sixties Scoop."[100] Theresa Stevens, who works in Indigenous child welfare services in Kenora, Ontario, was recently interviewed by the *National Post* on the devastating impacts of the Sixties Scoop in her community of Wabaseemoong (Whitedog First Nation) in northwestern Ontario. She said that child welfare workers would arrive in the community with a bus that they filled with local children who had been apprehended. The children were then flown to another isolated community and given away to strangers. "When the planes landed at the dock, families there were told they could come down and pick out a kid," she stated. So many children were taken from her community that teachers at the local school were laid off because there weren't enough children left to be taught. Stevens said that the process continued until 1990 and was only stopped at her home reserve when the band members openly defied the child welfare authorities. "They stood at the reserve line on tractors with shotguns saying, 'You aren't coming into our community and taking any more of our children,'" she stated.[101]

Children across Canada subjected to the Sixties Scoop were deprived of their cultural and familial identities. The trauma that they suffered paralleled and continued the damage caused by the residential schools. In recent years, a major class action lawsuit was undertaken by adults who are still struggling to restore links with their families after being separated from them for decades.

ONE LITTLE BOY

On October 21, 1974, thirteen-year-old Charlie Hunter and his friends headed out to go skating on the lake beside St. Anne's Residential School. There had been a flash freeze, and the first ice of the season presented an opportunity too good to ignore. The school staff were inside having a meeting, and it seemed like the perfect opportunity for boys to do what boys do. But with the weather starting to warm up again, the ice was not strong. As they chased each other on the ice of the lake, a partially blind student, Joseph Koostachin, fell through into the cold water.

Charlie came to his aid and pulled Joseph to safety. But in doing so, Charlie slipped under the ice. The children were now shouting for help. Joseph Kataquapit, a local groundskeeper, rushed down to the shore and tried to pull Charlie out of the water. By the time that the boy was pulled out, he had been under the water for at least fifteen minutes. The school's headmaster had the body flown to Timmins for an autopsy. Charlie Hunter's body was then sent to Moosonee, where it was buried.

But Charlie wasn't from Moosonee. His family lived over 500 kilometres away in the isolated village of Weenusk on the Hudson Bay coast. The family was never given an explanation of why the body was buried in Moosonee. Joyce Hunter was born after the death of her older brother. Nonetheless, she knows well how the death devastated her parents and older brothers and sisters. It left a lasting mark on the family. Charlie's older brother George, for example, had been inseparable from Charlie. The two had planned to go to high school together in Timmins. As Joyce mentioned, "my brother George was a year older than Charlie and had made a promise to Charlie that they would go to high school together, so he stayed home that year waiting for Charlie to finish school. After Charlie's death, he never went back to school."[102]

Charlie's parents had to rent a charter plane to go see the gravesite. They had to stop at St. Anne's Residential School to pick up the other children from the family. As Joyce recalled,

> They had to stop at the school to pick up my sister Christine and my brother Sam. The government had just taken Christine that year and cut off all her hair. My mother was eight months pregnant when Charlie died, and her eyes were swollen from crying with Christine being taken and Charlie gone. When my brother Sam saw my mother, he ran up to her and said, "See what you did." He blamed my parents for letting the children be taken. They were devastated. They had to give the children up because it was the law.[103]

After the funeral, Charlie's father, Mike Hunter, spent the next thirty-five years trying to bring his son's body home. One day he called his young daughter Joyce and told her, "I'm old, and I'm tired. I just want my son to come home. I am asking you to take this on."[104]

Joyce Hunter began the process of trying to have her brother's body returned to the community. "I went to see lawyers and the coroner," she said. "I called the minister of Indian Affairs. I spoke with Justice Murray Sinclair of the Truth and Reconciliation Commission. I called all the king's horses and all the king's men and said, 'All we want is for Charlie to be brought home.'"[105]

Joyce is a passionate young woman, and I came to know her well as she looked to my office for help. But the breakthrough came when she met *Toronto Star* reporter Peter Edwards and told him of her family's four-decade struggle to bring Charlie Hunter home to his people. The *Toronto Star* story galvanized the public, and donations came flowing in from Canadians to have the body repatriated to the village of Peawanuck.[106] One offered to pay for the casket. Another offered to pay for the tombstone.

The funeral service was held on Friday, August 19, 2011, in the community's St. Kateri Tekakwitha Roman Catholic Church. During the ceremony, Charlie's brother George sang a song that

The Hunter family gathered for the repatriation of the body of Charlie Hunter to Peawa-nuck. Joyce Hunter is standing in the centre behind the coffin. *Courtesy of Joyce Hunter.*

he had written in a raw moment to his aged parents—"Why Did You Send Me to School?"

At the little cemetery, relatives lowered Charlie into the ground. His father then loaded a shovel of dirt and began to fill in the hole. One by one, the family members, cousins, and then the entire community took their turns filling in the grave. Standing there at the grave weeping softly was Joseph Koostachin with his white cane. Charlie had given his life to save Joseph. Charlie's mother, Pauline, came to hug him and reassure him that it was now okay. Charlie Hunter, the little boy who had been taken away to St. Anne's Residential School, had finally come home.

The family was overwhelmed by the generosity of ordinary Canadians who saw the returning of Charlie Hunter to Peawa-nuck as one small step on the road to reconciliation. Joyce Hunter marvelled at what this gesture meant for her family:

What was done to my family was done on purpose. It was done with malice. It was done to erase what they were as human beings. But in the end all we wanted was to have our brother come home. It took the Canadian people just two weeks to do what the federal government wouldn't do for my parents in a lifetime.[107]

THE DARK LEGACY

St. Anne's Residential School closed in 1975, but it continued to cast a dark shadow across the communities of James Bay for years. Generations from the same families—parents, grandparents, great-grandparents—had suffered at the hands of St. Anne's staff. Some were victims of horrific crimes and assaults. The result was a multitude of intergenerational social problems stemming from alcoholism, low self-esteem, and perpetuation of family violence. Many of the survivors of this abuse had never even told the members of their own families what they had endured.

In 1992, survivors held a conference in Fort Albany to put together a picture of what had gone on at St. Anne's and to find new paths for healing. Over 400 survivors attended. The conference organizers included Andrew Wesley and Edmund Metatawabin. They reached out to former staff asking them to join with the survivors in coming to terms with what had taken place at St. Anne's. No former staff responded. However, in a hopeful show of reconciliation, the newly appointed Catholic bishop of Moosonee, Vincent Cadieux, attended. He said that, as painful as it was to hear these testimonies, the stories needed to be told. He then expressed his hope that the rich tradition of spirituality of the people would give them the strength to rebuild a relationship with the Catholic Church.

The evidence presented was grim—sexual abuse, rape, forced abortions, torture, and psychological trauma. The rapes were undertaken by support staff as well as the religious brothers. A nun handed over one fourteen-year-old victim to the brothers. After the rape, the girl was told that she would be whipped if she told anyone. She was later forced to have an abortion at the school infirmary.

After she told her story at the conference, Edmund Metatawabin and Andrew Wesley tried to comfort her. They walked her back to the school grounds to the site where she had been forced to have the abortion.

> "I miss him, I miss my baby," she said. She stared off into space, like she was lost in another world, the world where her baby still lived.
>
> ...Andrew [Wesley] said a prayer for the baby. Then we all took it in turns to hug Lucy. Afterwards, she said she wanted to be alone.
>
> ...The sun had started to set, and the spruces across the river had sunk into shadow, the rocks' reflections rimmed by darkness. I started to cry.[108]

Following the conference, Chief Edmund Metatawabin went to the Ontario Provincial Police (OPP) and formally asked for a full investigation of the allegations being raised by former students. Constable Greg Delguidice of No. 15 Division of the OPP in Cochrane agreed to undertake an investigation. The police investigation at St. Anne's came a full half century after the RCMP had taken the church's word on what had happened to the three little boys who had run away into the cold James Bay night.

But these were different times. In Newfoundland, a groundbreaking investigation had just taken place into the shocking revelations of sexual and physical abuse at the Mount Cashel orphanage. Across the United States, scattered investigations into sexual crimes at various dioceses were beginning to disclose a disturbing pattern of the abuse of church power to protect sexual predators.

A team of four investigators and one police sergeant opened a special investigation unit. Over a four-year period, the OPP undertook a thorough investigation and collected 992 witness statements that dealt with 860 complaints of abuse at the school. They uncovered a litany of crimes, including rape, beating, sexual assault, and the torture of children with whips, cords, and the school's electric chair.[109] They identified more than 180 perpetrators. However, when it came to pressing charges, it was determined that many of the perpetrators were dead or untraceable. In the end, the police were only able to charge eight perpetrators—all charges pertaining to the final years of the institution.

• • •

Following the criminal convictions in court, St. Anne's survivors continued to push for justice. The federal government agreed to set up a pilot project with the Department of Justice and the Catholic Church in an attempt to settle the claims. This process faltered in 2003 as both the government and the church took aggressive stances in denying the claims of 70 per cent of the people who came forward. "Even people who had suffered extreme abuse . . . were offered nothing," Edmund Metatawabin noted in a 2013 court affidavit.[110]

But St. Anne's was just one of 130 residential schools across the country whose survivors were agitating for justice. Numerous potential class action lawsuits posed a daunting prospect for the federal government and the various Christian churches implicated. In the end, the federal Liberal government of Paul Martin agreed to work with the survivors in an elaborate process of reconciliation, compensation, and remediation known as the Indian Residential School Settlement Agreement.

In 2006, the new government of Stephen Harper was given the task of implementing the agreement. According to Harper's senior adviser at the time, Bruce Carson, the new prime minister didn't want to live up to the agreement. As Harper told Carson, "If I had $5 billion to give away, I would give it to the farmers."[111]

Harper came from the Reform wing of the party known for its deep opposition to Indigenous rights and reconciliation. However, his new Indian Affairs minister, Jim Prentice, was from the old Progressive Conservative wing and pushed cabinet into accepting the moral and legal obligations to follow through.

In 2008, Harper decided to support the agreement. He made a historic apology in the House of Commons to survivors of the residential school system. He pledged that they would receive justice. It seemed like a watershed moment in terms of reconciliation with Indigenous people. As part of the prime minister's commitment, a legal process was put in place to deal with the criminal acts committed against children in residential schools such as St. Anne's.

The result was creation of the Independent Assessment Process (IAP) to adjudicate claims in a manner that survivors were assured would be non-adversarial. Under the IAP, Department of Justice lawyers wore two hats: they acted for Canada as the defendant, but they also had to prepare evidence for the hearings. The Department of Justice was obligated to seek out all documents and evidence regarding the history of abuse at each residential school. This "narrative" of evidence would be presented to the adjudicators, thus sparing individual claimants from having to provide proof to back up their claims. Thus, the narrative provided the basis on which the adjudicators judged the credibility of the stories brought forward by those seeking compensation. But the narrative provided by the Department of Justice was a lie. It stated that there were "no known incidents found in documents regarding sexual abuse at Fort Albany [Indian Residential School]."[112]

Neither the adjudicators nor the lawyers for the claimants were told that the government was sitting on thousands of pages of police and court testimony. Many of the claimants who came forward were self-representing because they were told that the process would be simple and "non-adversarial." They found it to be anything but. As they recounted being shocked in the electric chair or being forced to eat their own vomit, the government's legal representatives challenged their stories. Department of Justice lawyers pointed to the narrative to remind the adjudicators that there was no evidence to back up such allegations. Yet the federal government had evidence that identified the names of 180 perpetrators of physical and sexual abuse, rape, and torture of children at St. Anne's. These crimes were verified by nearly 1,000 witness statements.[113]

Edmund Metatawabin, who became a spokesman for the survivors, writes about the interference by the Department of Justice in his memoir *Up Ghost River*:

> When we tried to prove the issue of widespread abuse, the Department of Justice said they did not have any of the official documents, such as the OPP investigation and court records. And in the official narrative, they denied

that the abuse against us had ever taken place. "No known documents of sexual abuse at Fort Albany IRS," it said. . . . It was hard to understand how such a flagrant misrepresentation of the truth could come from Department of Justice lawyers.[114]

In the summer of 2013, I was approached by Edmund Metatawabin and lawyers Fay Brunning and Suzanne Desrosiers, who laid out the pattern of interference by the government lawyers. In any court process, the failure to disclose evidence or the attempt to suppress documents represents a serious breach of legal obligations. Yet this had been done under the Office of the Attorney General of Canada. I wrote to both Minister of Indian Affairs Bernard Valcourt and Minister of Justice Peter MacKay and reminded the government of its legal obligation to disclose evidence.

In a letter of response, Minister Valcourt admitted that "of course" the government knew all about the evidence but was under no obligation to "seek out" the files because they "belong to the government of Ontario."[115] And anyway, he assured me, the evidence was not admissible under the IAP rules. Both statements were false. The reality was that the government didn't need to "seek out" the evidence because it had already obtained it through a provincial court order when it first became apparent that it was facing major damages for the abuse perpetrated against children at St. Anne's. As well, under the IAP, the government was legally obligated to make the other parties aware that it had this evidence.

Department of Justice lawyers had pressed for access to the police files and court testimonies back in 2003 when they knew that the crimes at St. Anne's would eventually end up in court. At the time, they told a provincial judge that it would be "unfair" for the defendant, Canada, not to have access to evidence that implicated it in potential criminal actions.[116]

The Ontario Superior Court released the documents to them with the proviso that the evidence be made available to future plaintiffs as well.[117] This never happened. What was "fair" in protecting the narrow interests of the federal government as the defendant apparently didn't extend to the survivors who had been beaten, sexually assaulted, and tortured under its watch. The Department of Justice sat on those documents for ten years while

At a press conference in July 2013, Charlie Angus and Edmund Metatawabin hold up the false evidence narrative introduced by the Department of Justice at hearings related to criminal abuse at St. Anne's Residential School. *Courtesy of the author.*

telling the survivors of St. Anne's that there was no evidence to back up their claims of horrific abuse at the institution.

The defiance of the federal government in turning over the evidence to the Independent Assessment Process was brought to the Ontario Superior Court in December 2013. When pressed about why they had suppressed evidence and prepared a false evidence narrative, Department of Justice lawyers shrugged and suggested human error.

In a decision rendered on January 14, 2014, Justice Perell found that the government of Canada had compromised both the IAP and the survivors' ability to achieve justice.[118] He ordered the government to supply all police and court evidence to the hearings.

When the documents were finally turned over in the late summer of 2014, thousands of pages were heavily redacted. Tellingly, the names of criminals who had abused children were blacked out, as were the names of witnesses. This made the evidence virtually useless to the survivors.

In a heartfelt letter to Attorney General Peter MacKay, Edmund Metatawabin wrote on behalf of the survivors of St. Anne's. He asked why the government had done so much to undermine their basic legal rights:

> My god! We were just children, undergoing torture, abuse and neglect from abusers and pedophiles without the protection of our parents nor the government or its agents. It was against the rules for our parents to enter that total institution and therefore they can not be blamed.... The federal government was conspicuously absent and negligent to give us solace and protection.
>
> Now, in 2014, it appears that nothing has changed.[119]

In terms of the shameful history of treatment of the children of St. Anne's, the federal government was consistent to the end. Duncan Campbell Scott would have been proud.

JAMES BAY EDUCATION
AFTER ST. ANNE'S

I n 1976 J. R. Nakogee Primary School opened in the village of Attawapiskat. It was a time of great hope and change in the Treaty 9 territory. The bands spread across the vast reaches of the region had come together as a political entity known as the Grand Council of Treaty 9. This political entity was then transformed by the addition of communities of neighbouring Treaty 5, and it was renamed Nishnawbe Aski Nation (NAN).

On July 7, 1977, Grand Chief Andy Rickard delivered NAN's statement of independence to Premier Bill Davis. NAN saw its political power as resting in recognition of the treaties:

> We . . . declare ourselves to be a free and sovereign nation. We bring you a declaration of independence. . . . Your government has failed to live up to the terms, and the spirit of the treaty. . . . We agreed to share. We lived up to the terms of our agreement. . . . You agreed to share. You said our rights would never be lost. You did not live up to the agreement.[120]

In the village of Attawapiskat, a sense of change was in the air as planes landed daily at the local airstrip. Television arrived, and within three years the first direct dial phones would connect the community to the outside world.[121] Construction of the school encouraged families who lived out on the territory to move into town. Even though many houses lacked running water or indoor plumbing, the presence of a school encouraged the 1,000 people living in the village to think that better days were coming.

Families looked to J. R. Nakogee Primary School as a chance to be involved finally in their children's development. Compared with provincial schools being constructed in the rest of the province, J. R. Nakogee was bare bones, but to the parents who had suffered through St. Anne's it was everything that they could wish for. No longer would their children be taken away. No longer would their young ones be subject to arbitrary and abusive treatment.

After the disastrous residential school experience, the Department of Indian Affairs could have learned many simple lessons on the delivery of education from the provincial systems across the country. Those systems have provided Canada with some of the highest-quality public education in the world. In the provinces and territories, curricula are continually being overhauled by education experts. The delivery of education is legislatively enforced through defined formulas dictating everything from the physical sizes of classrooms to the funding envelopes for textbooks, school maintenance, and school construction. All of these individual line items are protected through "ring fencing," which makes it impossible, for example, to shift money meant for libraries to pay for perks for trustees. Ring fencing also prevents municipal or provincial governments from diverting funds meant for schools to unrelated projects.

The other key driver is that regional school boards, for all their warts and shortcomings, are accountable to parents at the grassroots level while also legally obliged to the provincial education departments above them. This doesn't mean that there aren't discrepancies between richer urban schools and poorer rural schools. And, though the trustee system is far from perfect, it does establish a baseline for input from parents and local communities.

These models would have been easily transferable to schools such as J. R. Nakogee, but that's not how the Department of Indian Affairs worked. As Paquette and Fallon point out, "in contrast to the rich complexity of provincial legislation framing public education across Canada, the legislative and policy bases for First Nations education in Canada is starkly threadbare."[122]

The Indian Act hadn't really been changed since Duncan Campbell Scott's time and had little to offer legislatively for education. Indian Affairs just didn't see itself as being in the business of educating children. The bureaucrats were accountable to their political masters, not accountable to the people whom they were overseeing. And, putting it as bluntly as possible, no government ever won votes by spending money on Indians.

But the fact that J. R. Nakogee began as a poor cousin of other schools in Ontario didn't bother the parents of Attawapiskat. The community finally had its own school and was determined to make the most of it.

As an isolated, fly-in community, Attawapiskat had to rely on diesel fuel for heating. The fuel was shipped there in summer on a barge from Moosonee. It was stored in massive tanks near the local Catholic church. Prior to construction of the school, pipes were laid to feed three 400-gallon underground tanks to supply the school and three 200-gallon underground tanks to supply the teachers' units. The total storage on site was 1,800 gallons of diesel fuel.

Local resident John B. Nakogee was involved in the original construction of the school before moving on to work for Indian Affairs in Moose Factory. After the school opened, it became apparent that there were problems supplying adequate fuel to the teachers' units. Nakogee was at a meeting with department officials when approval was given to run a larger fuel pipe to the teachers' triplex. Laying pipe in the subarctic ground requires an understanding of the impacts of continually shifting ground. The land of the James Bay lowlands is swampy. The term "muskeg" comes from the Cree word *mushkego*, hence the Attawapiskat Cree's designation as being part of the Mushkegowuk (Swampy) Cree of James Bay. An engineer would know that steps would have to be taken to keep the pipe from cracking.

"I was there when the pipe was installed," said Nakogee. "I witnessed the installation. They dug a trench and placed in the cast iron pipe and then back-filled it. There was no insulation whatsoever. It was just an iron pipe sitting in the ground."[123] Reports stated that the pipe was laid at a depth of just two feet in some places.[124] Then as the cold winter hit and the frost pushed into the muskeg, the ground began to shift. At some point, the pipe cracked, and fuel began spilling into the ground under the school. "Almost immediately after the school was built, community workers noticed a strong odour of petroleum fuel around the school and the townhouse unit," Attawapiskat resident Fred Wesley recalled.[125]

At the beginning of the 1980s, John B. Nakogee returned to the community to take a role with the Education Authority. He said that the complaints of illness and diesel fuel smell increased each year:

> During the early 1980s, students began complaining of headaches and nausea. Teachers complained of severe headaches. We checked the crawl space to see if oil had leaked from the furnace but couldn't find anything. But people kept complaining of the smell. It was when we began to dig out ground for an extension [to the school] that the fuel was discovered.[126]

In 1984, the Department of Indian Affairs sent in a team to assess the situation. They made a few suggestions, such as cleaning the base of the foundation and wall studs with detergent, hauling the contaminated soil out from under the school's crawl space, and putting an interceptor drain near the building in an attempt to divert the fuel.[127] Given the vast amounts of fuel leaking under the property, such measures were insufficient.

The problems persisted, and twelve years later, in 1996, Bovar Environmental was sent in to do another assessment.[128] It recommended scraping off the top eighteen inches of soil. Some remedial work was done, but the stench in the classrooms wouldn't go away. Band-Aid solutions were clearly not going to work on ground now heavily saturated with diesel.

• • •

Even as Attawapiskat was struggling with the ground contamination at the school, efforts were being made to move the community forward with numerous education initiatives. In the 1990s, Chief Reg Louttit invited Bill Blake, a former education director for the Timmins Board of Education, to work with the community on improving education outcomes for students. "We established the Education Authority as a separate corporation to handle all federal monies for education," recalled Blake. "We undertook comprehensive assessments of school programs led by former directors of education or supervisors with the provincial Ministry of Education. We established norms to hire teachers trained in Ontario so that they could meet the standards of the provincial curriculum."[129]

The community lacked a place for children to play, so Reg Louttit led a major fundraising campaign to have an arena built. Years of negotiations went into making the arena a reality. It served as a hockey arena, community meeting hall, and gymnasium for the students at the local school.

The Education Authority then set out to have a high school built in the community. Until then, students had to leave home at thirteen to go to school in communities such as Timmins. John B. Nakogee was part of the negotiations that resulted in the building of Father Vezina High School. "Indian Affairs didn't put a red cent into the construction of Father Vezina School," Nakogee recalled. "We built that school ourselves."[130]

The Education Authority secured a loan from the Bank of Nova Scotia to build the school.[131] It opened in 1999. It was named after Father Rodrique Vezina, the beloved Oblate priest who had dedicated himself to serving the families in the western James Bay region. The opening of this school should have been another landmark for the community moving forward with a positive education plan for its youth. But as the high school was opening, the contamination under the grade school had become too problematic to ignore any longer. The smell of diesel in the classrooms was now so bad that children were getting sick. The amount of diesel in the ground was estimated at 151,000 litres[132]—making the school grounds of Attawapiskat one of the largest brownfields in Canada.

An environmental firm, Acres International Limited, conducted an investigation and ranked the site as a level one threat to human health—the highest threat level possible. The call for "IMMEDIATE ACTION" should have raised a sense of urgency at the Department of Indian Affairs, especially since children are much more vulnerable to toxic exposure than adults.[133]

If such a spill occurred in the provincial school system, there would be a legal obligation for both the local school board and the provincial ministry to put a plan in place for ensuring the health and safety of students and staff. Students would be removed immediately from the school and transferred to other facilities. Remediation of the site would be undertaken according to the strictest labour and health standards to ensure student and staff safety. However, J. R. Nakogee Elementary School wasn't part of the provincial system. It was operated by the Department of Indian Affairs, which treated problems at schools the same way that it treated other problems on reserves. When the department is forced to confront a serious issue on a reserve, it seems to have a de facto four-point response:

1. ignore the problem;
2. if ignoring it doesn't make it go away, stall for time;
3. if forced to take action, pay for a study on the basis that the facts need to be determined first; and,
4. if the problem persists, repeat the pattern.

Such strategies are employed by a bureaucracy working with tightly defined spending caps that don't come close to providing the funding necessary to address the myriad of infrastructure shortfalls on reserves. But the fundamental problem with this approach is that saving the department money in the short term results in problems that become massive financial and structural liabilities in the long term. The cleanup of contaminated soil in Attawapiskat has now been listed as one of the largest and costliest brownfield remediation projects in Canada.[134]

In the community, there was increasing concern about the safety of the children. Teachers were quitting because of the side effects of being exposed to the contaminant both in their apartments and in the school. Children in the grade one classroom were passing out from the fumes. Frustrated with the stonewalling by Indian Affairs, the community hired an independent firm, Anebeaaki Environmental, in 1999.[135] Using a standard risk analysis of the threats facing the children, it confirmed that the school grounds constituted a class one threat to human health. Out of a threat ranking of 100, a class one threat is defined as anything over 75. The children of Attawapiskat were going to a school in which the health risk was identified as 89 out of 100.[136]

What did it mean to the children? Students went home with their clothes smelling of diesel fuel. But it wasn't just the smell

Families demonstrate against contaminated school grounds, Attawapiskat, 2000. *Courtesy of Shannen's Dream campaign.*

that was problematic. The children were exposed to a daily carcinogenic cocktail of benzene, toluene, ethyl benzene, xylenes, and TPH (gas/diesel). Symptoms were noticed across the school population—drowsiness, dizziness, headaches, rashes, and nosebleeds. Here's how one mother described the effects (in 2009) on her children:

> They have rashes all over their bodies.... My daughter, under her armpits, had a rash [that] started to smell like rotten meat because her skin was all torn apart, she was scratching it too much, and she was making holes in her armpits, and it smelled like rotten meat. I know the smell because my mom passed away with breast cancer, and I used to smell [the] discharge from her breast, and it smelled the same way as my daughter's armpits....
>
> My other son, my eight-year-old, since a year now he started having bleeding noses and complaining of a headache all the time. [When he wakes up] in the morning, his

face is all bloody because he had a bleeding nose while he was sleeping. I don't know how many pillows I have to throw away because I can't take that blood out.[137]

Such were the symptoms faced by children as young as five. Long-term exposure to these contaminants raises the risk of blood, bone, and liver cancers. Benzene also targets the brain, kidneys, liver, and bone marrow, leading to internal bleeding. As well, the chemicals attack the immune system, causing chromosomal damage and miscarriages.

Exposure to toluene is equally serious. The effects of this chemical were first noted among munitions workers in 1916. By 1949, it had been classified as a toxin, with telltale symptoms being fatigue and headaches. The long-term implications of such exposure include spontaneous abortions in women or babies being born with attention deficit disorders, brain disorders, and serious impacts to the central nervous system. The Canadian Centre for Occupational Health and Safety lists toluene as extremely toxic. Yet bureaucrats knew that children were being exposed daily to the largest toluene site in the country.

When the report was released to the community of Attawapiskat, parents did what parents anywhere would do—they pulled their children out of school and demanded action. Health experts were needed to assess the children. Also needed was a remediation plan that included a full cleanup of the site and the building of a new school. But the government did not send in medical experts to establish exposure levels in the students. As parents protested outside the school, the department offered to put a new roof on the contaminated building (the original roof had begun to leak) in order to encourage families to keep their children in the school.

On May 1, 2000, the band condemned the school and ordered it closed. Pressured to act, the Department of Indian Affairs agreed to send up seven duplex portables with another portable complex for band administration. The portables were set up adjacent to the large brownfield in the heart of Attawapiskat. Dust from the contaminated site blew into the portables and surrounding playing field.

Soon after the school closed, Minister of Indian Affairs Robert Nault attended a meeting with the chiefs of the Mushkegowuk

Tribal Council, which represented the James Bay communities.[138] John B. Nakogee was at the meeting and said that "Robert Nault assured us that there would be a new school built. It will go ahead, and we will do everything to make it happen, he said. The students were very happy, but nothing ever happened."[139]

Nakogee was told by the regional director of Indian Affairs that, despite Nault's promise, it would take at least ten years for Attawapiskat to see a school. The school that had been such a symbol of hope for the community was now abandoned, and it posed serious health concerns for the children being educated in its shadow.

PART II

FIRE AND WATER, 2004–06

n 2004, I was elected as a Member of Parliament in the riding of Timmins-James Bay. At the time, I knew very little of the history of Treaty 9, which covers the vast majority of the constituency. In the northern part of the riding, the James Bay communities of Moose Factory, Fort Albany, Kashechewan, Attawapiskat, and Peawanuck are members of the Mushkego (Swampy) Cree. They share a common history and language.

On my first trips to James Bay, I realized how development in the region was being hampered by a series of interrelated crises in infrastructure. Not only were housing, water treatment, and education badly underfunded, but also there were no enforceable standards for ensuring public safety. Unlike provincial jurisdictions, the reserves are under the Indian Act, and there are no legal benchmarks for ensuring safe water, adequate building construction, fire protection, health services, child welfare, and, of course, educational outcomes. The lack of enforceable standards has allowed the federal government to ignore serious threats to the health, safety, and general well-being of the citizens under its jurisdiction.

This section examines the catastrophic water crisis of Kashechewan of 2005–06 as well as the tragic fires and floods that plagued the community. On a political level, the magnitude of the crises that affected Kashechewan put the Fourth World conditions of the northern Treaty 9 region on the national agenda.

JAMES BAY JOURNEY

The immensity of the land of the Mushkego Cree is something to behold. James Bay is a massive drainage basin for the inland rivers of northern Ontario and Quebec. At the southern tip of James Bay, the mighty Abitibi and Mattagami Rivers flow into the larger Moose River that then empties into the bay just south of Moose Factory Island. A rail line connects the villages of Moosonee and Moose Factory with Cochrane to the south. There are no roads in this country (other than a temporary ice road that connects the communities in the frozen months of January to March). To get to the communities spread out along the western shore of the bay (Fort Albany, Kashechewan, Attawapiskat, and Peawanuck) requires a plane.

The first time that I flew over the Moose River toward the airport at Moosonee was with my provincial colleague MPP Gilles Bisson. We had come north to attend a Cree cultural festival being held at Moose Factory in the summer of 2004. Gilles had been representing these communities for a number of years. As our plane swayed and swished toward the airport, he sat eating a ham sandwich and talking about how much I would love the region and its people. As he spoke, I was clutching a barf bag in my lap, wondering what I had gotten myself into.

The Cree gathering was a week-long festival of music, meetings, and celebration. One night there was a large gathering at the local arena to thank teacher John Delaney for his years of service to the region. John had come north to Moose Factory in the 1960s as a young teacher. For decades, he had been a mainstay of the community with his dedication to youth leadership, academics, and sports. He married locally and raised his family in Moose

Factory. As it became known that he was dying of cancer, the community wanted to thank him for his dedication.

His former students, now leaders in their own right, came out to pay tribute to the man who had inspired them to succeed. They told stories and presented him with gifts. This was a good introduction for me to the James Bay Cree, who place such a high value on mentoring young people.

With the tribute to Delaney complete, the fiddlers went to the stage for the step-dancing competitions. Since the earliest days of the fur trade in the 1600s, James Bay fiddlers have been known for their prowess. Cree step-dance groups from both the Ontario side and the Quebec side of the bay competed against each other in a flurry of colour, sweat, and style.

During the intermission, Deputy Chief Charlie Cheechoo of the Moose Cree First Nation asked me if I would like to be introduced from the stage. He told me that this was the best way of getting known to my new constituents. I immediately jumped at the chance.

He went to the microphone on stage and announced, "Hey, everybody, we have a guest of honour tonight, our new MP—Charlie Angus." I was caught in the glare of a spotlight that singled me out in the dark arena. "We have another guest, Mr. Gilles Bisson, our provincial MPP." A second spotlight caught Bisson in its hold. "And," Cheechoo added, pausing for effect, "in our culture, the politicians have to dance."

With that, the band kicked into a high-octane version of "St. Anne's Reel." The crowd clapped rhythmically, and as much as we tried to slink into the darkness the spotlights acted as tractor beams on us. We had no choice but to move out to the dance floor and try to step-dance. Seated around the dance floor were elders. We begged some of the older women to get up and dance with us to ease our humiliating attempt to do-si-do. They were laughing so hard that some of them had tears rolling down their faces. After what seemed like an eternity, one old woman came out to join us and then another. The crowd roared approvingly. Soon there were a number of people up dancing with us.

When it was all said and done, Charlie Cheechoo came up and slapped me on the back. "Congratulations. You did more in five minutes than the last MP did in ten years. If you do nothing else up here, people will always remember that you were a good sport tonight."

His comments spoke to a deeper issue—the historical disconnect between this isolated region and political representation in Ottawa. I had worked for the previous three years before the election with the Algonquin Nation in Quebec and thought myself knowledgeable about First Nations land issues and funding problems with INAC (Indian and Northern Affairs Canada). But the issues of the James Bay communities were overwhelming. It was like landing in a foreign country. The landscape of bogs, stunted trees, and dramatic colourings of dark greens, greys, and tans was completely different from the thick boreal landscapes that I knew south of Moosonee. So were the realities of living in communities with substandard housing, health, and education.

As I travelled farther up the coast, it seemed as if I had left Canada behind and entered a veritable Fourth World. In Attawapiskat, nearly 2,000 people lived in poorly constructed and overcrowded homes. The community had little social infrastructure other than the local food and clothing outlet (the Northern Store), the Catholic church, and the hockey arena.

But the main issue that concerned people in Attawapiskat was the broken promise to build a proper grade school. It had been four years since the school had been condemned, and, despite the promise of former Minister of Indian Affairs Robert Nault that the portables would be temporary, the federal government seemed to be perpetually stalling on action.

There was a growing sense of hopelessness among the students that was a cause of worry for the parents. During a visit to the school, I met Councillor Andrew Koostachin, and we immediately became good friends. His children, including his daughters Serena and Shannen, were being educated in the portables. He spent his days encouraging students to keep up their studies even though some began dropping out as early as grade four.

"I saw a little boy walking in the field during school hours," he told me, "and I said to him, 'You should be in school.' 'What's the point?' the boy replied, pointing to the cluster of portables. 'It's not a real school.'"

Andrew's father-in-law, John B. Nakogee, was equally frustrated with the deteriorating condition of education in Attawapiskat.

"These portables," he explained, "are little more than sheds. Hangars where people store their planes are better than the portables our children are being educated in."

Clara Corbiere taught grade one in the portables. She recalled being shocked at the "horrible" conditions of the learning environment:

> There was a two-inch gap under the door, and the class faced the airport. Every time a plane took off, the class filled with the smell of air[plane] fuel. The children had to get bundled up in the cold or rain to go to gym class at the arena and then would sit soaking wet all day. The smell of the diesel contamination was all over the site. It was a horrible condition for educating little children.[1]

In these early visits, I knew very little about the history of the Mushkego Cree and their signing of Treaty 9. But people in the community knew the treaty well. Stan Louttit's grandfather had signed the treaty. As grand chief of the Mushkegowuk Tribal Council, Louttit spoke to me of the importance of honouring an agreement that promised proper education for the children. Now, a full century after that promise had been made and broken, the communities were still working to ensure that Canada respected the spirit of the treaty. As a newly elected MP, I was seeing how history continued to impact these communities. It was a history that I had not been taught in school.

THE WATER CRISIS

Kashechewan is a place of peeling paint and
smashed windows, of children with chronic skin
rashes who play on filthy mattresses, and of a
water supply that's so filthy, it has already made
half of its residents sick.
—CANADIAN PRESS[2]

As serious as the issues were in Attawapiskat, the situation in Kashechewan First Nation (100 kilometres to the south) was even starker. The people of Kashechewan were originally members of the neighbouring Fort Albany Band, but the communities broke apart roughly along religious lines (Fort Albany being Catholic and Kashechewan being Anglican/Protestant). Fort Albany was on the south side of the large Albany River; Kashechewan was established on the north side by the Department of Indian Affairs in 1957. The location of Kashechewan was problematic from the beginning because it was on a flood plain. A large dirt wall had been built around the community to hold back the annual rise of the Albany flood water.

The community was plagued by chronically underfunded infrastructure. The housing stock was in terrible condition. There was no fire hall. The police unit was set up in a badly deteriorated house, and the local medical station had been flooded out by backed-up sewage on a number of occasions. The water plant was seriously deficient, and the community was on a permanent boiled water advisory. Life on a flood plain created perpetual insecurity for the families.

Living within the ring of the large dike exacted a psychological toll on people since they couldn't even see the land and river
on which their culture was based. As we stood in the shadow of
the dirt wall, resident Rebecca Friday asked me a blunt question:
"How would you like to raise your children in a prisoner of war
camp?"

The image of the northern reserve as an internment camp also
struck a chord with Allan Teramura, director of the Royal Architectural Institute of Canada.[3] His mother spent her childhood in
an internment camp for Japanese Canadians, and he found haunting similarities to Kashechewan. "When I showed my mother
photographs of Kash, she recognized it as the same as where she
grew up in the internment camps. I had thought the days of putting people in camps were over," Teramura said.[4]

Teramura began to look into the architectural designs of
northern reserves to determine why such little thought has gone
into the development of sustainable communities. He found a few
examples of design innovation in isolated reserves that have been
successful.[5] However, despite these examples of how to make more
livable communities, the reserves across the Treaty 9 region have
been maintained in a depressingly consistent pattern of social
failure. At the heart of the problem, stated Teramura, is that the
reserve is constructed not as a community but as a holding camp:

> As an architect, I looked at the brutally pragmatic layout
> that had no sense of any Indigenous identity and the fact
> that everything has been constructed in the most miserly
> way. It made me realize that this was a camp. A camp has
> a finite lifespan and is created for a specific purpose. You
> don't make long-term investment. It is built and then left
> in a state of limbo. What are you trying to accomplish
> with these huge camps? If it is to demoralize people so
> they will leave and become assimilated, it is a policy that
> has failed. The people are still there, and they have shown
> themselves to be indestructible.[6]

Communities like Kashechewan have been compared with
Third World shanty towns, but Teramura believes that there are
fundamental differences between them. One crucial difference is

The community as a holding camp. Grade school portables at Kashechewan First Nation, 2014. *Courtesy of the author.*

the role played by the bureaucracy in any development on reserves. The Indian Act limits all manner of local control. According to Teramura, this creates a special set of dependencies:

> The camp is different than Third World housing. Shanty towns are self-built. They at least have some manner of cultural identity, whereas in the north there is no sense of local place or identity. It isn't just the physical conformity but the inability to control your surroundings. When you incarcerate a population you don't give them the agency to control their surroundings.[7]

This image of an internal displacement camp can't be applied to all reserves. Across Canada's more than 600 First Nations is a wide variety of differences in social, economic, and infrastructure development. But reserves, regardless of their locations, tend to be much lower on the scale of indicators for quality of life than non-Native communities. Certainly, the poverty in James Bay is exacerbated by isolation and lack of road access. As in so many northern reserves, though, the underfunded and failing infrastructure fosters a perpetual cycle of uncertainty and crisis. It is hard for a community to move toward economic sustainability when its citizens are continually living on the edge of crisis.

What offsets this cycle of perpetual crisis is an incredible sense of social solidarity that keeps the communities together. I was moved by this sense of warmth on my first visit to James Bay. Teramura was equally struck by the sense of community when he visited Kashechewan in 2014: "Going into Kash was overwhelming. What struck me was how welcoming and friendly the people were. They have every reason to be suspicious of outsiders, but the sense of optimism and humanity really struck me, despite the sheer crappiness of everything that was around them."[8]

One of the first people to welcome me in the community was Chief Leo Friday. He had been attempting to get the Department of Indian Affairs to sit down with the community and address the enormous shortfalls facing it. So far, most of his appeals had fallen on deaf ears. We worked together to try to engage Indian Affairs in a plan to begin addressing the short-term, medium-term, and long-term infrastructure problems plaguing the community.

One of its biggest concerns was water safety. The water treatment plant was only ten years old but began to fail soon after it was built. The community had been on a boiled water advisory for years. The fact that a new water plant had failed so quickly should have warranted an investigation into how contracts were awarded and overseen by Indian Affairs, but for that to happen Kashechewan would have to take a number and stand in line.

Between 1995 and 2003, Indian Affairs spent $1.9 billion on water and sewage plants for First Nations in Canada.[9] But there was little to show for such expenditures. In 2005, thirty-eight First Nations communities in Ontario alone were on long-term boiled water advisories. Many of them had already received significant investments in water treatment plants.[10] Despite the billions spent, the advisories remained in effect.

In a report prepared for the auditor general by the commissioner of the environment and sustainable development, the failings of the Indian Affairs approach were exposed. The report pointed to the example of a $3 million water plant built in a community where "people living in about half of the 500 houses . . . do not have running water, from pipes or cisterns, and some have to haul their water from watering points."[11] Although the investment in a new water plant looked excellent on paper, the department had failed to make plans to connect the plant to the houses. After government officials cut the ribbon at the new plant and left, people were still hauling water in buckets to their homes.

Numerous other factors had resulted in such a clear failure in basic water infrastructure. In determining the size of the treatment plant, Indian Affairs had based its capacity on a model that counted two children per family. This model was completely unsuited to isolated reserves, where families had many children and homes often contained multiple families. This meant that, by the time the plant was finally operational, it was already under capacity in its ability to provide quality drinking water to local families.

In explaining to the *Toronto Star* how water treatment plants could have been constructed on such a poor planning principle, Indian Affairs official Glenn Gilbert said that the department had been "surprised along the way" by higher-than-anticipated population growth in the affected reserves, but that the department was now "taking that into account."[12]

Most shocking was that, when approving contracts, Indian Affairs had no standards in place for ensuring proper design, construction, and operation of water treatment plants. There were no plans for training local people to operate the plants and no policies on regular inspection or upkeep to ensure that they operated safely.[13] In fact, the report by the commissioner of the environment and sustainable development pointed out that there was "limited evidence" that the projects approved by the department even met basic building codes.[14]

In the case of Kashechewan, the water treatment plant's intake pipe was placed 150 metres downstream from a sewage lagoon. Whenever there were heavy rains or spring floods, there was the threat of raw sewage leaking out of the lagoon and being drawn into the water system.

In July 2005, I visited the water treatment plant with NDP leader Jack Layton. As the former president of the Canadian Federation of Municipalities, Jack knew a fair bit about municipal water and sewage treatment. He was very concerned about water safety in

Kashechewan. He told national media that a potential threat to human health was looming.

I wrote to Prime Minister Paul Martin as well as Minister of Indian Affairs Andy Scott, calling on them to sit down with the community to address the infrastructure crisis. My letter was just one of many calling for action in various communities over the lack of access to clean water.

As these issues were playing out across Indian country, the government of Ontario was undertaking a massive overhaul of the province's water regulations. The Clean Water Act was brought in by the newly elected provincial Liberals in response to the Walkerton water crisis. In May 2000, E. coli contamination in the municipal water system at Walkerton made 2,800 people sick and left seven people dead. Following a major inquiry by Justice Dennis O'Connor, the province overhauled water regulations, training requirements, and standards for every community in its jurisdiction. But reserves, falling under federal jurisdiction, were not covered.

So, despite awareness of the dangers posed by the Walkerton tragedy, Ontario First Nations communities continued to be plagued by inadequate water standards. At Gull Bay First Nation, 150 kilometres north of Thunder Bay, concerns were raised about a water treatment plant that had failed soon after construction. The new plant was shut down because of health risks posed to residents. It was then learned that Indian Affairs had failed to obtain proper planning approval. Although the department had spent $5 million on construction, the plant did not meet basic regulations.

Interviewed by the *National Post,* Chief King of Gull Bay stated that "there is gross mismanagement in our community. How can the bureaucrats get away with this? The Minister is backing them up and saying they are doing an excellent job, but he is the one responsible for what his Department does."[15]

Money spent on failed water treatment plants was money directed away from equally pressing concerns on isolated First Nations communities, such as housing and education. The *National Post* pointed out that the failure to deal with mould and fungal contamination in housing at Gull Bay resulted in forty families having to live in hotels. While the band and INAC bickered over how to remediate the housing crisis, the hotel bill was more than $80,000 a month. If the government had developed a plan to replace the damaged housing stock, it could have alleviated the problem for less money than was being spent on the ongoing Band-Aid responses.

• • •

On October 14, 2005, Health Canada confirmed that a water sample sent from the water treatment plant in Kashechewan contained high levels of E. coli bacteria. Despite the lessons of Walkerton, though, Health Canada's recommendation was to maintain the status quo and simply call on people to boil water. The problem was that families had been boiling water for years. What about bathing children? Health officials didn't think that this would be a problem. In calls with officials from Indian Affairs and Health Canada, the local medical team laid out the serious health issues facing the community from dirty water—diarrhea, stomach pains (two telltale symptoms of E. coli contamination), as well as skin rashes and other ailments.

The tragedy at Walkerton opened the public's eyes to the serious dangers posed by E. coli contamination. Although many people exposed to E. coli suffer short-term bouts of severe stomach pain and diarrhea, the bacteria can lead to more serious problems among younger and older people, such as kidney failure, paralysis, blindness, and hemolytic uremic syndrome (HUS), a life-threatening condition that requires treatment in an intensive care unit. Health Canada's simple advice to boil water was clearly insufficient given the threats posed.

On October 17, 2005, I asked Minister of Health Ujjal Dosanjh in the House of Commons about the crisis in Kashechewan:

> This past weekend an E. coli outbreak hit the community. The school is closed, the health centre is closed, and a Health Canada official told the people that it was perfectly safe to bathe their children in E. coli–contaminated bathwater. That is like telling those Cree people to bathe their children in toilet water. Would the health minister or any of his staff be willing to come up to Kashechewan and bathe their children in this kind of water?[16]

Dosanjh promised to look into the issue. Nothing happened. On October 17, 2005, the band declared a state of emergency and called for an evacuation of the community until the extent of the contamination could be determined.

In Ontario, declarations of states of emergency are handled by the provincial agency Emergency Measures Ontario (EMO). However, since the declaration came from a reserve, EMO contacted Indian Affairs to see if the department would be willing to pay for the evacuation. Indian Affairs said no. In an attempt to reassure the community, the government offered to fly up bottled water, initially sending 250 eighteen-litre bottles. That was enough for one litre of water per person for two days.

In Kashechewan, people were enraged by the lacklustre response. More to the point, they were genuinely frightened. At a community meeting, a father held up his daughter to show the scabs and rashes on her arms. An old woman revealed the Band-Aids that covered her arms. These sores had come from exposure to water-borne parasites.

Rebecca Friday shared the community's anger with the national media: "We are so frustrated. I don't care what they say anymore. I don't care what INAC says. We are fed up—sick and tired and angry."[17]

As a newly elected MP in the fourth party, I was doing everything that I could to get the federal government to respond to the gravity of the situation. I was working closely with my provincial colleague at the Ontario legislature as well as the political and medical leaders of James Bay. Perhaps because the deprivation faced by people in Kashechewan was so stunning, the media began to push the government for an explanation. By October 19, 2005, failure of the government to respond had become a full-fledged media storm. The opposition Conservatives now jumped into the fray, pointing to the Kashechewan water crisis as yet another sign of Liberal incompetence. Aboriginal Affairs critic Jim Prentice challenged the Paul Martin government:

> This [the Kashechewan water crisis] did not happen in a Third World country. This happened in Ontario and it happened to Aboriginal Canadians. In just a moment the minister is going to tell us yet again that he is working on it.

The truth is that after two billion dollars and twelve years, Aboriginal Canadians are still drinking contaminated water. If the minister will not accept personal responsibility, will he tell the House who is accountable?[18]

Minister Andy Scott was likable but not very effective. He was also in charge of a ministry that had a long history of waiting out stories of squalor and departmental mismanagement on reserves. But perhaps because of the recent events in Walkerton the Kashechewan story had staying power. As the pressure mounted on Scott, the department sent more bottles of water, promising to keep nearly 2,000 people safe with daily flights of 1,400 bottles of water.

But then late on October 22, 2005, Dr. Murray Trusler, the chief medical officer at James Bay, stepped forward. He had just returned from a visit to the community, and he was willing to participate in a national press conference with regional leaders to discuss the health threats there. Trusler had decades of experience with far north health issues. He understood the issues of the region and had taken the important step of photographing what he had witnessed. He produced a PowerPoint presentation showing children afflicted with horrid skin ailments from their exposure to dirty water.

The obvious choice for this press conference was Ottawa, where Minister Scott was like a deer in the headlights of the growing Kashechewan crisis. But in a strategy meeting that I participated in with Chief Leo Friday, Grand Chief Stan Louttit, and MPP Gilles Bisson, it was decided to take the issue to the provincial legislature, Queen's Park. Given the political markers laid down by the provincial Liberal government in response to the Walkerton Inquiry, it raised the question why Indigenous people living in Ontario were not included in this new push for water safety.

The press conference was held at Queen's Park on October 24, 2005. Dr. Trusler spoke of the health impacts that he had witnessed, including his concern that hepatitis A and B could now be in the water supply. The reality was that, if E. coli and other possible contaminants were in the system, a serious overhaul of the whole water and sewage system was immediately required. Given the overall collapse of infrastructure in the community, it simply wasn't feasible to believe that this could be done without moving

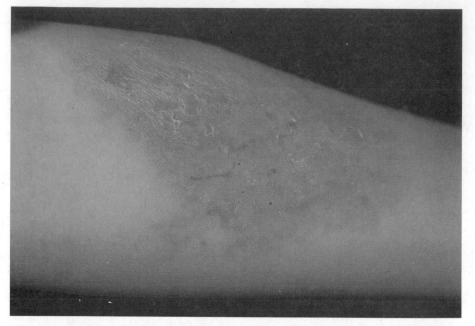

Open wound on child's arm from exposure to water-borne parasites in Kashechewan. This was one of the photographs used by Dr. Murray Trusler in his press conference on the crisis unfolding in the community. *Courtesy of the author.*

the community members out until the safety of the water could be assured.

What drove Trusler's point home was a slide show of photographs that he had taken of young children suffering from numerous infections and rashes. The most noticeable were the effects of a chronic bacterial infection caused by water-borne parasites that live under the skin. One particularly disturbing photograph showed a baby with a soother in his mouth, his body covered in horrific burn scars from an accident.[19] This child had to be bathed in the heavily chlorinated water that made the pain from the burns excruciating. Veteran media in the press gallery winced and shifted uncomfortably as Trusler spoke. The doctor stated that, if something wasn't done by either level of government, people could die.

At the end of the press conference, there was a stunned silence among journalists. Richard Brennan, a senior journalist with the *Toronto Star,* opened the media questions with one simple question: "Who is responsible for this?"

Gilles Bisson pointed out that since 2003 the provincial government had been sitting on a report showing that the Kashechewan water treatment plant was substandard and that the workers lacked basic training. "There's something wrong here.... Post-Walkerton, we would think something would have been done."[20] Bisson commented further on the government's inaction: "It's rather unfortunate that we have to drag people down from Kashechewan and have to show pictures to get this government to act on what I think is a most basic issue: the question of people's safety."[21]

The McGuinty Liberals were now drawn into the fray and scrambled for a response. David Ramsay, the provincial Aboriginal Affairs minister, initially responded to media calls by stating that the province was waiting on direction from Minister Andy Scott, who had stated that the federal government would be ready to respond in another ten days.[22]

This response didn't cut it. And as the provincial Liberals began to feel increasing heat from the media, Premier McGuinty ordered a full evacuation of the community. That the provincial government moved decisively while the federal government seemed to be trapped in inertia added to the political pressure on Paul Martin and Andy Scott. Opposition leader Stephen Harper accused the prime minister of dithering. He demanded that Scott resign for "one of the saddest and most disgraceful performances by a minister in the history of this House."[23]

As pressure mounted in the House of Commons, the national media focused on the question of how a community could be allowed to deteriorate so badly under a government's watch. A *National Post* column was typical of the coverage:

If there were an Olympics for government mismanagement, the Department of Indian and Northern Affairs would lead the medals table.... Yesterday, Indian Affairs Minister Andy Scott visited the Kashechewan First Nation, ... [where] there have been reports of diarrhoea, headaches and fevers, and residents are convinced that some deaths are related. Visiting officials were offered jugs of drinking water by residents at a community meeting but declined, and who can blame them ....[24]

The issues drawing attention were the collapsed infrastructure and the precarious state of a community living on a flood plain. Provincial minister David Ramsay suggested that the infrastructure was so broken that the community needed to be rebuilt from scratch: "From what we're hearing, the infrastructure seems in such bad shape, it doesn't seem reasonable to start rebuilding on that particular site."[25]

As the crisis dragged on, Andy Scott flew to Kashechewan and was clearly affected by the conditions he encountered. On October 28, 2005, he sat down in Ottawa with community leaders of Kashechewan to discuss a long-term solution. To get to this meeting, our delegation had to push our way through a wall of media cameras and journalists gathered outside the Confederation Building on Parliament Hill. We entered Scott's office to be greeted by the minister, senior bureaucrats, and representatives of the Privy Council. On our side were Chief Leo Friday, National Chief Phil Fontaine, and Grand Chief Stan Louttit. Scott looked drained and nervous.

The government offered to move the community to one of five possible locations (chosen by the community) on their territory. The work of choosing an eventual new community site would begin in the coming spring. Once the site was identified, the government would build fifty homes a year over a ten-year period until the new community of Kashechewan was fully established with a school, community centre, proper medical centre, band office, and functional water and sewage systems. In the meantime, the government would immediately begin moving in supplies to repair the water treatment plant and a number of homes.

When the agreement was put in front of the chief, it was noted that none of these verbal commitments was on paper. It was like Treaty 9 all over again. The only thing that the agreement committed to was building a new subdivision. The officials were quick to reassure the delegation of the goodwill of the government. Surely, with so many senior bureaucrats sitting at the table, we could take the government at its word.

Chief Friday needed the goodwill of the department because implementation of the agreement would be done over a long period of time. Advised by the national and regional leaders to support the accord, he signed it. The media were informed that the community of Kashechewan would finally be moved to safer ground.

• • •

Within two weeks of the Kashechewan agreement, Minister Andy Scott agreed to meet a delegation from Attawapiskat who had come to discuss the need for a new school. There was concern among the delegation that the financial commitment to rebuilding Kashechewan would drain infrastructure funds from other First Nations communities in Ontario. This was how Indian Affairs had always responded to a serious crisis—by reallocating resources from equally needy communities to respond to the crisis of the moment. If the government followed through on its promise to move Kashechewan, then it was unlikely that it would agree to fund the school in Attawapiskat.

Among the delegation from Attawapiskat were two youths from the grade eight class at J. R. Nakogee School: Serena Koostachin and Deanna Mudd. Before the meeting with Scott, they spoke at a press conference at which the educational crisis in Attawapiskat was laid out. When they went into the meeting with the government bureaucrats, these two young students seemed to be overwhelmed by the size of the room and the nature of the negotiations between their elders and the government. But they spoke passionately of the need for a school. Scott agreed with their sentiments and stated the government's intention to have the new school built.

After the meeting with Indian Affairs officials, I asked thirteen-year-old Serena if she had been nervous or frightened when she spoke to the government officials about the need for a school. She stated firmly, "I wasn't afraid because I was speaking on behalf of my people."

When the news that a school was to be built was told to the students back home, there was incredible excitement. Speaking to the *Timmins Daily Press*, Chief Mike Carpenter described the response of the children: "You should have heard the kids. I went to the school, I told the students by announcing it on the radio. They were all yelling. One of the teachers told me one of the kids had remarked, 'Gee, now I'll be able to graduate with a new school.'"[26]

What wasn't discussed at the meeting was how Indian Affairs would fund an expensive new project like the Attawapiskat school while committing to a full-scale rebuilding of Kashechewan. The department had strict funding caps on infrastructure projects, and when a new and unexpected spending issue came up (such as moving the community of Kashechewan) the money had to be poached from other projects already on the books.

• • •

Paul Martin fled the heat of the Kashechewan crisis to head to Kelowna, British Columbia, where he made even larger financial promises. At a summit of First Nations leaders, he announced the Kelowna Accord, which included $5 billion in infrastructure and development for First Nations communities over the next five years. The promises made at Kelowna came at the end of a thirteen-year run of government in which the Liberals had tightly squeezed budgets for First Nations.

Martin's promise was made on November 25, 2005. It was one among a number of huge promises made as his government stared down defeat in the House of Commons for the sponsorship scandal. As the Liberals were making promises to fund the Kelowna Accord, they also announced a $5 billion pledge to follow through finally on their long-promised national child-care program. They then promised to start getting serious finally about the Kyoto Protocol despite years of rising greenhouse gas levels in Canada.

All of these promises were dependent on one huge issue—the ability of Martin's damaged government to survive a looming election. Martin had promised to call an election thirty days after the final report by Justice Gomery on the sponsorship scandal; that election would happen in February or March 2006, before any of these promises could be enacted. He didn't make it.

Three days after making the Kelowna Accord announcement, Martin went back to the House of Commons and was defeated in a non-confidence vote. Whether or not he intended to follow through finally on the Liberal government's long-standing list of unfulfilled promises was moot. His political road had ended.

FIRE AND FLOOD

Leo Friday, chief of the Kashechewan First Nation, returned to his community and a hero's welcome yesterday after winning a promise from the federal government to build his people a brand new home. As his plane touched down on the reserve's bumpy gravel strip 400 kilometres north of Timmins, locals whistled and blasted air horns. Six men beat a traditional welcome on a moose-skin drum. Grateful residents, some of them near tears, lined up to shake the chief's hand as another plane waited to take sick and needy residents to communities in the south.
—JULIUS STRAUSS[27]

I n January 2006, Stephen Harper's Conservatives were elected with a minority government. Perhaps sensing how mishandling the Indian Affairs file had damaged the credibility of the Martin government, Harper appointed Jim Prentice to the portfolio. Prentice was one of his most trusted MPs and knew the issues well. Not surprisingly, in the wake of the Kashechewan debacle, he made the issue of establishing clean water on reserves a priority for the new Conservative government.[28]

In the James Bay region of Ontario, the big question was whether or not Prentice would honour the agreements made in the dying days of the Martin government to Kashechewan and Attawapiskat. Senior bureaucrats continued to negotiate with Attawapiskat on the school project. Prentice met with Attawapiskat chief Mike Carpenter in Timmins on June 27, 2006, where he reiterated the government's support to remediate the toxic school grounds and stated his commitment to push the new school project forward. He put these commitments in writing in

December 2006.[29] Officials from Indian Affairs followed up with a series of letters (as late as July 30, 2007) to confirm the process of negotiations for building the school.[30]

Leaders at James Bay were hopeful that Prentice might just have the political power at the cabinet table to get First Nations infrastructure funding on the agenda. But within the region, tragedy and crisis continued to plague the communities. Nowhere was the tragedy felt more than in Kashechewan. On January 8, 2006, a fire broke out in the community's makeshift police detachment. Two young men—Jamie Goodwin and Ricardo Wesley—were being held overnight in the jerry-rigged jail cells of the local Nishnawbe Aski Police station (NAPs). Like other services in isolated reserve communities, NAPs was cash starved even though the funding was shared between the federal and provincial governments.

The Kashechewan detachment was little more than a shack. As the fire spread through the building, NAPs officer Claudius Koosees tried in vain to unlock the padlock to free the men. He was badly burned but kept trying. It was to no avail. A second officer, Silas Reuben, pulled Koosees out of the burning building. "Claudius wasn't leaving. . . . He would have died too," stated a witness.[31]

Traumatized community members listened to the men screaming as they died in their makeshift cells. These deaths shook the community. The funeral service for the men was over four hours in length as anguished community members stood to speak about their feelings of grief and pain. Rebecca Friday explained the impact to national media: "We were just coming back with a little bit of relief from the water situation, but with this happening it is really devastating for all of the people. No one is functioning, and it is very, very hard. The community is so close together it is hard for anybody to smile for the past few days."[32]

At the inquest, it was noted that, if the unit had had a basic water suppression system, it might have saved the lives of the two men. Workable sprinkler systems are a legal requirement in any public building in Ontario, but Kashechewan as a reserve was not subject to this basic standard—even though the police unit was partially funded by provincial authorities.

Police in federal and provincial jurisdictions operate under legislative standards for ensuring the health and safety of officers with regard to resources and supports. Such standards, however, do not extend to First Nations police forces. So, for NAPs police who serve the communities of Treaty 9, some detachments were so substandard that officers often lacked backup, functional radios, and appropriate sleeping quarters. Some detachments were heated by a wood fire in an oil barrel. As one officer explained to me, "I've had to sleep in places that you wouldn't let your dog sleep."[33]

On April 12, 2006, a second tragedy hit Kashechewan when a fire swept through an overcrowded home of twenty-one people. All of them escaped except four-year-old Trina Martin, left behind in the chaotic panic to get out. She perished in the flames. The community had been negotiating with Indian Affairs for years for basic firefighting equipment and a proper fire hall, but plans sat in a bureaucratic file folder as the flames consumed Trina's home.

Like the deaths of Goodwin and Wesley, Trina's death hit the community hard. The family buried the little white casket in the graveyard on the flat lands leading to the airport. Barely was the last shovel of frozen dirt on the grave when the Albany River began to rise. As ice backed up in the annual spring breakup, the water rose fifteen feet in just two days. On April 23, 2006, an evacuation was declared, the third in a single year.[34]

This flood was a catastrophe. As water spread across the land, it flooded the graveyard, washing away the flowers that had just been laid. The water reached the airport, and the electrical system shorted out. Crews on the ground had to light fires to guide the planes in to the landing strip.[35] The water treatment plant, which had received major upgrades since the E. coli disaster, was badly damaged. Basements became full of dirty water, and the nurses' station was contaminated by backed-up sewage.

Indian Affairs spokesperson Deidra McCracken reassured the media that the government was still looking at plans to move the community to higher ground.[36] Given the amount of damage done to the community by the 2006 flood, the provincial government called on the federal Conservatives to accelerate the process of moving the community to the new location (known as Site 5). "We've just got to give these people a safe place to live," declared provincial minister David Ramsay.[37]

The move never happened. On May 25, 2007, Minister of Indian Affairs Jim Prentice announced that the government was not going to follow through on its commitment to move the community to a new location. The community would remain on the flood plain. Prentice promised to invest $209 million over the coming five to seven years to repair the dike and make the community more livable.[38] But that promise wasn't kept either. Homes were repaired, but the financial promises fell well short of what was needed. The government spent about $57 million between 2005 and 2014 on housing and infrastructure repairs.[39]

But for all of the money spent, conditions failed to improve, and the community continued to be flooded. The federal government spent more than $70 million during this period covering the costs of evacuations and repairs to damages caused by spring flooding.

The reality was that the community couldn't be made safe because it was situated on the flood plain. In the spring of 2014, Kashechewan was evacuated for the second time in two years. The nurses' station was filled with backed-up sewage, and forty houses were badly damaged by flooding. Families were flown to emergency centres across Ontario. As the days ticked into weeks, residents became increasingly frustrated. In July 2014, the government announced that 260 evacuees living in hotels in the community of Kapuskasing could not return to Kashechewan because their homes had been so damaged that they would have to be torn down and replaced.[40] It was estimated that it would take at least two years to rebuild this neighbourhood. The cost of the evacuation had been pegged at $21 million, and costs would continue to mount as the government dealt with the displaced families (including the need to set up a temporary school for the 100 plus children).

Since walking away from the agreement to move the community, the Conservatives had spent $14.8 million on dike repairs but still were unable to guarantee the safety of residents. "Even with these erosion protection measures [in place] the dike will not comply with all relevant dam safety standards because it does not meet the minimum height requirements," the government admitted in a statement signed by the Indian Affairs minister in June 2014.[41] An engineering report released just before the flood season of 2015 was even bleaker. The engineers noted that the dike failed all of the basic standards for dike and dam safety and that the ongoing deterioration of the structure had placed the residents at "intolerable risk."[42]

Flooded neighbourhood in Kashechewan in 2006. The same neighbourhood has been flooded many times, most recently in 2013 and 2014. *Courtesy of the author.*

The uncertainty around the safety of the dike forced the full evacuation of residents for nearly three weeks in the spring of 2015. Emergency centres were set up in Kapuskasing, Cornwall, Wawa, Kirkland Lake, and Smooth Rock Falls. The cost of moving and housing the evacuees ran into the millions. Once again the talk in the media was of the need to finally deal with the situation and move people to higher ground. But as the flood waters abated, the government flew the families back onto the flood plain to wait for another spring and another potentially catastrophic flood.

The impacts on the community have been traumatic. Chief Derek Stephens stated that, because of the continual disruptions, only one student was expected to have the classes needed to graduate from high school in the 2014–15 school year. Nearly ten years after the historic agreement to transform the lives of people in Kashechewan, the community was still at square one, living behind a dike wall that one spring just might fail completely.

PART III
ATTAWAPISKAT SCHOOL CAMPAIGN, 2007–09

I n 2007, a number of First Nations infrastructure projects across the country were cancelled in order to pay for the new Conservative government's budget promise to address water quality on reserves. The Attawapiskat school project was just one of many educational projects cancelled. The decision by the Conservative government to walk away from its commitment to build a school in the community resulted in a grassroots campaign kicked off by its young people. Grade eight student Shannen Koostachin emerged at this time as a youth leader for the right of the children of James Bay to enjoy quality education.

Shannen was part of the Students Helping Students campaign, which opened the eyes of many Canadians to the fundamental inequities faced by students on reserves. The campaign launched a modern civil rights movement.

This section looks at the remarkable success of the campaign and the impact of the emerging youth leaders from Attawapiskat. It also looks at how their youthful vigour and optimism would be tested by a series of emergencies in 2009, just as the campaign was growing into a truly national movement.

Of the many crises having impacts on the James Bay region in 2009, the most disturbing was a tragic epidemic of suicide among the youth. Their staggering death rates were intimately connected to the ongoing crisis of basic living conditions as well as the deliberate underfunding of basic education and child welfare services.

To non-Native youth across Canada, the Attawapiskat School campaign had become a positive story of young people making a difference. For the Cree youth of James Bay, it was a life-and-death struggle.

THE THIRD GENERATION

To the Students of J. R. Nakogee School,

We are students at a small alternative school in Toronto. It has come to our attention that students in your community have no access to a safe school of your own.... We firmly believe that every student in this country and around the world has the right to a safe, meaningful education. Our class is working on future action regarding this disgrace including workshops and petitions. We are willing to help in any way we can. Good luck and please be in touch.
—SIGNED, YOUR BROTHERS AND SISTERS AT
THE STUDENT SCHOOL, FEBRUARY 9, 2008

I received the call from Steve Hookimaw, chair of the Attawapiskat Education Authority, just before the parliamentary break for Christmas in 2007.

"The government has cancelled the school," he said.

I was stunned. There had to be a mistake. "What did they say to justify this?" I asked.

"Nothing. They just stopped taking our calls. We're going to fight this."

Even as the news sank in, it didn't seem possible. I had been at the meeting with Minister of Indian Affairs Andy Scott when the promise to build the school had been made. I had the trail of letters from his successor, Conservative minister Jim Prentice, and senior department officials supporting the project.

Now, just a few months after those promises were put in writing, the project was cancelled. How was this even possible? Prior to my election as an MP, I spent two terms as a trustee on the Northeast Catholic District School Board in Timmins. From my experience on a regional school board, it simply wasn't possible to walk away from a multi-million-dollar project at the last minute given the amount of planning involved in getting the project to the table in the first place.

The reality was that, as the Conservative government attempted to follow through on its 2006 throne speech promise to deal with the water crisis on reserves, money had to be diverted from other areas of the Indian Affairs budget. School projects that had been given the go-ahead were now being cancelled and the money redirected. The government pulled the plug just as the Attawapiskat Education Authority was completing its report to the department detailing the capital plan, school design, and classroom size.

In the Kafkaesque world of Indian Affairs, no explanation was forthcoming for this abrupt end to years of planning. First you see the commitment, and then you don't. The decision to kill the Attawapiskat school project was made on September 26, 2007,[1] just one month after Chuck Strahl was appointed to replace Prentice as the minister of Indian Affairs.

But even after learning that the government wasn't going forward with the project, the Attawapiskat Education Authority was confident that it could secure bank financing for construction of the school. This was how it had built the high school. The Education Authority had a track record with the bank and knew how to get this project off the ground. On October 31, 2007, its consultant, Leonard Domino, informed government officials that the Education Authority had secured $30 million in bank financing to build a school for 400 students. All that was needed was the signature of the minister on a long-term tuition agreement.[2]

The department was not willing to let this happen. In the bureaucratic speak of Indian Affairs, the government stated that "the Department is willing to work with the First Nation to explore alternative financing options but the current system does not allow much room for innovation."[3] No explanation was given for this decision either. But the translation was clear enough: the project was dead.

• • •

Attawapiskat students holding a protest over the government decision to cancel the school project, December 2008. *Courtesy of Shannen's Dream campaign.*

When news of cancellation of the project was delivered to the community at the end of November 2007, a heavy gloom fell on the students. April Wesley, who had studied in the portables, saw this as a continuation of the broken promises of education since the days of the residential schools:

> My grandparents survived the horrors of residential school. They were forced to move away from their families. My parents had no choice but to attend a contaminated school, and I am a third generation who has to endure my whole entire elementary school in a portable. How many more generations is the government going to victimize before we can get a quality of education like any other Canadian?[4]

The years in the portables had internalized a sense of failure in the students. This was articulated well by teenager Sky Koostachin:

> Before the school was condemned, we had three principals, twelve teachers, a PhD, and two pilots who graduated

The photograph that launched a campaign. Grade one class protesting the need for a proper education, Attawapiskat, December 2007. *Photo by Tyna Legault. Courtesy of Shannen's Dream campaign.*

[from J. R. Nakogee]. Since we have been in portables, nothing successful has come out of the portables. The old school was like a family. We felt connected. When they put us in the portables, we lost that connection with each other. The government's way of living is our way of dying.[5]

Grade eight teacher Carinna Pellatt had just arrived in the community. She was struck by the fact that few of her students would share their emotions after being told that they were not getting a school. "When they heard the school wasn't being built, they were very disappointed, but they didn't cry. They weren't going to articulate what they felt. Some of them felt the school was never going to be built in the first place," she recalled.[6]

Pellatt realized that the Cree youth responded to bad news very differently from students whom she had taught in non-Native schools: "They were a quiet class. It doesn't mean they weren't good leaders, but leadership is very different in a Native community.

Once a group decides something, they all support the move. It doesn't take a lot of talking. Someone will voice what everyone is thinking, and they will resolve to do it."[7]

One of the students who voiced concerns was thirteen-year-old Shannen Koostachin. Her sister Serena had been in Ottawa just two years before to fight for a school, and her advocacy on behalf of the schoolchildren had inspired Shannen. Minister Andy Scott had made a promise to build a school, and now that promise had been broken. Shannen thought that it was the duty of the graduating class of grade eight students to hold the government to its promise and stand up for their younger brothers and sisters.

Teacher Clara Corbiere recalled the leadership of Shannen from the beginning: "The students were thinking of what they could do, and Shannen said, 'We can write letters to the government. We will hold a protest.' She was an awesome, awesome individual."[8]

So the students held a rally on a bitterly cold day before Christmas 2007. They took photographs of the protest. An in-your-face advertising company

Attawapiskat campaign poster sent to schools, churches, and community groups, March 2008. *Courtesy of the author.*

couldn't have done a better job than the students did with their digital photographs of young children holding cardboard signs asking for fairness. There was an immediateness to the images that made the viewer want to respond. The most dramatic photograph was of the grade one students bundled up with scarves and mittens against the minus forty-five-degree winds. They carried a sign that read "We've never seen a REAL SCHOOL, If the government has its way, we NEVER will."

I was given copies of the photographs by the Attawapiskat Education Authority and asked to participate in a planning session to launch a campaign to bring the government back to the table. I knew that, if we focused our efforts on a fight with the bureaucracy of Indian Affairs, these incredible photographs would end up in some file folder soon forgotten. So the idea arose to take the fight beyond Ottawa. The urgency in these photographs could be used to reach out to schools in other parts of the country. Perhaps a public pressure campaign could be mounted. At this point, there was no identified youth leader for the campaign, but the photographs certainly made it seem that this quiet group of young students had what it would take to throw the government back on its heels.

STUDENTS HELPING STUDENTS

Attawapiskat plans to launch an aggressive
campaign to raise the public's awareness of what
is being described as the federal government's
"substandard educational apartheid for First
Nations students."
—RON GRECH[9]

The campaign was launched from the Attawapiskat
Band Office on January 24, 2008. A phone-in press conference had been arranged for regional and national
media. Press conference participants announced a
national campaign to stand up to Canada's entrenched
system of "educational apartheid" and get a school built in Attawapiskat. It was a bold claim. Backing up this promise were the political and educational leaders of the community and region: Chief
Theresa Hall, Grand Chief Stan Louttit, Ontario Regional Chief
Angus Toulouse, Steve Hookimaw, local school principals Stella
Wesley and Ron Pate as well as me.

Stan Louttit provided the political context for a situation that
he described as "very appalling":

Why should First Nation pupils in Ontario and Canada
expect anything less than what's provided in Timmins,
North Bay, Sudbury, and Toronto? . . . Education is a basic
right for any Canadian citizen. This is an international
right. . . . We're not going to stop talking about it locally,
nationally, internationally [because] it contravenes the

very basic right of human beings to have an education, a quality education.[10]

After the political and education leaders of the community spoke, I outlined the strategy that we had developed for a campaign called Students Helping Students. Rather than plead with Indian Affairs, this campaign would engage school groups across the country to raise public awareness of the systemic inequities faced by the chil-

dren in Attawapiskat. We were calling on students to flood the government with letters asking for a school for the children of Attawapiskat.

"How is it that in Canada in the 21st century we can have a standard that says everyone has the education right except First Nation students?" I asked. "This isn't Alabama in the 1950s [or] Soweto in the 1970s and this certainly shouldn't be the situation in Canada in 2008, that one segment of our society ... is being told that they don't have the same basic systemic rights for education as other communities."[11]

Attawapiskat child Janelle Wheesk protesting for the right to a proper education. *Courtesy of Shannen's Dream campaign.*

So the fight was on. The only problem was that we hadn't worked out a plan to make this campaign actually happen. Interestingly enough, even though the grade eight class had provided incredible images to launch the campaign, none of the young leaders had been invited to participate in the press conference. In this early stage of the fight, the issue was still considered one for adult politicians.

•••

The call for a national campaign to fight for a school was picked up in numerous national newspapers thanks to the interest of Canadian Press. By the first week of February, two schools had joined the campaign. Iroquois Falls Public School in northern Ontario immediately offered to write letters to the government asking it to reverse its decision. My daughter Lola's grade five class at St. Patrick School in Cobalt, Ontario, also joined the campaign. Lola's class speech about the situation facing the children in Attawapiskat kick-started a school-wide letter-writing club. A local newspaper wrote a story about their efforts.

Having two schools in northern Ontario writing letters to Minister of Indian Affairs Chuck Strahl was hardly indicative of a big wave of resistance, but nonetheless officials at Indian Affairs took note. An internal briefing note was prepared for officials that detailed my daughter's activities: "On, and around February 11, 2008, media reports indicated MP Angus' daughter Lola spoke to Grade 5 classmates about the school situation in Attawapiskat."[12] Perhaps the only thing creepier than department bureaucrats keeping tabs on a ten-year-old was the fact that they were doing so to contain the political damage of denying other ten-year-olds access to a proper education in a decent school.

Monitoring of the campaign was aided by the fact that the department obtained a copy of a February 26, 2008, email that I had sent to fellow New Democrat MPs discussing the strategy for "taking the battle digital!" The email laid out the strategy of using student organizers to put pressure on the government. I don't know how the Department of Indian Affairs obtained my email, but it appears to have been widely shared within the department and Prime Minister's Office.[13]

The first big breakthrough came from a phone call from teacher James Boafo at the venerable Catholic boys' school Neil McNeil in Toronto. The students there had been engaged in a fundraising campaign for a school in Africa, but after reading an article on the situation in Attawapiskat they decided to launch a local support group. Gaining a foothold at Neil McNeil provided a springboard for bringing other Toronto-area schools on board.

In early February, The Student School, a small alternative school in Toronto, made direct contact with the students at J. R. Nakogee School. The Toronto students were putting teams together to go to other schools in the city to build support. Attawapiskat student Marvin Kioke wrote back thanking them for their support. It was the first of many letters that the students would exchange with schools far away.

The Attawapiskat students were particularly impressed by a contribution made by a shy Indigenous grade five student at St. Patrick School in Cobalt. David Fraser had decided that, instead of writing a letter to the government, he would take the issue to YouTube. He sent the students at J. R. Nakogee School a link to his homemade video about the situation in Attawapiskat. "Dear St. Patrick School and David Fraser," wrote an Attawapiskat student. "Thank you for making the YouTube video. Your video touched us all. It's a great video for a grade five student."[14]

The idea of using YouTube might seem obvious now, but in 2008 it was still a new platform. Founded in 2005 by three university students, it had been transformed into a billion-dollar business within a year. However, despite the popularity of music and cat videos, the political implications of YouTube were still being tested as 2008 dawned. Thus, though few politicians understood the potential of this new platform, young people like David Fraser were driving its explosive growth.

His homemade video inspired students in Attawapiskat. Thirteen-year-old Shannen Koostachin responded by making her own PowerPoint presentation, to which she then added music ("I Will Remember You," by Sarah McLachlan). This project was posted to YouTube.

Carinna Pellatt believes that this first foray into new media gave Shannen the confidence to step forward as a leader:

> Shannen had a real spark of energy and charisma. Most students who have that energy just act goofy in grade eight, but Shannen believed she could improve things for the other students. Shannen was always concerned about others. When she started to work on her PowerPoint presentation, she became really excited because she realized that she had the power to speak up and actually have her voice heard.[15]

Her homemade YouTube video was the first time that she articulated what it felt like to be one of the "forgotten children" of Attawapiskat. YouTube offered the campaign a communications tool to get the message out to young people in a way that no other form of action (press conferences and faxed statements) could even begin to match.

Inspired by the potential of what the young people were doing, I sat down with my oldest daughter, Mariah, and tried to lay out a four-minute YouTube infomercial to provide students with enough information to start their own school outreach projects and letter-writing campaigns. The video was anchored by photos of the children in Attawapiskat juxtaposed with various photographs of Minister Chuck Strahl running a marathon, sitting on his tractor, or wearing a cowboy hat in a mock-up stagecoach.

The "Attawapiskat School Fight" video was launched at the beginning of March 2008 and immediately drew the attention of national media such as CTV, the *Toronto Star*, and Global National News. Within days, the number of views had begun to climb. By the end of the first week, the video had become one of the most watched political videos in the country.[16]

Speaking to the *Toronto Star*, I confessed my surprise at the speed with which the video took off:

> It would never have occurred to me in a million years [to use YouTube] but that's where they [students] go to look for information. Actually I didn't think we would get much out of it. I just wanted to put something [up] that any Grade 6 kid … would get enough information that they could go to their class and say "Why don't we take up the fight?"[17]

Soon the video hit 35,000 views, and the number kept climbing. The campaign was quickly spreading as young people in various schools and regions began sharing the videos and photos taken by the Attawapiskat students. It didn't take long for education leaders to focus on the Attawapiskat story as an example of unacceptable inequity. On March 14, 2008, the Ontario Public School Boards' Association (OPSBA) stepped into the fight by committing the full support of its 3,175 schools representing 2.1 million students.[18]

"All children have the right to a quality education, and we want the students of Attawapiskat to know their peers care about them," said Waterloo trustee Catherine Fife, vice-president of the OPSBA.[19] Fife became an active organizer in the campaign, participating in weekly organizing calls initiated to build support for the children.

Teachers' organizations such as the Canadian Teachers' Federation, Ontario English Catholic Teachers Association, Ontario Secondary School Teachers' Federation, and Elementary Teachers' Federation of Ontario threw their weight behind the campaign. All of these organizations had enormous resources with direct links to Canadian classrooms. As these educators began asking how it was possible that Canadian students didn't have access to a proper school, it was becoming clear that Indian Affairs faced a major problem.

The issue of chronic underfunding of schools and the huge disparity in per capita student funding between provincial boards and reserve schools had never received much attention outside First Nations communities. Now ordinary Canadians were learning about the inequity.

Within weeks of the campaign launch, Attawapiskat support teams were springing up at schools in Belleville, Trenton, Toronto, New Brunswick, and Manitoba. Clarke Road Secondary School in London put together a youth outreach team to start a city-wide campaign of support. The Associated Hebrew School in north Toronto flooded the department with letters while students from Glen Shields Public School in Concord, Ontario, sent in pages of names and signatures on homemade petitions.

Queen Alexandria Elementary School in east Vancouver started an outreach campaign on the West Coast. The great thing about the YouTube campaign was its portability—the video gave students enough information to start a class project and then launch a letter-writing campaign. Within a month, over 100 schools across Canada had become involved. By mid-spring 2008, it had become impossible to keep track of the number of school groups taking action.

CONTAINING THE DAMAGE

...deliver the lines. Stick to them to the letter!!
This is another one that just isn't going to go away.
—SUSAN BERTRAND[20]

The bureaucrats were scrambling to get their story straight. Indian Affairs was usually unfazed by controversy. But the story of the children of Attawapiskat was generating a great deal of political heat. Of all the federal departments, Indian Affairs saw protest and denunciation as part of routine business. On any given day, its monolithic office building in Gatineau, Quebec, was subject to protests by First Nations communities upset about broken agreements. Department staff were used to First Nations people and their allies occupying the large first-floor entrance of the building.

The department's communications team rarely lost sleep over such protests. When a First Nations community held a press conference outlining the latest act of government bad faith, Indian Affairs simply had to wait it out. At best, the story could hold its own in the media for a day or two, and then another issue in another First Nations community would inevitably replace it. This cycle created a blur of issues that department officials knew rarely breached the Ottawa "bubble."

Since the days of Duncan Campbell Scott, the Department of Indian Affairs had always been inscrutable in dealing with the media. It worked on the premise that the less said the better. If you don't feed the fire with oxygen, it will sputter and die out. When certain stories hung around and journalists pressed for more details, department spin doctors would bury them in obfuscations about investments and funding agreements.

But the Attawapiskat School campaign had blown the model apart. The photos and YouTube videos were raising questions about the treatment of children. The visuals were hard to argue with. This wasn't going to be a fleeting issue stemming from a one-day Ottawa press conference; it was in perpetual repetition on the Internet. It was as if twenty-first-century cyber kids were confronting the nineteenth-century Indian agent.

This letter from a grade six student to Minister Strahl indicated the problems facing the department:

Dear Minister Strahl,

. . . . As you read this [letter] there are hundreds of children in Attawapiskat jammed into portables and you are too lazy to do anything about it. . . . Even though we children are not old enough to vote we have many relatives. Aunts, Uncles, parents, grandparents and many people we can convince to not vote for your political party! I hope you change this problem because the United Nations say that all children have a right to education because it is a right not a privilege. You may not believe that this is a big issue but it is wrong and you know it. If you do nothing I hope you enjoy your next four years because they will be your last!

Sincerely,
Kyle[21]

The letter was framed in the language of the rights of children—particularly rights defined by international agreements. The students weren't interested in bureaucratic talk about budgets and priorities. They wanted to know why children were going to school in such terrible conditions.

Indian Affairs prepared talking points to explain the decision to cancel construction of the school. Its first line of defence was to claim that the school project hadn't really been cancelled but simply postponed. An internal memo warned communications staff to push back against media questions about school projects being cancelled: "Two media enquiries to INAC Ontario Region Communications (CP and Timmins Daily Press) enquired about 'a five year moratorium on school construction.' ... There is no moratorium in any of our capital budget areas, and INAC continues to provide funding for school projects in Ontario First Nation communities."[22]

But this wasn't true. Capital school project funding had been cut by over 50 per cent, and all Ontario school projects for the year were cancelled. Although four school projects had been completed in 2006–07, the number dropped to just one school to be built in Ontario over the coming four years. North Spirit Lake was informed that its school project had been cancelled just as construction supplies were about to be shipped to the community. Cat Lake and Fort Severn, also in Treaty 9 territory, were making do with temporary portables. Canadian Press accurately reported that school projects had been cancelled in areas across the country "despite a federal budget surplus that's expected to top $2 billion—even after sweeping tax cuts."[23]

Across Indian country, numerous schools were condemned or substandard. Many other schools required major upgrades and additions because of badly overcrowded classes. In some schools, children were being taught in the halls or even in the furnace room. At Rocky Bay First Nation in northwest Ontario, a school project was cancelled even though the department had reports of mould, asbestos, and the danger of a roof collapse if there was a heavy snow.[24]

Vince Hill, co-director of education for the Prince Albert Grand Council in Saskatchewan, told media that at least a quarter of the council's twenty-nine schools were nowhere near meeting the basic standard for quality. A school in Deschambault Lake in northern Saskatchewan burned down in 2004 and hadn't been replaced. Other schools were badly overcrowded. "We're involved in what's called the new paper wars. It's incredible how much paper is being shuffled back and forth to make it look like something's happening. But very little is transpiring on our end," Hill told CP reporter Sue Bailey.[25]

But while the situations were dire on many reserves across the country, it was the government's treatment of the children in Attawapiskat that kept the media's attention. As journalists continued to press for an explanation of the cancellation of the school in Attawapiskat, an ever-changing litany of excuses was trotted out. Front-line Indian Affairs staff were instructed to tell media that "a variety of national and regional factors have contributed to unusual funding pressures such as a skilled labour shortage, high fuel and steel costs and some emergency situations."[26] These excuses were more fabrications, but staff dutifully had to "deliver the MO [minister's office] approved line" in dealing with media.[27]

One person who didn't stick to the approved lines was the minister himself. Strahl had built his reputation as a Reform MP who spoke out for accountability in Ottawa. His stint as Speaker of the House had given him a more ceremonial and collegial role than his previous partisan approach with the Reformers.

Our first exchange regarding the school in Attawapiskat was in the House of Commons on January 31, 2008. It set the tone for what was to be, unfortunately, a bitter and personal fight between us. In my question to him, I stated that

> education is a universal human right unless one lives on a First Nation territory under the current government. . . . We have had three Indian Affairs ministers support the [Attawapiskat school] project, but the current minister told the community that First Nation schools are no longer a priority for his government. Why should the children of Attawapiskat have to put up with his fundamental disinterest in their health and well-being?[28]

Strahl tried to stick to his talking points but got thrown off: "They [students] have to put up with that [member's] sanctimonious attitude because the member knows . . . there are . . . extensive investments, record investments, in education across the country. . . . There are no health concerns in that school. He should not portray it otherwise."[29]

There were, of course, no "record investments" made by his government. But Strahl's decision to draw attention to the health and safety situation at these badly contaminated schoolgrounds overstepped the department's carefully constructed message box. The government had numerous internal reports describing the

Hand-drawn postcard sent by a grade school student from Holy Spirit School in Toronto to Minister Chuck Strahl, March 2008. *Obtained through Access to Information legislation.*

Attawapiskat schoolgrounds as a class one site, where the "risk potential for adverse impact on human[s] or the environment is high and action is required."[30] But now that Strahl had laid down the marker on health and safety, the department had to scramble to find ways to make a class one threat to children's health appear to be benign.

Within minutes of the minister's statement in the House of Commons, department staffers were emailing back and forth about the health and safety issue. Bureaucrats passed the text of Strahl's comments to both the communications and the political staff in the department. Deborah Richardson, the regional director general of Indian Affairs, sent Strahl's statement to Communications Manager Anne Van Dusen, saying that it was "not quite accurate ... we need more lines that clarify." Within an hour, the communications team had updated lines that "may do the trick."[31]

With Indian Affairs claiming that there were no health and safety issues at the Attawapiskat school, journalists began pressing for evidence to back up the minister's comments. The government was not telling the media that, internally, Indian Affairs had rated replacement of the school in Attawapiskat as one of its three top priorities for Ontario because of "health and safety requirements," "overcrowding," and the need for "extensive repairs" to existing portables.[32] So, even though the department knew that more than 400 children were being educated on a site poisoned by toluene and benzene, officials worked to protect the credibility of the minister.

On February 26, 2008, INAC's media relations manager, Susan Bertrand, warned the public affairs team that CBC journalist Sherry Huff was still asking for reports that had given J. R. Nakogee School a clean bill of health. The department didn't have any such evidence. As Bertrand attempted to explain away the lack of evidence, she noted in her report that "Ms. Huff then pressed that INAC would have copies of those reports and in a show of good faith should provide them. I noted that I would follow-up on her request."[33]

Eventually, Indian Affairs attempted to put the issue to rest by stating that it did have an inspection report on the school from Health Canada. The media weren't told that this report was not about the portables in question but about a visit to the nearby high school.[34] Nonetheless, even this prevarication brought little relief to the bureaucrats. "We've been digging into [the Attawapiskat school situation] for weeks," confessed Bertrand to Van Dusen, "and there is no straightforward, simple answer and it's not a good story."[35]

The government tried another way to change the channel on the health and safety issue. By early March 2008, the department began claiming that Attawapiskat wasn't getting a school because children on other reserves were even more needy.

During a March 6, 2008, CTV interview, Strahl stated that Attawapiskat children had to wait for a school because the government was forced to respond to the needs of children on the Pikangikum reserve, which had lost its school in a fire. He claimed that, following the burning down of Eenchokay Birchstick School, the government had stepped in and built a new school:

> There won't be a school this year [in Attawapiskat]. That's
> true. Last year in the same region the Pikangikum School
> burned down. That means there's no school at all for those
> kids. We had to move in. We built a new school. I was
> there for the opening of that here a month or two ago. We
> spent $13 million no one had even put in the budget. But
> it's [the school in Attawapiskat] not cancelled. There's just
> not enough money this year for that school.[36]

If the government wanted to find a community in greater need
than Attawapiskat, then it chose well in pointing to Pikangikum.
The community of 2,400 in northwest Ontario was a veritable
Fourth World. Over 80 per cent of the community lacked indoor
plumbing. As Strahl was speaking on television, Pikangikum was
in the midst of a horrific suicide epidemic among its young people.
Between 2001 and 2009, there were 481 attempted suicides and fif-
ty-eight deaths.[37] A staggering 273 of those attempts happened in
the three-year period 2006–09. The despair among young people
was so entrenched that the community had been given the unfortunate title of suicide capital of the world.[38]

A report by the Office of the Chief Coroner of Ontario identified
numerous factors affecting the sense of hopelessness among the
youth of Pikangikum. The number one recommendation was the
need to construct a proper school for the children: "Education will
contribute to the health and prosperity of Pikangikum's people by
giving them the knowledge and skills to control their life circumstances and problem solve. . . . When this happens, the unfathom-
able deprivation they face through poverty, lack of running water,
overcrowded inadequate housing, lack of a sewage system, and the
death of their youth through suicide, will finally abate."[39]

So, given the shocking despair among young people in Pikangikum, it was understandable that Strahl would talk of the need to
build a school there. But what Strahl didn't tell the national television audience was that the replacement "school" in Pikangikum
was really just a series of portables with no gymnasium—just like
Attawapiskat. And the children have been there ever since.[40] Politically, however, the department was hopeful that its claim about
having helped the children in Pikangikum would draw attention

away from its inability to back up claims that the Attawapiskat school had a clean bill of health.

Following Strahl's statement on Pikangikum, Anne Van Dusen wrote to a colleague: "I think we have successfully moved away from focussing on the HC [Health Canada] health and safety inspection message. Hope this helps."[41]

As a tactic, however, the Pikangikum gambit failed. Insinuating that Attawapiskat children were somehow queue-jumping in the misery line raised an obvious question: if there were children in a worse state than those in Attawapiskat, then for God's sake what was happening under this government's watch?

The minister's office was flooded with emails from angry Canadians of all political stripes. Even self-identified Conservative voters couldn't understand how a government could be so unwilling to ensure that children were provided with safe facilities for education. One citizen summed up the response to Strahl's interview:

> I was shocked by your cavalier attitude regarding the First Nations children of Attawapiskat on the CTV National News tonight.... You noted that you have 600 schools under your area of responsibility and that many of them are in greater need of repair than the school facilities at Attawapiskat.... If you can't, or won't, take responsibility for the plight of the First Nations people whose interests you are supposed to serve then you should resign your position.[42]

A *Toronto Star* editorial also attacked the government's handling of the situation. The editorial criticized Strahl, stating that his "lack of a sense of urgency" on the issue was "troubling." It pointed out that Attawapiskat was a sign of a much bigger credibility problem for the Conservative government: "A government that has the money for tax breaks but not for rebuilding and repairing decaying aboriginal schools is a government with a wrong sense of priorities."[43]

Given the growing outcry, the government had two options. It could smother the fire by taking away the fuel, or it could come out swinging. The first option was for the minister to declare his concern for the children and visit the community, where he would announce a new round of negotiations (which the government could then drag out indefinitely once the media lost interest). The second option was to double down. The government, in what was to become a signature move of the Harper regime, chose the second option.

In letters to the editor, Strahl challenged the claim that the school project had indeed been cancelled. "MP Angus is flat out wrong when he repeatedly says a new elementary school in Attawapiskat was cancelled. . . . The NDP MP continues to spread inaccuracies."[44]

The bureaucracy realized, however, that such claims weren't passing the nod test among the media. An internal memo outlined the problem: "More videos are appearing on YouTube in support of the Attawapiskat students' request for a new school. There continues to be extensive media coverage of this issue." The department's many changing storylines were not gaining traction and the memo complained that the media reporting was "poor and does not accurately reflect the situation or statements provided by departmental spokespersons."[45]

In an attempt to get the Attawapiskat story under control, Indian Affairs decided to bring in PR heavyweights Hill and Knowlton "to develop a communications strategy and related products to address this issue."[46] Indian Affairs was hoping that it could push back the questions about the situation in Attawapiskat by hiring professional spin doctors. But the government was about to meet a group of Cree youth who would blow its media strategy to pieces.

THE SPARK

Dear Mr Strahl,

Hello! My name is Shannen Koostachin. I am a student here at J. R. Nakogee School in Attawapiskat, Ontario. I just want to ask you: Why would you say our school is healthy? . . .

Our school is NOT and NEVER healthy!

The school is shifting, so that means that the doors and window shutters can't close very well. That causes our school to freeze inside. . . .

We use a mountain of snow for a playground. . . . We walk back and forth to the gym and computers and library. Well, it's not a real library. Kids would get sick from coming out in the cold from the gym. Healthy? NO!

. . . . I wish I could come up to you and make a speech. To be honest, you make me mad.

Thanks for reading this, Mr Strahl.

Sincerely,
Shannen. . . .

PPS. HOPE YOU WRITE BACK.[47]

In March 2008, James Bay youth rallied for education rights in Fort Albany. The protest showed just how far the campaign had come in a mere two months. In January, the campaign had been officially launched by the adults—chiefs, politicians, teachers. But even as political leaders of the region gathered in Fort Albany to show support for the Attawapiskat School

Shannen Koostachin holding some of the hand-drawn postcards sent from students across Canada, March 2008. *Courtesy of the author.*

campaign, it was clear that the youth were stepping up. Fort Albany's local school, Peetabeck Academy, had declared its intention to set up a sacred fire to show solidarity with the students in Attawapiskat. The fire burned throughout the week on the grounds of the school. On March 20, 2008, a youth rally was held at the school. The gymnasium was packed with energetic youth.

The Fort Albany rally was a perfect opportunity to build on the growing solidarity with schools in other parts of the country. The organizers invited school groups across the country to light a candle of support. Education Director Daniel Metatawabin called on Canadian students to show their support: "We know that children all across this province have taken up the fight for Attawapiskat. Their classes can join with us in lighting a candle and holding a moment of silence. The strength of this sacred fire can light a direction for all of us as we move forward."[48]

The sacred fire rally just happened to fall on Holy Thursday. With many Catholic schools looking for appropriate Holy Thursday activities, the symbolism of lighting a candle in solidarity had resonance. Public schools were also on board. The photographs of young Cree children filling a gym with lit candles added to the growing digital iconography of the campaign.

It was during this rally that Shannen Koostachin began to step forward as a leader of the young people. During the youth speeches, she and her fellow student representatives, Ashley Sutherland and Chris Kataquapit, read from prepared speeches. But Shannen's energy was infectious.

The students were thrilled to receive hundreds of hand-drawn postcards and handwritten letters from students in the south. The cards were clearly inspired by the imagery and simple language used by the students of Attawapiskat in the photographs taken during their first winter protest. Those photographs had been like messages in bottles tossed into the digital sea, and now the cards were proof that their voices were being heard. They were no longer third-class children. Chelsea Edwards, a twelve-year-old Attawapiskat student at the time, remembers the growing sense of confidence that they gained from the deluge of letters and postcards: "We were always the forgotten children, and then suddenly there was all this attention. We were this isolated reserve in the middle of nowhere, and suddenly we were getting letters from students in Toronto and the rest of Canada. It was awesome."[49]

There is a photograph of Shannen from that day. She is holding the hand-drawn postcards that had been mailed to the students. She is beaming in the photo. She had been telling her classmates again and again that they could be heard, and now it seemed as if her message was coming true.

SHANNEN MEETS CHUCK

Hi Mr. Strahl,

My name is Emma Wesley. Guess what? My friends in Grade
Eight and I have never been in a real school and I'm not gonna
let the younger kids feel the way we feel. I can't believe you're
not going to give us a new school. We're tired and fed up of this
fake school. I hate what Attawapiskat students have to do to get a
school. If you think that this letter is too harsh, come to Attawapiskat and tell me. I thought the government was nice but look
what you're doing to us. At first, I thought that kids broke promises, not grown men. If I was one of the INAC I would quit my job
and instead, actually help the natives.[50]

The campaign was never intended to be a long-term
fight. The plan had been to mount enough pressure
to bring the government back to the negotiating table.
There was no political upside for the Conservatives to
remain defiant as more and more attention was drawn
to the abysmal state of First Nations education. Yet Minister Chuck
Strahl continued to stick to the line that the Attawapiskat school
was not a priority because many other First Nations communities
were even worse off. He told reporters that, in terms of need, "the
facilities in Attawapiskat are not as high up as some unfortunate
schools that are in worse shape."[51]

Such a line might have had some credibility if he had shown
willingness to alleviate the situations of other schoolchildren
whom he said were in worse straits. After all, as the Minister
of Indian Affairs, Strahl was also the Minister of Education for

hundreds of thousands of First Nations children across the country. But school projects across the country were still being delayed or cancelled outright. Education had not been pegged as a priority for the newly elected Harper government. The Attawapiskat campaign had blindsided the Conservatives, but rather than try to alleviate the issue they became more entrenched.

By late spring, the campaign began to transform from individual class campaigns into much broader community-focused activism. A number of schools had moved from undertaking classroom-based letter-writing campaigns to holding public events that drew media attention.

In the Waterloo region, the English as a Second Language class at Sunnyside Public School was so upset about the situation facing children in Attawapiskat that they began to look for ways to build bridges between their school and the children of the north. Many of these students had come from countries torn apart by war. They were disturbed by the similarities between the conditions in Attawapiskat and those in the countries that they had fled. "I thought Canada was helpful and wanted to help people who wanted to come to school," said Sonya Keny, thirteen, unable to attend school until her family arrived in Canada five years before.[52] The students invited Attawapiskat student Robin Kioke to come and meet them. They then launched a public letter-writing campaign.

In Sault Ste. Marie, a local women's centre organized a gathering at which hundreds of old vinyl albums were broken and then signed by individuals as symbols of the government's record of broken promises. Strahl wrote to me after I had forwarded the boxes of broken records along with a package including 1,800 letters from students in Brampton:

> This letter is in response to your letter ... which was accompanied by two boxes of damaged albums.... For some reason you continue to tell members of Attawapiskat ... that I have intervened personally to ensure their school is not built. This is untrue, you know it's untrue, and yet you repeat it endlessly.... If you cared for students "at large" you should resist the temptation to call for

a Minister to fund projects based on who maximizes the YouTube coverage.[53]

Although Strahl seemed to take the issue personally, it just didn't make sense for the government to continue to dig its heels in with so much momentum on the side of the school campaign.

What would it take to put this campaign over the top? The impetus for the next step came from the students at J. R. Nakogee School. As they watched the campaign grow in other parts of the country, they became increasingly restless and wanted to take an active leadership role. When student Jonah Sutherland suggested that the class cancel the annual grade eight trip to Toronto and go to Ottawa instead to meet the minister personally, his classmates immediately agreed. They saw themselves as being on a mission to improve the lives of their younger brothers and sisters. They were convinced that, if members of the government heard what the conditions were really like, they would change their minds about the school.

The annual grade eight trip was a rite of passage for students at J. R. Nakogee School. It gave them the chance to see things that they might otherwise see only on television. The trip included visits to Canada's Wonderland, Niagara Falls, the Royal Ontario Museum, and the Eaton Centre. But this class decided that they had an obligation to speak directly with members of the government.

Shannen Koostachin, Chris Kataquapit, and Marvin Kioke wrote formally to Strahl requesting a personal meeting: "We want to talk about our new school. We were promised that three years ago. But in December you stopped the school project. We are asking to have a meeting with you. Please don't forget about us again." They signed the letter "The Forgotten Children of Attawapiskat."[54]

I didn't think that the minister's staff would allow the meeting to happen. Everything that the Harper government does is through the narrow political prism of political calculation. Why would the minister put himself in a face-to-face meeting with children only to tell them that they weren't getting a school? The optics would be brutal.

Strahl's office, however, confirmed by email that the minister was willing to sit down and talk to the students. This seemed like a very good sign. With the news that the meeting would take place, there was a growing sense of excitement. The trip to Ottawa just happened to coincide with the National Day of Action for Indigenous People on Parliament Hill. Thousands of people were going to protest, and when word spread that the now famous children of Attawapiskat were going to join the march there was immediate buzz among grassroots activists.

The synergy of the students arriving for a meeting with the minister on the same day as a major protest made it seem as if things were moving toward a resolution. There would be maximum media on the meeting between Strahl and the children. Surely the government flacks had done the political arithmetic and had decided to put him in the centre of the story only to maximize the benefit of delivering good news.

The youth believed that they had momentum on their side, and they felt like a children's army marching to Ottawa. "We've been doing a lot of work on this campaign," teacher Carinna Pellatt told *Timmins Daily Press* reporter Chelsea Romain.[55] She explained that the letters from students in other parts of the country had given the youth of Attawapiskat a sense of determination and hope. The students brought a gift for the minister—a jar full of contaminated soil from the playground that stank of diesel fuel. The grade eight class nominated three student leaders to represent the community: Chris Kataquapit, Solomon Rae, and Shannen Koostachin.

On May 28, 2008, a press conference was held on Parliament Hill at which the youth spoke to national media for the first time. The issue of educational disparities in First Nations communities was now firmly on the media radar. The student press conference drew a large crowd of Ottawa veteran reporters.

"We have been called the Forgotten Children of Attawapiskat," declared a very nervous but determined Kataquapit, "but we are forgotten no longer. Thanks to the efforts of thousands of students across Canada, the children have a voice."[56]

Solomon Rae didn't read from notes. He had memorized his statement, which sounded like a litany of broken promises to the children:

I am here on behalf of my younger sisters and brothers who don't know what a real school looks like.... I am here on behalf of the students who have already lost hope and dropped out because they have no hope, even before grade five. . . .

Our message is simple. We want what every other kid in Canada takes for granted—we want a school, a safe school, a clean school, a school that will give our young people hope.[57]

In her speech, Shannen revealed traces of the leadership role that she would soon take on. She was frustrated with adults who failed to live up to their obligations to the children:

As young people, we have been told to stand up for our promises, but our own government cannot keep a promise that they have made three times. Minister Chuck Strahl needs to keep his word. How can he tell us that we don't have a right to a new school? All students in Canada deserve a learning environment that they are proud to attend. That gives them hope. We want the same hope as every other Canadian student.[58]

After the press conference, there was a large luncheon at which the youth met political, First Nations, and education leaders. Jack Layton and National Chief Phil Fontaine were on hand to welcome them. A busload of students from St. Edmund Campion High School in Brampton arrived in Ottawa with thousands of letters and solidarity T-shirts that they had made for the students from J. R. Nakogee School.

The meeting with Strahl was set for the following morning, just prior to the national march of Indigenous activists and supporters. The youth leaders were part of a larger Attawapiskat delegation that included Chief Theresa Hall, Grand Chief Stan Louttit, and community elders Annabella Iahtail and John Matinas.[59]

The plan was for the youth to speak to Strahl about the conditions that they faced, and then Louttit would lay out options for getting the school project back on track. These options included putting the school back on the capital planning list or asking Strahl to commit to a tuition arrangement so that the community could get a bank loan and build the school itself. Louttit had enormous respect in the communities of James Bay as a negotiator for their rights. He was deeply involved in the Attawapiskat School campaign. Prior to the meeting, Grand Chief Louttit spoke with the three youth to prepare them for what was to come. "Speak from the heart, and speak the truth, and you will be fine," he said to them.[60]

The delegation was then ushered into a large, plush room with rich cornice mouldings. To break the ice, Strahl pointed to the surroundings and asked them, "What do you think of my office?"

Shannen didn't miss a beat. "I told him I wished I had a classroom that was as nice as his office that he met in every day."[61]

As they sat down, Strahl pre-empted the discussion by telling them matter of factly that the school wouldn't be built. It simply wasn't on the government's list of priorities. The delegation was stunned. What was the purpose of the meeting if the government refused to discuss options for addressing the educational needs of Attawapiskat students?

"We invite you to come to our community to understand our living situation," Chris Kataquapit offered.[62]

But the answer was no.

The elders began to cry. Shannen didn't want to cry in front of the government, so she stormed out of the meeting. Stan Louttit went out into the hall to find her. "This is not how the meeting ends," he told her comfortingly. "You need to go back in there and be a leader."[63] Shannen wasn't just sad but also furious. Nonetheless, she listened to him.

As she stepped back into the room, Strahl was telling the delegation that the meeting was over because he had to attend to other issues. Shannen stepped forward to shake his hand. And this is how she later retold the story to media and supporters:

> He told me he couldn't stay for more of the meeting because he had other things to do. We were very upset. The elders who were with us had tears in their eyes.... But when he was about to leave, I looked at him straight in the eyes and said, "Oh, we're not going to quit, we're not going to give up!"[64]

• • •

The delegation came out of the meeting into a bank of media cameras. Without having a chance to decompress, they were whisked through the cameras and into taxis to meet the rest of the students joining the march assembling on Victoria Island (a fifteen-minute walk from Parliament Hill). It was a fairgrounds atmosphere as thousands of people prepared for the big protest march. As soon as the rest of the Attawapiskat students on the island saw the delegation, they knew that something was wrong. The leaders looked tense, and the youth representatives were clearly stressed. Around them, protest marchers bustled and shouted excitedly for the rally to begin, but the students of Attawapiskat stood in the midst of the crowd, bereft and desolate.

Carinna Pellatt said that the students were determined not to cry in public: "How they express sadness is so different. We stood in that circle, and the elders were crying. I cried. But the students were so stoic. I always wondered why the minister agreed to meet them if he was just going to turn them down."[65]

As the Attawapiskat students tried to come to terms with what had just happened, the Brampton students stood with them. Pellatt said that the presence of these suburban students had a profound effect on the Attawapiskat youth: "When the students from St. Edmund Campion came to be with them, it really meant a lot. Both groups of students were shy, but words aren't necessary with the Cree. Just to know that students came to be there with them meant so much."[66]

National Chief Phil Fontaine was there to meet the delegation. He was shocked that the government had set up the meeting only to tell the students to their faces that they weren't getting a school. "This is shameful. What kind of man would tell these students they don't deserve a school? I am shocked. There is no honour here at all."[67]

Strahl later told the media that he had simply been honest with the youth. "I could have strung them along. But they have been strung along before."

As the march was getting under way, the delegation still hadn't had a chance to really think through their next move. The Attawapiskat students were asked to march at the head of the demonstration. I quickly lost sight of Shannen as she and her friends picked

Attawapiskat students leading the protest march to Parliament Hill, May 29, 2008. *Courtesy of Janet Doherty.*

up their placards and ran to join the protest march. They led the crowd in a chant of "How many schools can Chuck Strahl stall?"

Walking up to Parliament Hill, the leaders were troubled by how things had turned out so badly. It wasn't supposed to have gone this way. These were still early days for the new government, but clearly Harper's team was not responding the way that previous governments would have responded to the bad publicity of being perceived as so hard-hearted toward First Nations children. The Harper government had been pushed on the school issue and they pushed back hard. The government was likely to dig in on the Attawapiskat School campaign, and the momentum of the entire movement appeared to be in jeopardy. The question we asked ourselves was what effect would this rejection have on the Attawapiskat students? Was it fair to bring children down from James Bay only to have their hearts broken?

As we approached Parliament Hill, the rally organizers informed us that they would allow one of the young people from the delegation to speak during the protest. This was a moment to try to salvage something from what had been a very heartbreaking day. It was decided that Shannen would be the one to tell all assembled what had happened in the meeting with Strahl.

When she was informed that she would be the voice for the community, she seemed to be panic stricken. "I don't have my speech with me. I lost my notes. I don't know what to say."

"Shannen," I said, "this is the moment where you need to be heard. Just speak from the heart. You'll know what to say."

The youth stood on the steps of Parliament as one First Nations leader after another denounced the government. Shannen had her hair pulled back in a ponytail and seemed to be so small and so young as she stood beside these national leaders. She was shaking with nervous energy. She and her classmates were just thirteen-year-old kids from an isolated reserve who were now standing in the midst of a complex political struggle that stretched back generations.

One of the adults whispered to me, "Do you think she will be okay? What do you think she's going to do?"

"I have no idea," I replied, "but we're about to find out."

When the time came, the rally organizers announced that the youth activists from Attawapiskat were on Parliament Hill, and a huge cheer went through the crowd. Shannen stepped forward to the microphone, and immediately the nervous, frightened girl became very poised.

"Hello, everybody, my name is Shannen Koostachin, and I am from the Attawapiskat First Nation. Today I am sad because Mr. Chuck Strahl said he didn't have the money to build our school." She paused and then added, "But I didn't believe him." The crowd lit up. Shannen became more confident. She related the story of looking him in the eye and telling him that the children were not going away. "And," she said, "I could tell he was nervous." The crowd roared their approval.

It was a simple speech, but her heartfelt determination genuinely touched people. The news coverage across Canada became the story of the thirteen-year-old girl who had never seen a real school and had stood up to the minister of Indian Affairs. Speaking to the media afterward, she related the daily humiliations of being educated in substandard conditions. "I told him [Minister Strahl] that we will not quit until every First Nation child has a

Shannen Koostachin speaking on Parliament Hill with National Chief Shawn Atleo (lower left in ceremonial clothing) looking on, May 29, 2008. *Courtesy of Shannen's Dream campaign.*

school that they are proud of, that they can call their own." In terms of the political impact, Shannen hit it out of the ballpark.

The day had been a hard one for the students, who had been so hopeful that they were on the brink of victory but were now going home empty-handed. But there were those present who saw Shannen's two-minute speech on the Hill as a potential break-through moment. In what would be a nasty and long-term fight with an entrenched government, the Attawapiskat School campaign now had a face and a voice who could speak to the media. Was it possible that from a generation of forgotten Indigenous children a youth leader had emerged who could speak of their reality to Canadians?

Karihwakeron (Tim Thompson), the education director of the Assembly of First Nations (AFN), certainly thought so:

All too often the issue of education gets lost in the discussion of First Nations and the crown. Suddenly, there was this charming young lady who put a human face to the issue of education and showed that these issues are not just part of a basket of grievances—this is a real life-and-death issue, and you could see it in her face. It was undeniable. It resonated with people. What was clear with Shannen was her passion and natural charisma. Sometimes this is what it takes to put an issue of this magnitude into focus.[68]

Another person standing in the crowd that day was children's rights activist Cindy Blackstock. She had been leading the fight for Indigenous children's rights in the areas of health and welfare. Prior to the march, she went to meet the young people who were gathering on Victoria Island and saw Shannen for the first time:

I am not religious, but I am very spiritual. I saw Shannen on Victoria Island, and her power stood out. I didn't know then that she was going to speak at the rally, but there was something about her. I then saw her on Parliament Hill, and when I heard her speak I was convinced that there was something powerful and spiritual about this young woman. She was a leader.[69]

Blackstock believed that Shannen could play a role in helping to break through the bureaucratic wall that had allowed the injustices against Indigenous children to continue year after year:

The Cree youth had internalized the broken promises. Shannen saw how some of the young people had begun to believe that they were failures and they weren't worthy of education. But when she looked at her friends, she saw hope and potential, and she saw the injustice of what they were facing. This was the beginning of a profound social movement, not just for education rights but for all manner of rights for First Nation children.[70]

THE DISAPPEARING SCHOOL

Fyi—[Attawapiskat school] never in the plan. . . .
We need to be firm.
—DEBORAH RICHARDSON TO BOB MAGUIRE (12:59 PM)

I'm not trying to be uncertain. The problem is it
was in one plan in 2006 but it showed in a future
period Deborah.
—BOB MAGUIRE TO DEBORAH RICHARDSON (1:05 PM)

Future years is not fixed in the plan. This is
what gets us into trouble. We have told the mo
[minister's office] this al [sic] along.
—DEBORAH RICHARDSON TO BOB MAGUIRE (1:10 PM)[71]

How does a $30 million school project disappear off
the planning table as if it had never been there? This
was what was perplexing about the Attawapiskat
school issue. Could senior bureaucrats spend years
negotiating a major capital construction project and
then claim at the last minute that it had never been on the books?
When the issue first became public, the government vigorously
denied that the project had been cancelled—it had just been
delayed. But as the year moved on, the government line hardened
as officials began to claim that there had never been a plan to
build a school in Attawapiskat in the first place.[72] They based this
new line on the claim that Attawapiskat had never been on the
government's list of priorities.

In an article entitled "School Never Was in Plans," INAC bureau-crat Joe Young attempted to explain this abrupt change in the government's line: "A capital committee looks at all different proposals. [The list] is reprioritized every few years based on a number of factors, such as overcrowding, health and safety . . . and we plan around that over X number of years." He then added a caveat: even if the school had been approved on paper, it had to compete with numerous other needs, such as water treatment plants, sewage treatment plants, and other infrastructure problems.[73]

In the provincial education system, the capital expenditure process for schools exists as a defined budget line. Such earmarked money doesn't get erased or transferred to other columns at the last minute. The capital costs of building the school, as well as the replacement investments for maintaining school infrastructure, are built into long-term provincial planning. It simply isn't possible for a mayor, school board official, or premier to pull funding dedicated to school construction and spend it on road or bridge construction. This is because all funding envelopes associated with education from teachers' salaries, to construction and maintenance costs, to class resources are protected by "ring fencing" for each line item.

Within the Department of Indian Affairs, however, there is no specific line item for school construction. Spending on education is rolled up in the overall Capital Facilities and Maintenance Program, and whenever Indian Affairs finds itself squeezed for funding it can dip into the capital budget.

Work by the parliamentary research department revealed that, from 1999 to 2007, a total of $579 million was taken from the capital construction envelope to address a number of other costs, such as "education, social development, economic development, federal responsibilities in the North and internal services." These "internal services" included spending on financial management, legal fees, and "public affairs/communications services."[74] So funds that should have been spent on school construction were being used to pay for spin doctors and lawyers. The capital fund served as a money pot to alleviate spending pressures within the department—over half a billion dollars in an eight-year period.

In 2009, in response to the Attawapiskat School campaign, the newly established Parliamentary Budget Office (PBO) undertook a major study of First Nations school construction and education funding. The report revealed a disturbing lack of accountability. The department had no idea of the conditions faced by students under its watch: "In the absence of Parliamentary appropriations specifically for funding First Nations schools, and which can be tracked through Parliamentary reporting tools such as the Estimates, it is impossible to determine how much Parliament intended to appropriate for school infrastructure funding and consequently, how much was actually spent on schools."[75]

This lack of due diligence in overseeing school construction made it difficult to get a clear picture of the state of Indigenous schools across the country. In some regions, the government undertook inspections of school facilities. In other regions, there were no data at all. What data existed painted a dismal picture. Of the 803 federal reserve schools across the country, less than 50 per cent were listed in good condition, and 21 per cent had not even been inspected. Seventy-six per cent of the schools in Alberta and British Columbia were found to be in "'poor' conditions." The report also noted that seventy-seven schools were listed as "temporary structures."[76]

The PBO found that the government's own targets for education construction were being shortchanged between $169 million and $189 million a year. It pointed out that dipping into school construction projects was possible because the government refused to protect school funds by ring-fencing them. Whenever the department had shortfalls in its budget, school projects could be delayed or cancelled.

Promising money for school projects and then taking the money back are long-standing practices. In a 2013–14 report, the department noted that, of the $320 million promised for school construction, the government sat on $86 million (over 25 per cent).[77] This habit of continually short-changing school construction has created a massive financial hole. A 2013 internal report prepared by the department identified the infrastructure backlog in First Nation school facilities at a staggering $878 million. Even then, the department admitted that the figure was likely to be low as "some school needs have not yet been identified."[78]

Speaking at a youth conference on the Attawapiskat School campaign, Terry Waboose, deputy grand chief of the Nishnawbe

Aski Nation, explained that the arbitrary treatment faced by the students in Attawapiskat was par for the course across Treaty 9 territory:

> I have seen letters from the Department of Indian Affairs that tell a community and the students we have a crisis in capital, and so even though you are approved you will have to stop your school and wait another four or five years if you are lucky. This is a problem because we don't have a government that sees us as equal. They see us as a drain.[79]

During the Chrétien-Martin years, these shortfalls had become increasingly problematic for First Nations schools. In 1996, Minister of Finance Paul Martin imposed a 2 per cent cap on all spending for Indian and Northern Affairs Canada. However, with a rapidly growing population and already underfunded services in Aboriginal communities, this cap had a huge impact on the delivery of services in them. In the two decades since the cap was imposed, the population grew annually by an average of 4 to 6 per cent. The 2 per cent spending cap left a shortfall of $1.54 billion in First Nations education dollars between 1996 and 2008.[80]

Education was the department's largest delivery cost (representing 20 per cent of annual spending). Yet, in a series of successive investigations, the auditor general could find no coherent method for how the department determined priorities or targets for education investments. In 2000 and then in 2004, the auditor general delivered a scathing rebuke of the federal government's handling of First Nations education: "We reported that Indian and Northern Affairs Canada could not demonstrate whether it was meeting its stated objective to assist First Nations living on reserves in achieving their education needs. . . . We could not find any formal document that clearly defined the Department's roles or responsibilities in education."[81]

Although the auditor general "recommended that action plans be implemented promptly," prompt action didn't happen.[82] Just as with the failed investments in water projects, so too with the failed investments in education. The department spent money with no targets or defined outcomes. The auditor general's review of INAC's education budget between 2000 and 2004 found that the government had not even taken steps to determine whether the money was being spent in areas that would improve learning outcomes:

> In 2000 we found that the Department did not know the actual education costs; nor did it have a cost comparison of the different delivery mechanisms used.... At present [2004], the Department does not know whether the funding provided to First Nations is sufficient to meet the education standards it has set and whether the results achieved ... are in line with the resources provided.[83]

The most disturbing finding of the auditor general was that, between 1996 and 2004, the huge gap between First Nations students and the rest of the population actually widened. It was determined in 1996 that it would take twenty-three years to close the education gap between reserve students and students in the provincial systems. By the end of the Liberal reign in 2006, that gap had increased to twenty-eight years.[84]

So, in simple terms, the government of Canada ran an education system that allowed the potential of tens of thousands of children to be squandered. And despite investigations and calls for accountability, the conditions were getting worse, not better. If such a terrible report card were given to a provincial education ministry, there would be firings and a huge shake-up of the ministry. But for Indian Affairs it was just another day at the office.

Karihwakeron, the former AFN education director, said that the lack of accountability lies in the fact that Indian Affairs simply doesn't see itself as being in the business of delivering education:

> First Nation communities come to meetings with government officials to talk about education that delivers quality education, that ensures accessibility. But to INAC it is just an issue of program management. You have some good people in INAC trying to do good things, but they aren't educators. Other governments look at education as a social good. To the department, it is just another program tool.[85]

Failure begins with the per capita student funding formula. In the provincial systems, this formula allows school boards to engage in long-term planning and investment for educational development. First Nations students are underfunded between 20 and 50 per cent compared with students in the provincial systems. This underfunding puts First Nations education at a huge disadvantage.

In the case of Attawapiskat, Indian Affairs provides the community with per student funding of approximately $8,000. If the student leaves Attawapiskat to attend school in Timmins, the department subtracts the $8,000 from the Attawapiskat education roll, and the money is transferred to the provincial school board with a top-up to meet the $16,000 per capita standard for schools in the Timmins area.[86] Thus, the federal department will pay the full cost of educating an Indigenous student in a provincial school yet will only provide half of this money to the reserve school. The result of this disparity is that students who leave Attawapiskat to be educated in Timmins will be educated in schools with full theatre facilities, science labs, and robotics programs, while the students who remain on the reserve face profound obstacles.

As Attawapiskat student April Wesley explains, "my education is all about isolation; isolated portable, isolated community, minimal resources, and minimal funding. . . . My teacher has to photocopy math chapters—we don't even have math textbooks."[87]

Karihwakeron points out that, when the government is under pressure to improve education outcomes, the response is a "mishmash of short-term programs that do not respond to the need for quality education."[88] But in terms of long-term commitments to education, the department doesn't pay for physical education instruction, computer training, or education in First Nations languages for on-reserve students.

Indeed, the government won't cover the costs of library books or librarians. In 2003, provincial and territorial governments invested anywhere from $2,113 per school (Newfoundland and Labrador) to $7,886 per school (Yukon) for library resources. The cost of providing library resources for First Nations schools would be about $4 million a year,[89] but with the 2 per cent funding cap in place such an investment has not been possible.

Students at Vezina High School in Attawapiskat. Underfunded First Nations schools result in cramped classrooms without proper teaching resources. *Courtesy of the author.*

The situation is particularly dire for students with special needs. In Ontario, when a child is identified as having special needs (e.g., a learning disability, a visual or hearing impairment, a physical disability, autism, etc.), the school board is legally obligated to meet with the parents of the child and establish a program that will meet that child's needs. No such provision exists on reserves because there isn't the funding to ensure that such plans can actually be realized. In 2005, *Toronto Star* reporter Louise Brown told the story of nine-year-old Kayla Rae from North Spirit Lake First Nation in Treaty 9 territory. She was identified as a potential math genius with a photographic ability to remember numbers, but she couldn't read. Lacking access to a literacy consultant or special education teacher, she was beginning to fall behind and fail in school. As Brown writes,

> this is ground zero of the growing education gap between Canada's native and non-native children.... Local communities say they are left to run schools with empty bookshelves, loose teaching requirements, rampant turnover,

no mandatory curriculum, no system for checking how well students are doing and no money to fly in experts to determine why even bright students like Kayla sometimes can't learn.[90]

In a report on conditions faced by children at Webequie and Mishkeegogamang First Nations in Nishnawbe Aski Nation (Treaty 9) territory, it was noted that Indian Affairs refused to support special education provisions for children, even after an assessment by a doctor:

> One child with identified special needs has been unable to attend school for a few years due to her high needs and the lack of supports available to support her. This child is currently not enrolled at school and is receiving no educational supports. This is one child, of many, who fall through the cracks. Professional assessments conducted by doctors and consultant are being ignored.[91]

In 2005, Attawapiskat principal Vince Dumond identified 31 per cent of the student population of 333 as having some form of special needs. This included spina bifida, ADHD, speech defects, pervasive developmental disorders, and intellectual delays. Dumond believed that the exposure to contaminants and toxins had a noticeable impact on the development of the children. Certainly, the physical problems that he identified in the student population correspond with the symptoms of long-term exposure to toluene and benzene. As a result of these needs within the school population, the Attawapiskat Education Authority had to divert already stretched classroom resources to try to meet the basic needs of these children. In a letter that Dumond released publicly, he wrote that the Education Authority received less than $300,000 a year for special education support and had to pay more than $900,000 out of other budget items to help special needs students.[92]

The impact of this is that some children are not able to attend school at all. According to John B. Nakogee, there were fifteen Attawapiskat children with special needs in 2014 who were not able to attend school because of shortfalls in funding. "There is no funding for hiring the specialist teachers needed to help these students, so they are forced to stay home and do not get any education."[93]

If those children were in a provincial school, plans would be worked out between the school board and the parents to ensure that the children had the full-time, in-class support required. The Attawapiskat Education Authority, in contrast, did not have the funding to dedicate one-on-one support, so the money was divided among a number of children with needs, which meant that they were able to go to school only part time. How long before such children become frustrated, fall behind, and give up?

Given such fundamental inequities, how can an educator make a difference that counts? It often comes down to the dedication of the local education authority and front-line teachers. Although many communities have high turnover rates of teachers, those who stay play vital roles in ensuring that these underfunded schools provide the best education possible under the circumstances.

As I was writing this book, I received a letter from Lawson Bate, who had taught grade school for three years in Kashechewan First Nation. Like its neighbour, Attawapiskat, Kashechewan has no proper grade school—just a smattering of portables. Lawson said that the experience of teaching in a fly-in community had a powerful impact on him:

> As a teacher in Kashechewan ... you are surrounded by many young, energetic, creative and caring teachers who are in the same boat as you. This causes the teachers in Kashechewan to lean on each other for support both at home and in the classroom and creates one of the most inspiring, interesting and supportive environments to begin your teaching career. Everybody in Kashechewan was pulling for me to succeed.[94]

Lawson was amazed at the sense of community spirit, particularly noticeable at Halloween and Christmas. The reserve came together to make such moments as magical as possible for the children:

> Kashechewan has a spirit and courage like nothing I have ever witnessed. The amount of students who have experienced more heartache and grief before the age of ten than

I have witnessed in my thirty years is humbling, and yet they still show up and try their best. This is what pushed me to create the best learning environment I could and dig deep to find compassion when feelings of frustration were strongest.[95]

These words could have been written about so many First Nations schools across this country. Imagine what could be accomplished if their students were put on a playing field level with the rest of Canada's student population?

THE FIGHT GOES INTERNATIONAL

Each year the Nobel laureates choose one child in the world who advances human rights, not only for children but for us all. . . . Shannen Koostachin . . . embodies all that is important in the Nobel Prize movement. . . . This is how one girl from a northern community in Attawapiskat First Nation said "I'm going to, with the company of other children, change the world," and she did.
—CINDY BLACKSTOCK[96]

In the days following the march to Parliament Hill, it became clear that the Attawapiskat School campaign was becoming an increasingly bitter fight with the government. There was no backing down for anyone involved. The meeting with Strahl had shown just how intransigent the new government could be when challenged. New strategies needed to be considered if the campaign were to move forward. This is where Cindy Blackstock came in. She had started out as an academic specializing in First Nations child welfare issues but had emerged as the leading voice on equity for First Nations children.

I was aware of her work in leading the Jordan's Principle campaign. Jordan River Anderson, from the Norway House Cree Nation in Manitoba, was born with complex medical needs. He remained in hospital for over two years until doctors said he could live in a family home in Winnipeg. The plan was to wait until he stabilized medically, at which time he would live with his family in Norway House.

But Jordan wasn't able to leave the hospital since the governments of Canada and Manitoba couldn't agree on who was responsible for paying for his care at home. The only way that the federal government would pay for his care was if the family put him in foster care. The Anderson family reluctantly agreed, but still the provincial government and the federal government continued to argue, and the little child remained in limbo.

As Blackstock described in an editorial in the journal *Paediatrics and Child Health*, "days turned into weeks, weeks turned into months and months turned into years, and governments kept arguing as Jordan watched the seasons change outside of his hospital window."[97] He died in hospital at the age of five, having never spent a day at home with his family.

Jordan was just one of many First Nations children who fell through the cracks because the federal government refused to pay for basic services for children on reserves. Such children had been ignored for decades. Cindy Blackstock set out to change this situation. Her organization, the First Nations Child and Family Caring Society, was established to provide research, professional development, and policy support to First Nations child and family service agencies across Canada. Through this work, Blackstock became increasingly concerned about the systemic pattern of obstruction by the federal government in responding to its legal obligations to First Nations children.

The provinces set the standards for children's entitlements to medical, social, and home-care support. But the federal government, which is obligated to cover the costs, simply ignores many of these benchmarks. The result is a two-tiered system of child welfare in Canada. What makes it even more discriminatory is that individual cases are subject to ad hoc decisions by bureaucrats focused on the bottom line.

Blackstock explained that, all too often, decisions are made by civil servants with no background in child welfare issues:

> First Nation people are always being asked [by the federal government] to demonstrate our capacity to deliver services. But nobody ever looks at the officials who are making the decisions about funding child welfare programs and asks what their qualifications are. My experience is that the vast majority of staff working in the federal government on First Nations children's programs have no

education or training in the area, and as a result they make arbitrary decisions that fail to consider the needs of the child or the requirements of the law. There are officials who make funding decisions that simply negate whole swaths of provincial legislation regarding Indigenous child welfare issues.[98]

Blackstock realized that, if individual child welfare agencies or families fought these issues on a case-by-case basis, nothing would change. In 2007, the First Nations Child and Family Caring Society, along with the Assembly of First Nations, launched a human rights complaint against the federal government for systematic discrimination against First Nations children in care. This historic case at the Canadian Human Rights Tribunal marked the first time that the federal government was held to account for its systemic mistreatment of First Nations children before a judicial body with the power to make enforceable orders.

The federal government did not want evidence of discrimination to be aired publicly in front of the tribunal. It attempted repeatedly to have the case thrown out. It then cut funding to Blackstock's organization. And then, several weeks into the hearings, the government was caught withholding tens of thousands of pages of documents prejudicial to its case.[99]

Blackstock also took the fight to the larger Canadian public. Along with the family of Jordan River Anderson, she launched the Jordan's Principle campaign calling on government agencies to put the interests of First Nations children ahead of jurisdictional disputes between federal and provincial bodies. Blackstock worked with NDP MP Jean Crowder to bring the Jordan's Principle motion to Parliament for debate. Jordan's father and sister were in the House of Commons as the motion passed unanimously on December 7, 2007.

Ernest Anderson, Jordan's dad, pleaded that Canada actually follow through and "not let the good done in my son's name just become a moral victory."[100] But despite the unanimous will of Parliament supporting Jordan's Principle, there was a huge uphill battle to transform the long-standing financial, departmental, and legal impediments that had been put in place by the federal government.

As Blackstock was pushing to make Jordan's Principle a reality, she became increasingly interested in the Attawapiskat School campaign. The underlying issues of systemic discrimination were the same. But what made the Attawapiskat campaign potentially transformative was that there were identifiable youth leaders who could speak to the inequity from their personal experiences. Blackstock recognized the potential of launching a truly Indigenous children's social movement.

She contacted me in the days following Shannen's speech on Parliament Hill to discuss possible strategies. She was particularly captivated by the young woman who had spoken with such determination on Parliament Hill. "Do you realize what these young people have accomplished?" Blackstock asked me. "This has become the largest youth-led, children's rights movement in Canadian history. These young people have put the issue

Shannen Koostachin as a young human rights leader. This photograph is now part of an exhibit at the Canadian Museum for Human Rights in Winnipeg. *Courtesy of Janet Doherty.*

of First Nation children's rights on the map in a way that has never been done before."

As Blackstock saw it, this fight was bigger than the fight for a school. Shannen's defiance on Parliament Hill had the potential to become a watershed moment in the fight for Indigenous children's rights. To move the yardstick forward, Blackstock thought that the issue should be framed in the context of Canada's international human rights obligations. She suggested taking the campaign to the international level through action at the United Nations.

Canada, as 1 of 193 signatories to the Convention on the Rights of the Child (CRC), had made commitments to protect children's rights, including the right to education. The CRC, the most widely ratified human rights treaty in history, sets out the obligations that countries have to children and their families. Countries are obligated to provide education to, and to respect the cultures of, Indigenous children in non-discriminatory ways.

Every five years the CRC requires states that have ratified the convention to report formally on their implementation of its obligations to an expert body called the United Nations Committee on the Rights of the Child. Canada was preparing for a periodic review, and Blackstock suggested that the Attawapiskat youth go to Geneva and participate in the review.

The Attawapiskat School campaign had drawn the support of a number of academics and educators who could provide the research needed to challenge Canada's failure to live up to the commitments of the CRC. Following through on Blackstock's suggestion, a youth team from Attawapiskat sent a formal letter to the Canadian government on July 11, 2008, to give notice that they would challenge the Canadian government at the upcoming review at the United Nations High Commission. They vowed to create a "shadow report" to expose the "systemic discrimination" that comprised "a breach of the key clauses of the UN Declaration of the Rights of the Child."[101] The letter was signed by Shannen Koostachin, Solomon Rae, Chris Kataquapit, and Jonah Sutherland.

Blackstock also suggested nominating Shannen for the International Children's Peace Prize. It celebrates children and young people who lead change in children's rights in areas such as education, housing, and child labour.

Nominating a student from Canada was certainly beyond the traditional focus of the prize, which historically recognized children from Third World countries. However, Blackstock believed that doing so would draw attention to Shannen's inspirational leadership and Canada's failure to meet its obligations to Indigenous children. As well, the nomination would link social justice fights in the developing world with conditions faced by so many Indigenous children in Canada.

In Attawapiskat, there was some concern with the idea of singling out Shannen for recognition when so many of the grade eight class were involved in the campaign. Blackstock, from the

Gitxsan First Nation, understood their reservation. First Nations value collective leadership over individual recognition. Blackstock pointed out that group nominations were not allowed, so it was agreed that Shannen would be the ambassador, not just for the community, but also for all First Nations children.

• • •

When Shannen learned that she was being nominated, she was dealing with the most tumultuous summer of her life. She had just turned fourteen and was preparing to leave home and family to attend grade nine in a completely foreign environment. She and her sister Serena were moving south to the Timiskaming region of northern Ontario to attend high school. They were going to stay with my family.

Having Shannen move in had never been part of any plan on my part. I knew that the Koostachin family was looking for a home for Serena so that she could finish high school in the provincial system. I wanted Serena to succeed and began talking with my wife about the possibility of having her stay with us if she left Attawapiskat. As soon as her parents heard that we were considering taking in Serena, they set up a trip for her to visit us. Younger sister Shannen came too but just, her parents told me, "to make Serena feel less awkward as she makes her decision."

Serena and Shannen visited the regional high school in neighbouring New Liskeard in the spring of 2008. The sisters were a study in similarities and contrasts. Serena was tall, graceful, and demure. Shannen wasn't shy at all. She looked you right in the eye. She radiated energy. But there was also something very compelling about her, as if she had stepped right out of a different place and time.

We took the girls on a tour of Timiskaming District Secondary School. Serena carefully took in the surroundings. Shannen was like a coiled spring of excitement. When we met teachers, she didn't hold back, always stepping forward to introduce herself with energy and determination.

Serena and Shannen were invited to speak to students at the local St. Patrick School, one of the first schools to launch a support campaign. The students were excited to have two representatives of the Attawapiskat School campaign visit, so they hosted an assembly.

During the assembly, Shannen blurted out to the students, "I like it in this town. I am moving here too with my sister." The children clapped loudly while my wife and I looked on in shock. She was just finishing grade eight. This was much too young for anyone to leave home, we thought. We also hadn't reached an agreement in which we (and my wife in particular) would become parents to two more teenage girls. But, truth be told, we were so surprised by her forwardness that we didn't even challenge Shannen.

There is one more story from this visit that merits telling. As we went on the tour of St. Patrick School, Shannen kept lagging behind or disappearing. I finally excused myself to go find her. She was at the far end of the hall staring into a classroom window festooned with cut-out pictures and children's poems.

"Is there something wrong, Shannen?" I asked.

She continued to stare at the children's art and replied, as if to herself, "I wish I had my whole life to do over just so I could be in a school like this."

I looked at this girl staring at the classroom window and suddenly understood the school campaign in a whole other light. Shannen wasn't barging through the doors of life because she was bold but because she knew that, if she didn't, opportunities might vanish for good.

In a letter that Shannen later wrote as part of her nomination for the International Children's Peace Prize, she described the underlying spirit that drove her determination. She wrote the letter in both English and her native Cree. She introduced herself as Mushkegowuk Innanu (Cree) from an isolated village that had never seen a real school. She told the committee that she wanted to be a lawyer. She then spoke of her message to other young people: "I would tell them not to be afraid. . . . I would tell them to think about the future and follow [their] dreams. I would tell them NEVER give up hope. Get up: pick up your books, and GO TO SCHOOL. But not in portables."[102] She signed the letter with two hand-drawn smiley faces.

EDUCATION IS A HUMAN RIGHT

Throughout the summer and early fall of 2008, the Attawapiskat School campaign retooled for what now appeared to be a long fight with the Harper government. The spring campaign had benefited from the huge wave of momentum in schools across the country. It was time to solidify this support by planting the roots of these fledgling campaigns into school culture and curriculum.

The campaign had the support of many educational institutions and teacher organizations in various regions of the country. They had enormous resources and connections to students. The strongest support was from school boards in Ontario. It was decided to bring some cohesion to the large number of student groups that had been working in relative isolation. The plan was to host a student forum in Toronto so that Attawapiskat youth leaders and student groups from southern Ontario could organize for a longer-term campaign. The forum would also serve as a teach-in, explaining the history of the struggle for education rights at James Bay as well as the larger international implications for human rights.

To make this project possible, a partner school board in Toronto was needed. The Toronto Catholic School Board stepped forward to provide on-the-ground logistical support. But from the beginning, it was agreed that students from all school boards in Ontario would be invited to participate. A planning team began developing the logistics for this forum. The team included representatives of various teachers' organizations, school boards, the AFN, and the Attawapiskat campaign team. Since the hall where the forum would be held could hold only 600 students, schools were asked to nominate small teams of youth leaders. In no time at all, every spot was taken.

On November 26, 2008, the Education Is a Human Right Conference was held at the Ontario Institute for Studies in Education (OISE). Numerous Toronto schools were represented. Students were bused in from schools in Trenton, Barrie, Waterloo, London, and Simcoe County. One group from the tough north Toronto neighbourhood of Jane and Finch showed up with a sign that read "JANE AND FINCH SUPPORTS ATTAWAPISKAT."

A series of educational and political experts led panel discussions on the education rights of children. However, it was the young people who shone that day. The youth hosts for the event were a grade nine student, Alex De Pompa from Mary Ward High School in Toronto, and Shannen's childhood friend, thirteen-year-old Chelsea Edwards. She had been chosen by the students at J. R. Nakogee School to represent the Attawapiskat youth.

Chelsea had never spoken in public before and was very nervous. During the press conference, she began to tell the media about what it was like to be educated in the portables. She kept pausing nervously while Shannen sat beside her whispering answers and advice in her ear. Finally, Chelsea started to laugh and handed the microphone to her mentor. Shannen took the microphone and didn't lose a second in telling the media about the humiliations of poverty through the eyes of an adolescent girl. She explained how the washroom was right in the classroom separated only by a little stall. "It's gross [in the classroom]," she stated as her classmates giggled. "I'd like to have the washroom moved out so they aren't right in the classroom. When you're in the washroom, all the students are right there, and they can hear what you're doing." She then looked at the reporters: "Anything else?"[103]

The conference displayed the growing confidence of the Koostachin sisters as youth leaders in the movement. They were featured as speakers. Serena told the story of Rosa Parks and put the Attawapiskat school fight in the context of a modern civil rights movement:

> Rosa Parks ... stood up for her rights, and she helped change America. All across Canada, First Nation children go to school in crappy portables or in buildings that are condemned. This is the way things have been done ... ever since the days of the residential schools. But the children

in our community stood up and said, "No. We aren't willing to sit at the back of the bus anymore."[104]

Shannen was always at her best speaking to other students. She was energized by their enthusiasm:

> I would like to talk to you about what it is like to be a child who would never see a real school. I want to tell you what it is like to never have the chance to feel excited about being educated.
>
> It's hard to feel pride when your classrooms are cold and mice run over our lunches. It's hard to feel you can have the chance to grow up [to be] somebody important when you don't have proper resources like libraries and science labs. That's why some of our students begin to give up in grade four and five. They just stop going to school. Imagine that! Imagine a child who feels they have no future even at that young age.[105]

Cree human rights activist Jocelyn Formsma presented the youth teams with a four-point list for spreading the campaign:

1. establish a local Attawapiskat support group;
2. start a letter-writing campaign to the prime minister;
3. call on the local MP to take a position on the issue of education rights; and
4. start organizing students at other schools to get active.[106]

These organizing principles were simple and easily replicable by students everywhere.

The students treated the event as if it were a campaign rally. Young people lined up at the microphone to declare their commitment to spread the fight throughout the province. But underlying the energy and enthusiasm was the sense of a much bigger issue to be dealt with in terms of Canada's own Third World.

Grand Chief Stan Louttit provided the historical context of the signing of Treaty 9. He told the students how the government had made a promise to provide education and teachers to the children of James Bay. Now, a full century later, the children were still waiting. "Canada, I am ashamed of you," Louttit declared.

> Parliament, I am ashamed of you. Indian Affairs, I am ashamed of you for doing this to our people. I am ashamed. . . . All we're asking is a simple thing. We want a proper school. We want a nice school like any other community so that the kids can be proud when they get up to go to school in the morning. Next time you hear Mr. Strahl speaking about all the things he is doing for our community, they are lies. They aren't true. You need to come to our community to see for yourself.[107]

Chuck Strahl had been invited to the forum but didn't attend. Instead, staff from Indian Affairs were sent to monitor the activities of these young people and report back to the department. In what was becoming a pattern every time the Attawapiskat school issue came up in the media, Strahl sent a letter to the *Timmins Daily Press*: "While MP Charlie Angus ... continues in full campaign mode (complete with all the rhetoric and the wildly-false accusations you might expect), Indian and Northern Affairs Canada (INAC) officials continue to work with the community. . . . Discussions are taking place right now. . . . Thankfully, the demolition of the closed elementary school is nearing reality."[108] Only in the world of Indian Affairs would the announcement that a school was being torn down be seen as progress.

GRADE NINE

Every day I walk through a big comfy school with a lot of
friendly people. Every day I walk through those hallways
thinking how lucky we are to be in a proper school. But
we also thought about the children back home. They,
too, deserve a better school as much as we do. That is the
reason why we are here today, to build this fight for a new
school. . . . We want our younger brothers and sisters to
go to school thinking that school is a time for hope and
dreams of the future. Every kid deserves this.
—SHANNEN KOOSTACHIN[109]

Shannen didn't want to be a leader. Not really. She
wanted a locker. She wanted to hang out with her
friends, sending text messages and kibitzing in the
science room when the teacher wasn't looking. She
wanted to go to school dances and join the archery
club. She wanted the chance to be an ordinary teenage kid. But
there was one thing that she wanted even more. She wanted the
"little brothers and sisters," the other children in Attawapiskat,
to have the same opportunity. And the fact that they didn't have
these things haunted her.

As she tried to acclimatize herself to grade nine, she was burdened by guilt about the increasing difficulties faced by the friends
whom she had left behind. The first time that she walked through
the doors of Timiskaming District Secondary School (TDSS) she
started to cry. She couldn't believe that she was finally in a "real"
school. In terms of modern high schools, TDSS in the small town
of New Liskeard wasn't much to write home about. Unlike schools

in larger communities that boasted theatre facilities and open gathering places with natural light, TDSS was a stripped-down institution. But to Shannen it was everything that she had hoped for in a school.

Even under the best circumstances, grade nine is often the worst year for an adolescent. Shannen began the school year in a completely foreign world far from family, friends, and the culture that had comforted her since she was a child. She found herself in an academic environment with a curriculum for which she wasn't prepared. "I feel like a grade four kid in a grade nine class," she wrote to a friend back home.[110]

For many reserve students, transferring into the provincial system is like jumping into a fast-moving stream without knowing how to do the strokes to stay above the waterline. In Shannen's case, the big stumbling block was homework. In Attawapiskat, just showing up for school set a student apart for high marks.

Shannen was considered a leader at J. R. Nakogee School because, no matter how dispiriting the conditions in the portables, she never missed school. But in the provincial system, showing up for class was only the first part of succeeding. Marks were based on completing the numerous homework assignments in English, math, and science. She had no grounding in the discipline of homework. It was a foreign exercise. Her failure to follow through on what other students had been doing for years resulted in her first-term marks taking a dive.

What made the transition to this alien world possible was the presence of her sister. As lonely as Shannen was, her big sister was always there. The two were inseparable. Serena at sixteen was graceful and put her time into artwork and sports. She hung out with the First Nations students bused in from Timiskaming First Nation thirty kilometres away in Notre Dame du Nord, Quebec, and from Bear Island, sixty kilometres south in Temagami.

Although the Algonquin and Ojibwe students came from backgrounds different from the tightly knit Cree of James Bay, Serena found a familiar rhythm in the laid-back approach of the First Nations students. They were making plans to hold the first-ever powwow at the school. Serena threw herself into organizing this celebration of Indigenous drumming and dancing.

Shannen didn't have Serena's ability to go along to get along. Some teachers found her chippy and bold. The skills that allowed a thirteen-year-old girl to stare down a minister of the crown weren't exactly the skills that won over teachers of grade nine students. Nonetheless, Shannen found a small group of friends, drawn to her irrepressible enthusiasm. To her, just walking downtown was a big adventure.

Her days always began the same. Shannen was a no-show at 7:15 AM when Serena went to the washroom and prepared for the coming day. Shannen was still missing at 7:30 when her sister went downstairs to get a little breakfast and get her homework together. There was no stirring as the clock ticked on to 7:55, which necessitated my wife or me going to the staircase in our rambling old two-storey house and shouting, "Shannen, are you coming down? You are going to miss the school bus."

Shannen Koostachin with the author, March 2008.
Courtesy of the author.

The bus arrived at the end of the concession road to pick up students along a rural route on the outskirts of Cobalt. From there, it was a twenty-minute ride to the regional high school in New Liskeard. If Shannen missed the bus, she would miss school. But every day, at the last possible second, she came flying down the stairs (no breakfast, hair askew), grabbed her backpack, and headed out the door.

"Did you do your homework?"

"Yes."

"Shannen, did you do your homework?"

"Yes," she replied, as she pulled her winter boots on.

"Shannen, the teacher called about your homework. Did you do it?"

"No."

"We need to sit down when you get home and work on your homework. Okay?"

She'd shrug. "Okay." And with that she'd bomb down the road, combing her hair as she went. In sunshine, rain, or snow, in sickness or health, Shannen never missed that bus. She never missed going to school. Even if she was struggling to find her academic way in this foreign environment, school was the dream that she had fought for, and she was determined to make the most of it.

SIX BOYS, ONE GIRL

Our country prides itself on education being a
right. Yet we are the only ones who send their
kids away to school. Nobody else puts up with
this, so why do First Nations?
—DEPUTY GRAND CHIEF TERRY WABOOSE[111]

The difficulties that Shannen faced in adjusting to the
provincial school system were part of the trial by fire
faced by First Nations students when they leave an
isolated community for education elsewhere. Across
Nishnawbe Aski Nation (NAN) territory are many communities in which there are no high schools or only substandard
programs. For James Bay youth, the destination tends to be the
provincial high schools in Timmins and Cochrane. NAN students
from isolated communities in northwestern Ontario often go to
school in Thunder Bay or Sioux Lookout.

Deputy Grand Chief Alvin Fiddler of Nishnawbe Aski Nation
left his isolated community of Muskrat Dam at the age of thirteen to live in a boarding house in Thunder Bay in order to attend
school. Now a successful political leader, Fiddler understands
what these students are going through: "The academic piece
is just one part of the shock awaiting these students when they
leave home. They need to adapt to a strange community, a strange
home, different peers, and different rules. We need to do a better
job addressing the needs of these students who are leaving home
at age thirteen or fourteen."[112]

Shannen and Serena during their first year away from home. *Courtesy of Brian Thornton.*

Transitioning into schools off reserve can undermine the confidence of an adolescent coping with the loneliness of being in a completely foreign environment. Journalist James Murray operated an Internet café in Thunder Bay that was a hangout for many students from isolated fly-in reserves. He believes that the culture shock results in the high dropout rates and troubles in which these young people sometimes find themselves:

> The talent level of these students is very high, but they often don't get the full orientation of what to expect when they leave home. Often they find themselves left high and dry. I worked with a student who arrived in grade nine and hadn't been taught how to write a sentence. All of a sudden he finds himself in a very fast-flowing education stream, and he doesn't want to stand up and admit he doesn't know what's going on. Some students then just start skipping class. In this student's case, he taught himself how a sentence worked. This is an extraordinary achievement.[113]

Jethro Anderson wasn't so lucky. The young adolescent went to Thunder Bay from Kasabonika Lake First Nation, an isolated fly-in community 450 kilometres north of Sioux Lookout. The community had no high school. He left his family and moved to a boarding home in the city. On November 11, 2000, his body was found in the McIntyre River near Thunder Bay. His family received few answers from the police as to what could have happened. He was only fifteen.

Anderson's aunt Dora Morris was not pleased with the police investigation of the death of her nephew: "It was just a really quick answer we got that he died from drowning. . . . They be telling me 'no' or 'he's just out there partying like any other native kid.' Those are the kind of comments I was getting."[114]

A second teenager, Curran Strang, from Pikangikum First Nation, was found floating in the McIntyre River on September 26, 2005. There was little explanation of what could have caused this death. On November 11, 2006, the body of Paul Panacheese was pulled out of the McIntyre River. He had left his home in Mishkeegogamang First Nation (formerly Osnaburgh House), where the signing of Treaty 9 had occurred in 1905.

Robyn Harper died on January 13, 2007, from what appears to have been an alcohol-related mishap. She was from Keewaywin First Nation and had been attending high school in Thunder Bay for only three days before her death. Later that year fifteen-year-old Reggie Bushie's body was found in the McIntyre River. Bushie had been a quiet boy who had left his family in the isolated fly-in community of Poplar Hill First Nation. He had never been outside his reserve before landing in Thunder Bay for school.

The next teenager to die was Kyle Morrisseau, who came from the same community as Harper. His body was found in the McIntyre River on November 10, 2009. Kyle was seventeen and the grandson of world-renowned artist Norval Morrisseau. Like his grandfather, Kyle had been an aspiring visual artist.

On February 7, 2011, Jordan Wabasse vanished after getting off a city bus. He was fifteen years old and was walking back to the boarding house where he lived. Jordan had moved to Thunder Bay from the isolated community of Webequie First Nation (500 kilometres north of Thunder Bay) to develop his skills as a hockey player. Many volunteers tried to find him. Months went by before his body was found floating in the nearby Kaministiquia River.

Six of the seven young people had attended Dennis Franklin Cromarty High School, a federally funded school for First Nations students. Teacher Greg Quachegan told the *Toronto Star* that local Native gangs might have targeted some of the students: "Students get harassed for not joining. They get homesick. They miss traditional foods—wild meat. A lot don't have money."[115] Vice-Principal Sharon Angeconeb stated that the teaching staff became surrogate parents. "We tell all our staff they have to be committed, they need to come for the students. We are their moms and dads. Our school work doesn't end when the bell rings."[116] The teachers signed up for night work travelling the city in a van checking in on the students until the early hours of the morning.

The First Nations communities of the region weren't pleased with the police investigations of the mysterious deaths of the six young men. Alvin Fiddler said that the police response seemed to be "almost non-existent."[117] Six Indigenous young men were found floating in the river over a seven-year period, and the story barely touched the national media. Some journalists who did cover the story speculated that these deaths were part of an epidemic of Indigenous suicides.

Yet all six youth had grown up along the river systems of northern Ontario and were no strangers to water. Fiddler said that there was no evidence one way or another to say what had caused these mysterious deaths. "Six students were found in the river. I don't know how you commit suicide by jumping in a river. The families need answers as to what happened to their children."[118]

Journalist James Murray said that the deaths speak to an underlying issue that plagues the disappearances of First Nations people: "There just doesn't seem to be the same sense of urgency when a First Nation youth goes missing. Imagine if six blond teenagers were found drowned in any city in Canada what kind of response there would be."[119] Fourteen years after Jethro Anderson's death, families are still waiting for answers. In 2014, the Ontario Coroner's Office stated its intention to move forward with an inquiry, but delays have held up the investigation. Christa Big Canoe, the director of Aboriginal Legal Services, told the *Toronto Star* that people need to know what happened: "There is a haunting similarity between these deaths."[120]

Joyce Hunter has reflected a great deal on the loss of these young people. She lost her older brother Charlie at St. Anne's Residential School. Joyce works for the City of Thunder Bay and says that these deaths were a wake-up call for civic officials. As a result, they came together with police, First Nations, and educational organizations to begin addressing the need to provide a more nurturing environment for students coming in from isolated reserves. The mayor and council pushed forward a plan to ensure that young Indigenous students aren't overlooked when they come to Thunder Bay for school.

"There is a strong commitment in this city to be welcoming and nurturing so that young people who come here will be able to navigate their way through the city as they should," Hunter explained. "All the key organizations in the city are trying to find new ways to help kids navigate a city when they have come from communities where there may only be a dirt road and a stop sign."[121]

On the day that I spoke with Hunter, two young First Nations men were hospitalized because of apparently race-based attacks by groups of white youth. She admits that the transition to a more inclusive city is a work in progress: "People ask me if race relations have improved since the city began to implement its plan. We aren't going to undo 500 years of craziness overnight, but people do want to make this place a more nurturing and supportive place for the students."[122]

THE YEAR OF EMERGENCIES

[This] would never stand in Toronto. It's a dangerous, dangerous thing and they [the federal government] are ignoring them. Would you risk your kid up there [in Attawapiskat]?
—BRENDA STEWART[123]

March 2009 was marked on the calendar for teacher development in Attawapiskat. A team of educators from the Toronto Catholic School Board was slated to visit the community to implement an early learning strategy in the primary classrooms. This process of teacher development is common in education systems across the country. But reserve teachers are rarely able to access such professional skills development. Stella Wesley, principal of J. R. Nakogee School, was always trying to enhance the skills of her teachers. It was difficult. In a school made up of portables, physical isolation and deprivation made teachers feel cut off from a supportive work environment. And, working in a fly-in reserve, they were cut off from the professional development opportunities that other teachers elsewhere took for granted. Just as young students dropped out of the portables, so too did teachers.

The educational relationship with the Toronto Catholic School Board had been developing for a number of years. It began with groups of primary school teachers from Attawapiskat going to Toronto to see how the early learning strategies were used. But implementing strategy in a Toronto classroom was one thing, while implementing it in the portables of James Bay was a whole other reality. Thus, it was seen as a real opportunity when resource teacher Brenda Stewart and a team of three educators brought their literacy program training to Attawapiskat.

The teachers arrived there just as the government's demolition of the abandoned J. R. Nakogee School building was getting under way. A series of community meetings had been held with representatives from Health Canada to discuss the safety precautions related to demolition. Tearing apart J. R. Nakogee School would be like pulling the lid off a cesspool of fuel-based contaminants. Exposing the diesel mixture was just one part of the health threat. The abandoned building was a veritable bomb of toxic mould. Health Canada had previously issued warnings to the community that contamination was so high that no one could enter the site without full protective gear: "[Accessing the old school is] by Health Canada standards ... Totally Un-acceptable. All areas of the old school are affected by mold. Walls, floors and ceilings again were inspected ... and all areas exceeded the limits of the testing unit. We recommend that staff that must enter this area [wear] personal protective face mask and clothing."[124]

Nonetheless, Health Canada assured the residents of Attawapiskat that it was safe for students to attend classes even though the demolition was taking place next door. The school officials had been informed that protections would be in place. However, as the giant scoop shovel tore into the side of the building, things began to go wrong. Dust, debris, and mould started to blow across the schoolgrounds and surrounding houses.

Stewart said that the only barrier put up to contain the mould and debris was a temporary fence: "They put up a chain link fence right beside where kids were playing with their toy trucks. The only thing holding back the dust was a six-foot tarp. It was ridiculous."[125]

As the red dust settled on the schoolgrounds and teachers' apartments, people began to experience headaches and nausea. As one teacher explained,

The dust was flying. There was paper from the classrooms ... flying. [There was] no consideration for our safety. I started getting sick. The snow started turning pink-brownish from the dust. I actually went over and told them, "Listen, you are demolishing the building, you are loading up the trucks—where is the fence?" It was under piles of snow.... The workers and the supervisors, they themselves had helmets on and masks on ... , and they were maybe twenty metres away from ... my house.[126]

As the dust spread, so did the stench of diesel. Rose Koostachin's family lived near the school property. They began to get sick soon after the demolition commenced. "We were getting dizzy. And outside ... we could smell the stink of the contamination.... We could see the mud, the blowing dust right in our yard.... We were feeling sick and we started throwing up, started getting diarrhea. Even the baby had diarrhea."[127]

In the school, both children and teachers began to feel nauseous and have headaches (telltale symptoms of toluene exposure). Brenda Stewart had brought her daughter with her to Attawapiskat, and she became sick from the exposure. Government officials, however, told them that nothing was wrong: "Health Canada came into the classrooms while the dust was flying everywhere and said the air was at acceptable levels. They told us to just close the windows.[128] The fumes were all over the school. Toxic mould was being released in the air. We all had headaches." She said that an inspection of the teachers' residence consisted of a cursory walk-through by an official who gave them the all-clear, even though her daughter was upstairs sick from the fumes and dust.[129]

With the building torn down, the scoop shovels began digging into the upper three feet of contaminated soil. The stench in the community was now overwhelming. The abandoned school had sat on the toxic soup like a cork. With the cork gone, the contaminants were fully exposed in the heart of the community. Dealing with this septic wound required a full site cleanup of the soil, not possible until spring.

With more children getting sick, the Attawapiskat Education Authority ordered the schools closed. On March 25, 2009, the community declared a state of emergency, asking Indian Affairs to send in health teams to assess the situation and evacuate the families who lived closest to the site.

Principal Stella Wesley said that closing the school was the only option: "We are very very concerned ... that our children are really losing out on their education, but ... the health comes first. . . . It wasn't an option that we had to close the school. It was a matter of a health and safety issue."[130]

Indian Affairs refused the request for help. When asked by the media about the decision to close the school, Minister Chuck Strahl's spokesman, Ted Yeomans, blew off the reports of children getting sick in the classrooms as a case of "NDP photo ops and political grandstanding."[131] Strahl said that he was "perplexed" by the community's response: "Why they're pulling their kids out of school at this moment is unclear, given there's no indications that there's a health problem."[132]

The problem for the government was that there were witnesses. The Toronto teachers returned to the city and spoke to media about what they had seen. Comments from Brenda Stewart were syndicated through the Sun Media chain. She denounced the government for putting children at risk:

> We were there during the demolition. We experienced the awful smell, the headaches, the nausea, noise, and the shaking of the buildings and homes we stayed in—all while the students were in the school. As someone raised in Toronto, I know that . . . no child would ever be put in such a dangerous position as to sit in a classroom or play in a schoolyard steps away from a toxic waste site.[133]

Three weeks after the demolition, the stench of fuel and contaminants hung in the air despite a strong wind coming in from James Bay. Knowing that the government was dismissing the health concerns of residents as a publicity stunt, I took a camera to Attawapiskat to document what was happening. A public meeting was held at which residents spoke of nosebleeds, headaches, and nausea. A number of young students came forward to state the situation that they were facing was real. Grade six student Summer Shisheesh was one of them: "It is true about the gas smell because my brother L. J. gets sick when he goes to school. . . . The government doesn't believe we have problems in our community. It feels like they don't care about the children of Attawapiskat. We are Canadians, and also we were promised three times that we would get a new school. So what's going to happen now?"[134]

Chief Theresa Hall requested that independent health teams come into the community to assess the situation. MPP Gilles Bisson called on the province to step in to address the risks posed to the students. "Our community members have been exposed to contaminants," Bisson said. "They have been sick. The schools are too unsafe to go back into. We need a team of independent medical and environmental experts to come in and work with the community to address this situation. . . . We are talking about chemicals known for causing leukemia, bone marrow damage, and kidney failure."[135]

Nothing was done by either level of government. After three weeks, the Attawapiskat Education Authority realized that the students were in danger of losing their year if the schools stayed closed for much longer. With the smell of benzene, toluene, and ethyl benzene still in the air, the students resumed classes. They went back to a schoolyard that had been covered in toxic dust and mould.

The federal government had decided to simply ignore the problem until the people gave up. This attitude was noted by an editorial in the *Timmins Daily Press:*

> It doesn't matter to him [Strahl] that community leaders have declared a state of emergency or that parents have pulled their kids out of classes. . . . It doesn't matter that . . . teachers visiting from Toronto were appalled by the Third World conditions. . . . In the face of all this chaos, Strahl is like a befuddled bystander, wondering what the fuss is about. . . . Ultimately, it is a sad state of affairs when saving political face is more important than acting in the best interests of a community. . . . The only hope for Attawapiskat is that Strahl is eventually removed.[136]

THE DARKEST PART OF THE NIGHT

Death taunts Krystal Shewaybick like a schoolyard bully. She thinks of it now as she hunches over a sheet of paper in the school library, carefully writing the names of her four sisters. "Just the 5 of us 4-ever.". . . And she thinks of it again after school when she gets home, bursts through the door with its broken window and gaping hole where the doorknob belongs, and sweeps her year-old sister into her arms. . . . Since her 15-year-old cousin committed suicide last winter . . . she has lived in fear of death. Not only her own, but that of her four little sisters, whose pictures are plastered across her bedroom wall.
—MARGARET PHILP[137]

The second crisis to rock NAN territory in 2009 had been building for some time. It began to manifest itself in early January when seventeen-year-old Thomas Trapper from Moose Factory killed himself. And then another teenager died. And then another. In Moose Factory, as in all tightly knit Cree communities, the death of a loved one brings all activity to a standstill in order to allow for mourning. When the death is a suicide, the impact is like a shock wave.

As the bodies began to be shipped down to Timmins, funeral director Mike Wilson was stunned by what he was seeing: "As a funeral director with twenty-five years experience I thought I had seen it all, but, to be blunt, the trail of teenaged bodies that has passed through our facility in the past eleven months has been sickening. . . . There were times the bodies came in in twos." What rattled him the most was that nobody outside the First Nations communities even seemed to notice. "This is a sad statement on our society, when this is happening and nothing is done," Wilson said. "If this were happening somewhere else, people would be screaming."[138]

Front-line workers at James Bay were scrambling to contain the ever-expanding number of suicide attempts, but the stress was taking its toll. One responder told me that, even as she was still grieving a suicide in her own family, she was expected to go out and deal with the next one. Among first responders, there were high levels of post-traumatic stress disorder. One Nishnawbe Aski police officer described the isolation that they felt when dealing with the traumas of youth suicides:

> I've stopped counting the deaths I've dealt with. . . . I have had to deal with them alone. This is when you realize how helpless you are. You go in and clean things up. Nothing changes. Nobody comes in from the outside. You're sup-posed to just carry on. But after awhile it seems that we [front-line police officers] start imploding and killing our-selves but nobody seems to hear.[139]

The crisis at James Bay shouldn't have been a surprise to the provincial Liberal government. It had been sitting on a report on the conditions faced by front-line child welfare workers in Treaty 9 and Treaty 5 territories. The report prepared by the Barnes Management Group, *Northern Remoteness: Study and Analysis of Child Welfare Funding Model Implications on Two First Nations Agencies*, documented the conditions faced by child welfare workers at Payukotayno James Bay and Hudson Bay Family Services in northeast NAN territory and Tikinagan Child and Family Services in northwest NAN territory. The report carried the same prophetic alarm as the Peter Henderson Bryce report on the treatment of Indigenous children a full century earlier:

> Nothing could have prepared the consultants for the impact of what was experienced in visiting the first com-munity. In twenty-five years of Child Welfare Service, this consultant had never witnessed such appalling con-ditions. . . . A tour of a community reveals the appalling

conditions of some of the homes. Given the severe winters,
it is remarkable that more people do not freeze to death.[140]

The report also noted the heavy emotional impacts on communities that had lost children to either suicide or the foster care system:

> The pain and despair in the voices of the Elders when they
> tell the stories of their grandchildren, who have either
> died through suicide or have been removed by the CAS
> [Children's Aid Society], are heartbreaking. The despair is
> so great and the feeling of hopelessness so overwhelming
> that there is little energy to even attempt minimal steps to
> improve conditions, even if the resources were available
> to do so.[141]

And the report pointed out that, in addition to dealing with poverty and isolation, the staff are burdened with caseloads far exceeding anything else in the province:

> Given the reality that there are few resources to support
> families, the family service worker must carry more of the
> responsibility to ensure the safety of the children on his/
> her caseload. Caseload size alone does not do justice to the
> work involved for a worker. Since the average family size
> is much larger than [in] the rest of the Province, it is very
> conceivable that a worker, responsible for 22 cases, might
> in reality be involved with over 200 children.[112]

These overworked and undersupported front-line workers were yet another manifestation of the jurisdictional black hole that impedes the ability of First Nations communities to receive equitable service delivery. The First Nations child welfare agencies are mandated under the province and, like other provincial agencies, must meet provincial standards for ensuring child protection. However, the costs for servicing youth on reserves are charged to the federal government, and Ottawa is very arbitrary in terms of which costs it is willing to cover.

In Ontario, the provisions for child welfare services on reserves were laid out in the 1965 Indian Welfare Agreement. Under this agreement, the province assumed responsibility for administering child welfare programs on reserves, while the federal government compensated it ninety-three cents on the dollar for their delivery.[143] But in the half century since this agreement was signed, Ontario has updated its legislation to more fully respect the unique needs of First Nations children, while the federal government has refused to update the 1965 agreement in accord with these new statutory realities. The result is a legislative catch-22: First Nations child welfare agencies must meet provincial obligations, yet federal government bureaucrats can decide which program expenditures will be covered.

This catch-22 is exacerbated by the fact that the two key federal departments involved (Health Canada and Indian Affairs) refuse to take responsibility for the growing gap in child support services. Thus, front-line workers attempting to get help with a growing suicide epidemic faced a bureaucratic game of pass the buck.

"In Ontario," Cindy Blackstock stated, "the federal government wouldn't fund counselling for suicidal youth. These costs were deemed ineligible. If you wanted funding, you had to apply to Health Canada, be rejected, then appeal, and be rejected again, and then maybe Indian Affairs would consider reimbursing the costs. Sometimes they'd say yes and sometimes no."[144]

While the bureaucrats were shrugging their shoulders over who was responsible, young people were dying in staggering numbers. The Barnes Report noted that, in a six-year period (2000–06), Tikinagan communities suffered 41 non-suicide child deaths, 484 suicide attempts (208 in Pikangikum alone), and 128 suicides, with the majority of victims under the age of twenty.[145]

Youth suicide, of course, is not just a First Nations issue. Educators and public health teams across North America have worked for decades to establish protocols for dealing with youth depression, suicide, and copycat attempts. The best practices include support counselling, school programming, skills training, "healthy school" initiatives, and a trained crisis intervention team when a suicide has taken place.[146]

In any community, the first response to a youth suicide is to bring in professionally trained counsellors to help prevent copycat

actions by providing support and comfort to the friends and relatives of the victim. But without access to trained therapists and
this kind of on-the-ground support, child welfare workers have
few tools at their disposal to help at-risk youth. Under provincial
legislation, they have a legal obligation to keep the youth from
harm, which all too often means pulling them out of their communities and putting them into either foster care or institutions
far away. Young people know that this fate might await them if
they come forward for help, so they often keep quiet, making the
work of local counsellors even more difficult.

In an in-depth investigation of the horrific suicide epidemic at
Pikangikum First Nation, the Ontario coroner noted that, though
many factors were involved in the high rate of death of children,
what stood out was the lack of basic child support systems, such as
a proper school and intervention programs, that are the norm in
the rest of the province. This lack of resources put enormous pressure on front-line workers, who "find themselves in the unenviable
position of trying to mitigate a series of compelling difficulties such
as domestic violence, crime, parental substance abuse, or solvent
abusing suicidal youth, with limited to no community resources
or supports to assist them. They have become the default provider
for many absent services, which are easily accessible and exist in
southern Ontario."[147]

Pikangikum was just one of numerous communities across
Nishnawbe Aski Nation and across Canada with substandard
schools, high levels of poverty, and little or no access to counselling for youth. In northwest Ontario, the crisis facing children was
so serious that in 2007 the international children's rights organization Save the Children flew to NAN territory to assess the situation.
Barbara Ammirati, who had led Save the Children US relief efforts
following Hurricane Katrina, landed at Webequie and Mishkeegogamang First Nations. She was joined by Nicholas Finney of
Save the Children UK. Both were shocked at the crushing poverty,
hopelessness, and hunger in the communities. "There's been no
sudden disaster here. It's a gradual disaster that has emerged,
unfolded and been propagated, whether it's intentionally or by
negligence, by people that should know better, by people in power,
over a long period of time," Finney stated.[148]

The other international NGO to step up to the plate was Feed the Children. It had been contacted at its headquarters in Oklahoma by the principal of the grade school at Mishkeegogamang over the high level of hunger among local children. The agency shipped 100,000 pounds of food to Sioux Lookout to help. Hunger is often an unspoken issue facing families on isolated reserves. The cost of food at the Northern Store (often the only food location on a reserve) is extremely high. In Mishkeegogamang, there was no local store. The report noted that

> the high costs make it difficult to afford the essentials required to cover basic needs such as food, heating and good shelter. Groceries are most commonly purchased at the Northern Store in Pickle Lake (30–50 km away); however, many families do not have access to transportation and a taxi to and from the town costs approximately $160, adding substantially to the cost of living.[149]

By December 2009, the Mushkegowuk Tribal Council had declared a state of emergency because child support workers and first responders were unable to deal with the enormity of the suicide crisis. Neither level of government responded.

Health workers, school counsellors, and elders in each of the communities did what they could to try to reassure the young people living with the nightmare of death around them. High school principal Ron Pate announced that he would keep the school open all night for any student who wanted to come in and talk or play a game of basketball. Pate, who had grown up in Harlem and was a Gulf War vet, promised to stay at the school every night if youth needed someplace to go. "I'm not going to lose a child on my watch," he announced.

Outside the trauma-struck communities, these appalling death rates barely made a blip on the political radar. On December 12, 2009, as the crisis was at its height, regional chiefs met with senior staff in Minister of Indian Affairs Chuck Strahl's office to discuss the funding crisis facing child welfare teams in the north. They brought with them Cindy Blackstock. As director of the First Nations Child and Family Caring Society, she was an expert on the implications of federal funding arrangements for First Nations children in need of child welfare programs.

The group hoped to find a resolution to the federal government's refusal to show leadership on the funding crisis in child welfare services. They arrived at the minister's office to find a security guard waiting for them. Blackstock was singled out by political staff and told that she wasn't allowed in the meeting. She was shocked to realize that her work on the human rights case had marked her as a political threat to the Harper government. Left to sit in the outer part of the minister's office, she was watched by a "rather large male security guard [who] stood directly on the other side of the coffee table while I read the newspaper."[150]

While Strahl's staff were focused on keeping Blackstock out of the meeting, Payukotayno faced layoffs of its front-line workers. Thirteen youth were dead at this point, and eighty more had tried to kill themselves. The child welfare agency had spent its annual budget by the third quarter as it vainly tried to respond to the epidemic. It was now being scrutinized by provincial bureaucrats because of its "deficit." And, if the province didn't cover the shortfall in the budget, the agency faced layoffs of all staff at the height of the crisis.

The provincial Liberal government knew from the 2006 Barnes Report that Payukotayno lacked basic funding to provide proper child welfare services in the region. The suicide crisis had pushed the agency past the breaking point. MPP Gilles Bisson challenged the provincial government to take action. His work, along with an exposé on the situation in the Toronto Star, forced the government to make a commitment that no staff would be laid off. "It is unfortunate it always takes a crisis to get the province to respond. In this case, thirteen kids have committed suicide. It is the only time we hear from these guys [the provincial government]," Bisson told the Toronto Star.[151]

In response to the political pressure, the Liberal government agreed to pay for four additional emergency workers at Payukotayno. But these were only short-term positions. The government's long-term solution to the suicide crisis was explained in a Toronto Star article noting that provincial Aboriginal affairs minister Brad Duguid was heading to James Bay to promote hockey: "Duguid is hoping to instil self-confidence in aboriginal teens in remote

communities through sports. He will launch the Play Program
..., a joint government and corporate venture to bring hockey to
poor, isolated towns."[152] Encouraging youth to play hockey in a
region already hockey-mad might have had some positive benefits
if the government was willing to address the terrible resource gap
facing Ontario's northern First Nations child welfare providers.
The Barnes Report had given the provincial government a clear
picture of the crisis as well as the solutions needed. But the report
was shelved. In 2012, the Liberals announced a $1.7 million cut to
the budget of Payukotayno. This resulted in the layoffs of twenty-two child welfare workers and the closure of two group homes.
The overstretched agency was told that it was time "to live within
[their] means."[153]

PEOPLE IN TENTS

"Nothing ever changes. Nothing ever makes a difference."
Shannen drew her knees to her chest. "I give up, Serena.
Winning this fight is impossible."

"Nothing's impossible, ShanShann. You said it yourself,"
Serena said, through her own tears. . . .

"But we said exactly the same thing a whole year ago.
We were sure that the government would promise a new
school. It was just a matter of time. . . . And look what happened—nothing. In fact, the situation in Attawapiskat is
worse. Much worse!" . . .

"Do you remember when I felt like giving up?" Serena repeated her father's words. "You get up, pick up your
books, and keep walking in your moccasins."

"I'm tired of walking, nimis [big sister]."
—JANET WILSON[154]

The third state of emergency declared at James Bay in
2009 was the result of failing infrastructure. On July 11,
2009, the sewage lift station in Attawapiskat failed, causing raw sewage to back up into eight homes. In the overcrowded homes of the community, this flood of human
waste left ninety people homeless, including many infants and
elders. Even for families who could have handled their own repairs,
the nearest construction supply store was 500 kilometres away by
air. Cleanup of the homes would be expensive and take months.

The homes were too contaminated for people to stay in them
without becoming sick. There was no place to put ninety residents
in a community already under pressure from an ever-growing

backlog of people waiting for housing. Over the previous decade, the population had grown by 40 per cent,[155] while the number of new houses didn't come close to replacing even the aging and deteriorating housing stock. The local arena lacked the facilities to provide safe housing for people over an extended period of time.

With nowhere to house the displaced families, the band council declared a state of emergency and asked the federal government to have residents flown to Cochrane until a remediation plan could be put in place. Indian Affairs refused to support the request. Although government officials stated their willingness to repair the homes, they told the community that it was on its own in dealing with the homeless people.

On July 25, 2009, the band council paid the cost to fly the displaced families to Cochrane to be housed in hotels. The costs of the flights and accommodations created serious financial drags on the band's limited budget. As each week passed, the band fell further into debt.

Attawapiskat wasn't the only James Bay community struggling with infrastructure collapse that year. Fort Albany was also in the midst of a major infrastructure crisis. It started in 2007 when community members began raising alarm bells about excessive levels of black mould in twenty-six houses recently built in the community. Like so many other approved infrastructure projects, this development fell well short of the required housing needs of the James Bay region. The basements were built without drainage weeping tiles even though, given high groundwater levels, they were sitting in the water table.

As well, sewage lines from the homes lacked back-flow valves to stop sewage from coming into the homes in case of a sewage system failure. High levels of humidity and mould had created health hazards, particularly for young children, who developed rashes and had breathing difficulties.

I was invited to inspect the mould damage along with MPP Gilles Bisson, band officials, building experts from Mushkegowuk Tribal Council, and James Bay health officials. The doctors noted that the levels of mould posed serious health threats to the children and elders inhabiting these homes.

Under political pressure, Indian Affairs agreed to send an inspector to examine the problem. Fourteen homes were examined and approved for remediation, while twelve homes that had equally high levels of mould and water damage were not examined or approved for remediation. A Sudbury-based company, Mould Clean, was hired to begin remediation of the fourteen approved homes. Andrew Solomon was a young chief recently elected in Fort Albany. He was faced with the dilemma of leaving the other twelve homes in conditions that would soon make them uninhabitable. He met with regional Indian Affairs officials to press the case for doing the job properly. Believing that he had verbal support from the department, Chief Solomon instructed the company to begin cleaning the unauthorized twelve homes along with the approved fourteen homes.

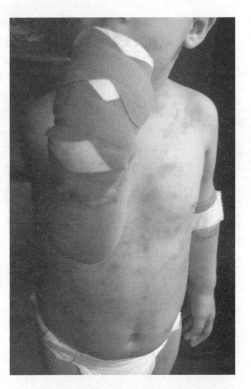

But as the mould remediation was taking place, Fort Albany's substandard sewage system collapsed. A number of homes began to fill with raw sewage and methane gas. The smell of methane was so strong that families lit candles in the basements to burn off the gas—a very dangerous and potentially explosive situation.

An infant exposed to high levels of mould in a home on Fort Albany First Nation, summer 2007. *Courtesy of the author.*

Since Mould Clean was already in the community, Indian Affairs approved it to take on the sewage restoration as it continued with the mould remediation. The company flew in pumps and began cleaning out the clogged sewage pipes. The costs were being charged to the company credit card as it put together invoices to give to the government. But then things began to go off the rails.

Attempts by the contractor to get paid fell into a bureaucratic abyss as department officials argued over how and what to pay.

One year went into two. As the company racked up debt, frustrated officials in the community called for the department to release the funds. Internal documents obtained under Access to Information legislation show the back-and-forth arguments with the department over the non-payment of bills:

> What's going on here [is] the pumps and hoses were flown in at the expense of Mould Clean, so the shit and piss can be emptied out on the ditches so the houses with basements can be liveable.... An arrangement was authorized and guaranteed by the [Regional Director General of INAC] ... and the amount owing ... is still accumulating at the First Nation's expense and possibly on the credit card of Mould Clean.... Let's quit playing games and get the people who did the job ... paid in full.[156]

In the end, Indian Affairs agreed to pay for partial cleanup of the homes and restoration of the sewage system. It denied having made any verbal commitment to cover the costs of the other homes as well as any accrued interest and other charges. The company, now out $2.3 million, was forced to take the band to court to recover costs.

A frustrated Chief Andrew Solomon wrote to Indian Affairs regarding the trail of broken promises:

> There have been several meetings between INAC and Fort Albany regarding these twelve houses and we have received repeated assurances to help provide funding. After repeated promises and commitments, INAC has never followed up. This has left Fort Albany liable for all the costs. The contractor has a judgment by the Ontario Superior Court and can begin seizing our bank accounts for the nearly $2.3 million.[157]

The company secured its money through a court order, and the band was forced to pay it. Company officials told me that they didn't blame the band for what had happened, but they simply couldn't carry millions of dollars of unpaid bills.

Over in Attawapiskat, the bills were also piling up. Unlike in Fort Albany, frustrated residents decided to make their protests public. A group of protesters went to Timmins to the office of De Beers, which owned a huge diamond mine on their territory. Building the massive Victor diamond mine near Attawapiskat had been promoted as a chance finally to bring James Bay communities into a twenty-first-century economy.

De Beers had been the focus of many regional protests. Despite jobs being offered to local residents and a complex benefit agreement with the various James Bay communities, the shanty town nature of the region remained. The reality was that a single mining operation wasn't sufficient to redress years of chronic infrastructure underfunding. Frustrated community members also protested De Beers because it was a visible symbol, whereas they had little ability to put pressure on a relatively faceless and distant federal government. Grand Chief Stan Louttit told the media that the public protest had been undertaken because nobody seemed to be taking the issues in Attawapiskat seriously. "A people can only take so much. Why is it that we have to resort to some form of civil disobedience to have our voice heard?"[158]

De Beers president Jim Gowan met with Chief Theresa Hall and the protesters. He wrote a public letter to Minister Chuck Strahl calling on him to work with the community to deal with the homeless families. As well, the company sent in a number of construction trailers from its mine site to be used as emergency housing for the short term.

The protest group then went to Ottawa in an attempt to meet with Strahl. He refused to meet with them. Chief Hall was clearly frustrated at having come over 1,000 kilometres by plane and bus. She said that the INAC officials sent to meet the delegation were "confrontational and disrespectful." She stated the case for action:

> Our people are suffering in Third World poverty while living next door to one of the largest and richest diamond mining operations in the world. We have made efforts with De Beers as well as Ontario and Canada for many months in an attempt to address our issues of poverty because our people are suffering, our infrastructure is crumbling, and our patience is running out.[159]

By late September, the band had run out of funds to keep people in hotels in Cochrane. The homeless were returning to tents without running water or to the construction trailers provided by De Beers. Winter was coming. Strahl reassured the House of Commons that the situation was under control: "In the meantime, people who are in those homes have been taken out and put into safe facilities, if that is where they would like to stay."[160] The reality was that the housing crisis in Attawapiskat was getting worse, and the lack of action would soon boil over into a major crisis between the Harper government and the James Bay Cree of Treaty 9.

LABOUR JOINS THE FIGHT

Organized Labour will ensure that no MP
in this country sleeps soundly at night
until these young people get justice.
—WAYNE SAMUELSON[161]

Terry Downey noticed them as soon as she arrived at the park. How could she not? They stood apart from the crowd, two young Indigenous sisters looking out on the blue water lapping along the shores of picturesque Lake Timiskaming. The rest of the assembled crowd was familiar enough—hydro workers, nurses, and union members. They had come out for an organizing event put together by the Ontario Federation of Labour (OFL). It was called Drive to Work, a pit-stop tour organized by Downey to galvanize labour organizations while making short YouTube clips of labour activists across the province. Shannen and Serena had been invited by local nurse Marta Sauvé to come to the event. Always game for new experiences in their new home, they had agreed.

Downey was intrigued by the sisters. She went over and sat with them on a park bench. They were shy and soft spoken. She had no idea who they were, so she asked them to tell her their story. Downey was stunned by what they told her. She couldn't believe that what these young women described was possible in Canada. She invited the two youth to come up to the microphone and tell their story to the rest of the group.

"Serena began to speak and then seemed to get shy," Downey recalled. "Shannen then lifted up her voice and started telling us about having to leave their homes. She started telling us about the conditions of the portables. I just started to cry. I knew we had to get this story out."[162]

Downey was vice-president of the OFL, representing over 1 million workers. She had been a union activist involved in social justice issues for years. But she had never heard a story like Shannen and Serena's. "I couldn't believe the story I was hearing," Downey said. "I had never heard anything like this before, and it was happening here in Ontario. In the labour movement, we hear about unfairness and bad conditions in places like Guatemala but not in Canada. I had no clue this was happening in our backyard."[163]

Downey began to "badger" (as she called it) OFL president Wayne Samuelson to get the union movement involved to help these two young leaders. Samuelson said that he had heard about the sisters and agreed to get the power of organized labour behind the Attawapiskat School campaign.

By the fall of 2009, the OFL had begun sending its various labour affiliates regular updates on the youth campaign under way in Attawapiskat. As a new school year began, the campaign was becoming increasingly embedded in school curricula, with resources and video materials now being produced by educators. The fight by Attawapiskat youth was becoming part of the educational discussions on how young people could effect change in Canada.

For the young people in Attawapiskat, however, things looked much less hopeful, for it seemed that their hopes for a new school had been defeated. Katrina Koostachin, Shannen's younger cousin, remembers having to force herself to get up and go to school in the portables. Since Shannen had moved away, it felt like the fire of hope had also left.

Feeling lonely and dispirited, Katrina called Shannen long distance. She tearfully described the frozen class windows and the frozen pipes, which meant that no water was running to the classroom toilet. She said that she was sick of breathing exhaust fumes in class and tired of believing that she had no future. "I called Shannen because I was having a hard time in grade eight, and I was crying. I told her 'Shannen, I want you to be here with me.'" Shannen didn't betray her own fears to her younger cousin. The children had to be strong. They were going to win. They had to win. Katrina recalled that Shannen told her, "'Don't be sad. . . . We will fight till we get a real school and a real education.' ... I have never been so proud in my life of a person [as I am of] Shannen. She was one of a kind."[164]

It was hearing from friends back home that pushed Shannen and Serena to keep fighting even as they attempted to fit into life at a provincial school. Through-out the fall and winter of 2009, they became increasingly dis-illusioned by the conditions still faced by their friends in Attawapiskat. The campaign had gone on for so long, and nothing seemed to be chang-ing. Winter winds were hit-ting the community, and they knew families who were living in tents because of the lack of adequate housing. They were also affected by the stories of youth suicide. It had been a long and difficult year, and they were feeling lonely and distant from their home.

The sisters were invited to address the annual convention of the Ontario Federation of Labour at the Sheraton Cen-tre in Toronto on November 27, 2009. Delegates at labour conventions are used to fiery speeches. Perhaps that is what they expected from the sisters, introduced as leaders in the fight for Indigenous justice.

Proud young leaders. Shannen and Serena in their powwow regalia. *Courtesy of the author.*

But Shannen and Serena didn't bring a prepared speech. On stage in front of 600 delegates, they looked vulnerable but deter-mined. Shannen radiated the same nervous tension as in her first speech on Parliament Hill. But something had changed in her since then. Going up to the microphone stand, she insisted that the microphone be unwound and enough cable provided so that she could walk the stage. She began with a friendly introduction: "Welcome, everybody. . . . *wâciyê*, my name is Shannen Koostachin. I've done this before, speaking on behalf of the younger students of Attawapiskat. . . . I recently moved to New Liskeard for a proper education. . . . I had to go away from home. I also had to leave my home and my family." She then stopped speaking, overcome with emotion. The hall was silent. She looked down at the delegates and began to tell her story. Her voice was almost a whisper.

> I've been going to school in portables for eight straight years. . . . You know it's still sad to hear that Indian Affairs hasn't done anything for us to this day [long pause]. So I ask myself, why aren't they doing anything at all? Aren't they supposed to be acting like governments? . . . Those younger students are still thinking that those portables are real schools—poor scattered buildings.[165]

I hadn't seen Shannen or Serena in a number of months since they had moved in with another local family for their second year of high school. They had grown up a great deal in that time. Shannen seemed to have changed the most. I remembered how she had always fed off the energy of young people when she spoke. But as she spoke to this room of adults, her frustration and anger came to the fore. Adults were supposed to make things safe for children. Why had they failed in their responsibility to the children? Shannen declared her intention to keep fighting until they saw justice:

> Every day I would have to call home because at times I would get homesick. . . . Every time I hang up I get that cold feeling that I'm on my own. But I have to put my heart aside and put my head into what I have to accomplish. . . . But this time I am not going to put my heart aside. I'm going to put my heart *and* my head into this [fight]. . . . We are not going to give up until we are given a new school. This school campaign is growing. . . . It's never going to stop. We're not going to give up.[166]

Shannen then handed the microphone to Serena. Her older sister was normally the more diplomatic of the two, but this time she was equally blunt:

> Year after year we have been asking for a new school. . . . I have made speeches before . . . and, honestly, it's starting to get frustrating. . . . Let me ask you something: what did they ever do to deserve this? They are just kids starting their lives and it's not off to a very good start. . . . I want them to lead successful lives, to be known by their culture and traditions and to live on their dreams. . . . If you want us to pursue our dreams, then make it happen![167]

There was a moment of silence in the hall, and then the delegates responded with a sustained standing ovation.

Terry Downey noted the response to the Koostachin sisters as she looked out into the packed hall:

> As these two young women started telling their story, it just blew people away. You had blue-collar workers looking at each other in shock. They were thinking of their own children who weren't facing such deplorable conditions. They were thinking, "What the fuck is our government doing to these children?" It was like a bolt of lightning through the room of that convention.[168]

Representatives of unions from across the province lined up at the microphones on the convention floor. They pledged the support of their locals with resources, organizers, and dollars. Blue-collar unions, health-care workers, hydro workers, all stood to say that the time had come for union workers to join the children in their fight for justice.

Downey said that the Koostachin sisters touched the labour movement in a personal way: "People got the message. This doesn't happen very often in the labour movement because we are very diversified and there are so many issues vying for attention. But this was one issue that people felt they just couldn't let go of. . . . They [Shannen and Serena] turned a story of children without a school into a potent political force."[169]

ATTAWAPISKAT WINS

The Attawapiskat issue dogged Minister Chuck Strahl. As 2009 rolled on, he had a difficult time establishing a narrative for the success of his government on Indigenous issues. The failure to address the inequities of First Nations education was increasingly obvious. And the stories of other "Attawapiskats" were beginning to be heard. At Bunibonibee First Nation in Manitoba, mould forced the school to be closed. At Lake St. Martin First Nation, students had been in portables for a decade because their school was prone to flooding and overrun by snakes.[170] Students in Kashechewan were going to school in portables. In Pikangikum, children were still waiting for the school that the government claimed to have built. Even for reserve schools in good condition, the gaps in resource support compared with the provincial systems were growing year by year. A 2009 report by the First Nations Education Council pointed out that, between 1997 and 2004, the funding per student in the provincial system had risen 24 per cent, while the funding for First Nations children had been capped by Paul Martin's 2 per cent limit.[171]

Frustration was also growing at the Assembly of First Nations. The AFN had been pushing for years for reform of the education system. A number of First Nations education councils had spent fruitless years negotiating with the federal government on agreements to transfer decision making to the councils. Strahl was pushed by national chiefs on his failure to deliver on education, but it was his combative stance toward Attawapiskat that kept the story in the media.

Just as the Ontario labour movement began pledging financial and organizational support to the Attawapiskat campaign, the government threw in the towel. Walking into a fractious meeting of the Assembly of First Nations in December 2009, Strahl promised to work with the chiefs on education reform:

> I have no problem saying, as you heard me say before, that education makes everything else we are going to talk about easier. Everything else—the preservation of your languages, the preservation of your culture, economic opportunities, ability to engage in national-international discussions—all those things become easier with education—standard of living, every measurable social indicator. It's hard to find something more important than education. I absolutely agree with it and I am eager to engage with you on those discussions.[172]

As proof of his goodwill, Strahl announced that the children of Attawapiskat would finally get their school. The government wouldn't fight over its size. Although Indian Affairs routinely builds reserve schools to a more meagre standard than those in the provincial system, the government agreed to build the school in Attawapiskat to provincial standards.[173]

After the meeting with the AFN chiefs, Strahl came up to me to personally deliver the news. He seemed to be relieved to have the Attawapiskat school issue finally addressed. I thanked him and shook his hand.

Shannen received a text message from her parents that simply said "Attawapiskat wins." This was the best Christmas present that Attawapiskat had ever had. For Shannen, it meant that she could now be what she had always dreamed of being, just an ordinary kid like everyone else. The long battle appeared to be over.

PART IV
SHANNEN'S DREAM, 2010

Shannen Koostachin was killed in a car accident not long after the government announced the building of a school in Attawapiskat. Her death not only had a huge impact on her community but also galvanized the resolve of a larger activist movement that had seen her as an emerging youth leader. Out of the outpouring of grief over her loss, the Shannen's Dream campaign was launched to fight for equity for all First Nations youth.

Shannen had been known as a fighter for a proper school for the children in Attawapiskat, but this new campaign wasn't focused on a fight for a single school—it sought to address the fundamental inequity faced by Indigenous youth across Canada. Shannen's Dream was established as both a grassroots student campaign and a parliamentary political fight.

This section looks at the launch of the campaign, which came at a time when awareness of the systemic discrimination faced by Indigenous children was finally breaking through in the public realm. This awareness was driven by the legal battle at the Canadian Human Rights Tribunal as Cindy Blackstock pushed for justice for Indigenous children discriminated against in matters of both health and child welfare.

TRAGEDY

Shannen was a crystal and you BROKE
Her. So why did you do that?
And she had a very strong heart.
Never give up hope that's what Shannen said.
Never give up faith to the last of all.
Every one should be able to
Never give up. SHANNEN changed the country.
—POEM WRITTEN TO PRIME MINISTER HARPER
BY A STUDENT[1]

The stretch of Highway 11 from North Bay to New Liske-ard boasts some of the most ruggedly beautiful land in Ontario. The highway weaves through imposing rock cuts, white pine forests, and glacial blue lakes. But this stretch is also among the most dangerous in the prov-ince, especially at night. Highway 11 is known as the "trucker's route," with the two-lane asphalt ribbon acting like a conveyor belt for a staggering haul of merchandise, lumber, and machinery across the country. There is an endless convoy of eighteen-wheelers speeding along the twisting, narrow highway. If you are tired, if you aren't paying attention, this road of beauty can be a road of death.

Shannen was on that road in the evening of May 31, 2010. Her family's friend, Rose Thornton, had invited her and two other teenage girls to take a weekend trip to southern Ontario. It was meant to be a celebration of a year of success. Shannen had found her sea legs in high school. Having seen the victory of the school campaign, she had turned her attention to improving her marks.

Shannen was looking forward to graduating from grade ten and capping off the year by playing the part of the lead dancer in the June school powwow. Serena had been the lead dancer the year before. Shannen had been practising hard to follow in her sister's graceful steps. She wanted to be a dancing butterfly on the schoolgrounds when the powwow began.

But the butterfly never made it. At some point on the trip, Shannen unbuckled her seat belt, perhaps to be more comfortable as she slept. At 10:41 PM, Rose Thornton's minivan went around a bend at Jumping Caribou Lake and was hit head-on by a southbound transport truck. In a second, it was all over. Rose and Shannen were both killed. The other two girls survived. I received the call the next morning at my office in Ottawa from Shannen's father. The only thing I managed to make out was "There was an accident. . . . It was Shannen. . . . She didn't make it." I don't really remember what else was said. It was a blur. As I hung up the phone, I sat at my desk and wept.

Over the next few days, as word spread about her death, I began to receive calls from people across the country who had been touched by Shannen. Calls came in from political, human rights, and education rights leaders. Many were crying. It was hard to believe that this young girl who had shown so much fire was gone. Each of them said, "We need to do something. There has to be some way to honour her life." I agreed. But what? In a region where we had lost so many young people to suicide and tragedy, the loss of this bright light was just too much to comprehend.

Shannen's body was brought home to a community in shock. At the time, Attawapiskat was struggling with a series of youth deaths. It had started the previous April when fifteen-year-old Brendon Kioke, a popular hockey player, died of gunshot wounds. In the early spring of 2010, twenty-one-year-old Ian Kamalatisit went through the ice on the Attawapiskat River as he was coming back from hunting for his young family. Shannen's friend, Chris Kataquapit, led the rescue teams that went out every day for five weeks until they managed to bring the body home.

Two days after Ian's death, Shannen's schoolmate Dakota Nakogee died from kidney failure after giving birth to a baby. Chronic kidney failure is a noted symptom of exposure to the hydrocarbon contaminants that had polluted their schoolgrounds since

Roadside memorial for Shannen Koostachin on Highway 11 south of Temagami, Ontario. *Courtesy of the author.*

they were children. On May 15, 2010, twenty-two-year-old Dwayne Hookimaw killed himself. And now the firebrand youth leader of Attawapiskat was being brought home to be buried in the little cemetery.

The funeral was held in the local Reg Louttit Arena. The event took six hours. The grief was so heavy at times that I wondered if it would be possible to continue with the funeral. When the family members came up to close the coffin, they just stood there holding on to each other, seemingly unable to say the final farewell to Shannen.

A number of eulogies were given. Shannen's young friend Chelsea spoke. "Shannen, whatever I choose to do is because of you. You inspired all of us. You proved to us anything is possible." She then asked the community to keep the flame that Shannen had lit alive.

The family had asked me to speak. It was the second eulogy that I had given in my life. The first one had been just a week before for my father. But this one was much harder.

> When we say goodbye to an adult, we can look back at a life of accomplishments and celebrate a life fully lived. However, when we confront a death such as the death of our dear young Shannen, we are forced to ask, "What could have been? What might have been?"
>
> If Martin Luther King or Nelson Mandela had died in a car crash when they were fifteen, would the world have ever known what it had lost? With Shannen, we had a glimpse of what might have been.
>
> But we see the footprints where Shannen was walking, we know where she wanted us and her community to go. And so the greatest tragedy of these events would be if we didn't continue walking in the footprints Shannen laid down for us. She told us again and again, "I am not giving up," and so we can't give up.

In the weeks following the funeral, I found it very hard to concentrate on anything. I just couldn't get my head around the fact that we had lost a young woman with so much potential for leadership. The Ontario Federation of Labour called—it wanted to plant a memorial tree. Various education leaders called about establishing a memorial fund for James Bay graduates. There was talk of a posthumous human rights award. There was discussion about establishing a bursary fund. But then I began to receive emails from Chelsea Edwards in Attawapiskat. She didn't want Shannen's dream for change to die with the accident.

Chelsea set up a Facebook page called "Shannen's Dream." As Chelsea kept reminding us, "Shannen had a dream that First Nation children had a right to go to 'comfy schools' that gave them hope and made childhood a time to dream." Shannen had put her heart and soul into fighting for a school. In doing so, she had inspired youth across the country. But even though they had won the fight for Attawapiskat, the bigger issue of fundamental inequity remained.

As the summer wore on, a team of volunteer planners coalesced to find a way to honour this young woman's life. Shannen had inspired young people to stand up for justice, so it seemed fitting to honour her by launching a campaign on behalf of all the children denied equitable education on reserves across Canada. The Shannen's Dream team included (among many others) Grand Chief Stan Louttit, Cindy Blackstock, Terry Downey (Ontario Federation of Labour), Chelsea Edwards, Catherine Fife (president of the Ontario Provincial School Boards' Association), Karihwakeron (Tim Thompson) of the AFN, plus representatives from various teachers' unions. Shannen's parents were kept in the loop but weren't involved in planning the campaign since they were focusing on their family and the healing journey ahead.

It was decided to launch a national campaign to galvanize young people across cultural lines to carry the movement forward. The fight was on to finally deal with the fundamental inequity faced by First Nations students across Canada.

A LITTER OF PUPPIES

It's a pattern that looks a lot like the pattern under residential schools. . . . The removal appears
not to be driven directly by an intention to "kill
the Indian in the child" but the consequences
are nonetheless the same.
—SHAWN ATLEO[2]

As plans were made to launch the Shannen's Dream campaign, systemic discrimination against Indigenous youth was becoming an increasingly hot political topic thanks to the work of Cindy Blackstock. She was pressing forward with the human rights complaint against the federal government over its discriminatory treatment of First Nations children in foster care. The government, however, was working hard to have her case thrown out by the Canadian Human Rights Tribunal.

Her work on behalf of First Nations children had put Blackstock on the Harper government's list of political enemies. Soon after she had been stopped from attending the meeting in Minister of Indian Affairs Chuck Strahl's office in December 2009, the Departments of Justice and Indian Affairs began to spy on her. They kept track of all her public speeches and international work on Indigenous children's rights. A number of bureaucrats were even assigned the task of monitoring her private Facebook page. Screen shots of baking recipes, Mother's Day greetings, and her online conversations with a twelve-year-old supporter were passed around among officials in both departments.[3]

Cindy Blackstock with students at a rally for First Nations children's rights. *Courtesy of Janet Doherty.*

The pettiness in the internal reports is striking. "Our girl's on a roll" wrote one official. "Our dearest friend Cindy Blackstock" was how another sarcastically described her.[4] The spying campaign was revealed when Blackstock, acting on a hunch, made an Access to Information request for government documents that mentioned her. Over 2,500 pages of documents were turned over, revealing a spying campaign that seemed to hearken back to the Red Scare days. To Blackstock, this surveillance was completely over the top: "I have never had a parking ticket, let alone a criminal record, and I have never conducted myself in an unprofessional manner.... I'm a common sense girl. Rather than spending money following me around, spend it on the children."[5]

Blackstock asked the Canadian privacy commissioner to investigate the government's spying on her. In 2013, the privacy commissioner ruled that the government had broken the law in its invasion of her privacy.

Why was the government so obsessed with a woman who advocated for children? Journalist Tim Harper pointed out that, in the current climate in Ottawa, her work for First Nations children had made Blackstock "an enemy of the state."[6] The *Toronto Star* described the vitriol in the documents on her as an example of the "meanness" that had become a hallmark of the Harper government.

Blackstock was politically problematic because she refused to walk away from the human rights case even after the government cut off funding to her agency. In pushing the case forward, she was shining a light on the negligent treatment of the most vulnerable children in Canada. She was exposing and explaining to the public the complex factors having such negative impacts on child welfare on reserves.

To be certain, the appalling poverty, isolation, and precarious living conditions on some reserves put many children in difficult situations. For the better part of a century, these factors have been compounded by interference (and indifference) from federal and provincial agencies. For generations, Indigenous children have been denied natural bonding with parents and relatives in a familial environment. Hence, basic parenting skills have not been passed on as families have suffered from government obstruction of the natural process of child rearing.

Theresa Stevens, executive director of Anishinaabe Abinoojii Family Services in Kenora, Ontario, was a special witness at the Canadian Human Rights Tribunal's investigation into discrimination against Indigenous children in government care. She spoke of the efforts to restore child-rearing skills in communities that had been devastated by both the residential schools and the Sixties Scoop:

> So if the majority of our on-reserve families, their parents or grandparents attended residential school and there was that family breakdown or the knowledge of parenting and traditional child-rearing practices, if that knowledge was broken or severed because parents or grandparents were sent to residential school . . . , it definitely had and continues to have an impact on the children and families.[7]

The ability of Indigenous child welfare agencies to respond to this trauma continues to be hampered by a multitude of institutional factors, particularly a lack of resources and chronic underfunding. Speaking to media, UBC professor Shelly Johnson said that First Nations-based child welfare agencies cannot bring about improved outcomes because of the huge discrepancy in funding compared with that provided to provincial child welfare agencies: "I don't think the answer is turning over [to Indigenous organizations] a broken and flawed system and then paying Indigenous people 22 per cent less than everybody else to manage that misery."[8] This chronic underfunding is exacerbated by the fact that First Nations children continue to receive child welfare services based on legislation nearly half a century old. The result in Ontario is that these children are many more times likely to go into foster care than other children.[9]

In 2011, Census Canada determined that, of the nearly 30,000 children in foster care in Canada, half are Indigenous, "a number that exceeds even the grimmest estimates."[10] This means that there are more children in the hands of the state now than at the height of the residential school system. John Beaucage recently completed a report on the crisis in Indigenous child welfare for the Ontario government and referred to the huge number of First Nations children in foster care as the "Millennium Scoop."[11]

When you drill down into these numbers, many reasons begin to appear why so many Indigenous children are being apprehended by the government. In 2003, Blackstock was part of a group that undertook a groundbreaking study of the apprehension of Indigenous children by child welfare agencies.[12] The group found little statistical difference between child welfare interventions involving on-reserve versus off-reserve children when it came to threats of sexual or physical abuse. In fact, sexual abuse was identified in only 2–3 per cent of the cases of children apprehended in either category.

The big disparity between the two groups was the issue of "neglect." Over half (56 per cent) of the cases of intervention in First Nations families were because of neglect, as opposed to just over 25 per cent in non-Indigenous families. The conditions deemed to constitute neglect of children include poverty, lack of food, unsafe living conditions, and parents with addictions. These are all problems responsive to targeted and culturally based interventions. But while such support programs are available in the provincial systems, often they are non-existent for on-reserve families.

Researcher Nico Trocmé, who helped to author the report, told First Nations leaders that the word *neglect* is not synonymous with bad parenting: "This is not a study that says that First Nation families are worse or are more abusive or more neglectful. This study says that First Nation families are living in far worse situations and under that stress, aren't able to meet the needs of their children as well as they would like to do."[13]

When non-Native children are identified as suffering from neglect, provincial child welfare agencies equipped with higher levels of funding are more likely to provide home support for the families. On reserves, however, such support is not available. Thus, child welfare agencies are often forced to take children away from their parents. Sometimes it is because of drug issues, but other times it is simply because of poverty. In cases of parents fighting drug addictions, the backlog of treatment for on-reserve patients is so long that many families cannot get the support that they need when they need it.

An investigation of Alberta child welfare policies by the *Calgary Herald* and the *Edmonton Journal* found that the large number of First Nations children in the child welfare system was connected to the huge discrepancy in resources provided to First Nations child welfare organizations compared with child welfare agencies off reserve. The papers reported that "Eighty-two percent [of First Nations children at risk] had been apprehended while 18 percent received services at home. In comparison, of the 5,005 non-Indigenous children in the system, only 54 percent had been apprehended, while 46 percent were receiving services at home."[14]

The papers also reported that, from 1999 to 2013, in Alberta, 145 children in foster care died. Nearly 75 per cent of them were Indigenous.[15] The provincial government later admitted that the real number was much higher: there were actually 741 deaths of youth in that period. The 145 deaths initially reported were those of youth in actual care, but when the deaths of children in families involved with child welfare agencies were included the number jumped dramatically. The actual number showed that children on the radar of Alberta's child welfare system were dying at the rate of more than one a week for thirteen years, but nobody outside the system seemed to notice. Twenty-four infants died in this period, including ten from sudden infant death syndrome.[16]

At one of the subsequent inquests, it was pointed out that the federal government did not supply funding for families on reserves to deal with infants suffering from fetal alcohol syndrome. Would these infants have had a better chance of surviving if there was at-home support?[17]

In an inquest into the death of "Baby K" from the Samson Cree First Nation in Alberta, Justice Bart Rosborough identified numerous problems that contributed to the infant's death from pneumonia. He raised warning flags about misdirected funds at the child welfare agency, poor management, high staff turnover, and the huge discrepancy between funding for off-reserve child welfare agencies compared with on-reserve child welfare agencies. As he noted in his final report, "it would appear that there is a significant disparity in the level of funding provided for children 'off reserve' as opposed to those 'on reserve.' An archaic funding arrangement with the latter results in considerably fewer resources made available to them."[18]

Raven Sinclair, of the Faculty of Social Work at the University of Regina, told the Calgary Herald that there was nothing accidental about the shocking number of deaths in the child welfare system: "There are an incredible number of kids dying in care each year. This isn't just an accident. It is not a fluke of statistics. It is happening year after year."[19]

In 2014, the issue made it onto the national agenda with the brutal murder of fifteen-year-old Tina Fontaine of Sagkeeng First Nation in Manitoba. On August 17, 2014, police found her body wrapped up in a bag at the bottom of the Red River. Sergeant John O'Donovan expressed his horror that Tina had been allowed to slip through the cracks so easily: "She's a child. This is a child that's been murdered. Society would be horrified if we found a litter of kittens or pups in the river in this condition. This is a child."[20]

Tina Fontaine's story was depressingly familiar to people working with Indigenous youth on the street. There is a huge correlation between the foster care system and the high rates of Indigenous youth who end up in gangs, the drug trade, or trafficked into prostitution. Tina is remembered by her family as a happy and well-adjusted child, but following the murder of her father she became increasingly distraught. She was removed from her extended family, placed in the provincial child welfare system, and moved to Winnipeg. Within a month of landing in the city, she was missing.

Even more shocking was that police were not searching for Tina when they dragged the river and found her body. They were searching for a man who had been feared drowned in the area, but their search ended with her name being added to the list of more than 1,200 murdered and missing Indigenous women in Canada.

• • •

Given the huge social problems in some communities, hard questions need to be asked about which system should be in place to ensure the safety of children living in deprivation. Blackstock believes that programming has to be completely rethought by moving control out of the bureaucracies and empowering grassroots community teams:

> One of the things that was stolen from us by colonization was the ability to dream for our kids. The vision, where it exists, is fragmented. Many communities have pragmatic solutions, but there is no predictability in funding. The funding programs are always annual. Agencies are always struggling to meet the annual funding program applications or objectives. There is no holistic vision for the delivery of child-centred services.[21]

Two key programs designed to create a more holistic approach to supporting children and young families on reserves are Health Canada's Building Healthy Communities program and Brighter Futures program. They have been in place since the early 1990s, and their success to date lies in their being organized and administered at the local level.

And, given the serious crisis facing Indigenous children in foster care, the government has recognized the need to take action. In 2008, the Department of Indian Affairs acknowledged that "a fundamental change in the funding approach of First Nations Child and Family Service Agencies to child welfare is required in order to reverse the growth rate of children coming into care, and in order for the agencies to meet their mandated responsibilities."[22]

Kitigan Zibi Algonquin youth lead march for children's education rights on Parliament Hill. *Courtesy of Janet Doherty.*

But such changes require serious investments. The federal government has stated that over the past fourteen years it has doubled the funding for Indigenous child welfare. But the vast majority of this increased spending was the result of increased "maintenance" fees charged by provincial and territorial child welfare agencies to the federal government, so this increase did not reflect new money to ensure that children stayed out of child welfare.

In fact, spending on First Nations child welfare agencies remained relatively flat over that period.[23] The exception was in 2011, when the government increased funding for some additional support programs. But they were not available in all areas of the country, including Ontario. As well, the auditor general noted that, when the department augmented funding for child welfare, it was, once again, robbing Peter to pay Paul. The increased child welfare costs were being covered by funds diverted from other capped programs, such as education and infrastructure.[24]

To Blackstock, the treatment of First Nations children cuts to the heart of the government's commitment to follow through on reconciliation in the wake of the historic apology for residential schools: "If the federal government's lacklustre efforts to fully redress inequities in child welfare funding are any indication, there are serious and important questions about the federal government's commitment ... to engage in reconciliation.... Reconciliation requires not just *saying* the right thing but *doing* the right thing."[25]

• • •

Blackstock's case at the Canadian Human Rights Tribunal wasn't simply about systemic underfunding of child welfare. Despite having voted for Jordan's Principle in the House of Commons, the Conservative government has continued to fight basic issues concerning child equity. In 2011, Maurina Beadle of the Pictou Landing First Nation of Nova Scotia went to court to try to force the government to cover the costs for home care for her badly disabled son, sixteen-year-old Jeremy Beadle. He suffers from cerebral palsy, hydrocephalus, and autism. He responds to feeding only by his mother and can be physically abusive to himself if other adults intervene. "They did an assessment on us, and say Jeremy is at the level where he should be institutionalized. I told them, over my dead body. I'm the only person he will eat for. If you put him in an institution, that's it," she said.[26]

After two years of fighting in court, the federal government lost the case. The judge cited its commitment to Jordan's Principle and ordered it to pay the health-care costs that had been draining the limited funds of the Pictou Landing First Nation. The Conservatives challenged this decision in the Federal Court of Appeal. They asked the court to order single mother Maurina to pay the government's legal fees. After putting her and Jeremy through the stress and cost of preparing for the appeal, the government dropped it on July 11, 2014, just weeks before the hearing was scheduled to take place.

Jeremy's case is far from being the exception, for the federal government routinely refuses home support for Indigenous children that would be available to non-Indigenous children. Hundreds of children on reserves across the country are denied basic medical and home-care support.[27]

Let's look at the case of a four-year-old child who suffered cardiac arrest and anoxic brain injury while undergoing a routine dental extraction. The trauma created "mobility [and] cognitive" disabilities that left her "totally dependent for activities of daily living."[28]

A Health Canada memo dated November 21, 2012, described the responses of a dozen government and social service agencies involved in assessing what the child required in terms of support to be released from hospital. The plans included a wheelchair ramp, hydraulic lift, bath chair, wheelchair, and specialized Hill-Rom bed to ensure that she could continue to breathe as she lay down. However, the federal government balked at paying for the specialized bed. The memo noted that the representative of Health Canada's Non-Insured Health Benefits Program said "absolutely not" in response to the request for the bed.[29] "Absolutely not." The two words jump off the page. They imply a feeling of bureaucratic effrontery as though this child, who hovered between life and death, was some kind of chiseller to the taxpayer.

In the end, the medical director of the hospital offered to pay for the bed because otherwise the child would have been left in limbo in the hospital. The document, released as part of the Child and Family Caring Society's human rights case against the federal government, is just one of many that show the tragic consequences for children and families of the government's systemic refusal to put the needs of Indigenous children ahead of saving money.

The evidence at the human rights hearing revealed that in British Columbia First Nations children in care are denied access to dental coverage, "even in emergency situations."[30] It was further revealed that the government sometimes refuses to pay for certain medications even after a pediatrician has declared their necessity.[31]

One dismal example provided to the Canadian Human Rights Tribunal was that of a child with multiple needs requiring a wheelchair, stroller, and lift/tracking system to move in and out of bed. According to the evidence, the federal government agreed to pay for only one of the three needs. If the family chose a lift/tracking device, the government would not pay to have it installed. If the family opted for a wheelchair, it would have to be a manual one since the government wouldn't pay for a motorized one, even for a child with severe disabilities. The manual wheelchair would then have to be fitted with inserts if the child was too small for it.[32]

Witnesses at the hearing described funding for Indigenous children as "woefully inadequate" and contributing to "circumstances [that] are dire," in which children are unnecessarily placed in child welfare and, in some cases, might even die.[33]

•••

On June 2, 2010, the federal government appeared before the tribunal with its third motion to have Blackstock's case thrown out. The new argument put forward was that the government could not be found guilty of discrimination because it merely provided funding for child welfare and did not have established programs for First Nations and non First Nations youth. It would be unfair to compare federal government spending with provincial programs. Blackstock said that this motion was another attempt at "splitting hairs—it is clear to any reasonable person that child welfare services cannot be provided without funding. More importantly, this argument does not prioritize concern for children over concern for government interests."[34]

On March 14, 2011, Chair of the Tribunal Shirish Chotalia sided with the federal government and ordered the case dismissed. Blackstock was devastated and vowed to launch an appeal. "In issuing this ruling, Shirish Chotalia in effect legalized racial discrimination against vulnerable children on reserve," Blackstock said.[35]

The Canadian Human Rights Commission joined Blackstock and committed to fighting the decision in the Federal Court. Senior counsel for the commission Philippe Dufresne stated that the ruling had to be overturned: "We are disappointed with this ruling because it has the potential of limiting access to the Human Rights Act to some of the most vulnerable. It is a concern for us."[36]

On April 18, 2012, Justice of the Federal Court Anne Mactavish found that the tribunal had "erred in failing to consider the significance of the government's own adoption of provincial child welfare standards in its programming manual and funding policies."[37] She overturned the ruling and ordered a new hearing overseen by a new chair. The federal government fought the ruling at the Federal Court of Appeal, where it lost again. The issue was now very much in the public eye as a result of the government's offensive against Blackstock.

The *Toronto Star* wrote that

> Cindy Blackstock has spent more than five years trying
> to hold Ottawa accountable for a funding gap on the wel-
> fare of Indigenous children on reserves. Instead of deal-
> ing with that funding gap, Ottawa has spent nearly as long
> searching for dirt on Blackstock. In total, it spent more
> than three million dollars trying to derail her bid to have
> the government's funding policy ruled as discrimination
> against native children.[38]

Blackstock said that the government's stonewalling was a national
shame: "This case strikes to the conscience of the nation."[39]

This stonewalling wasn't cheap. It was part of a much broader
pattern of legal obstruction used by the federal government to limit
Indigenous rights in areas of education, child welfare, resource
development, and treaty entitlements. Journalist Doug Cuthand
noted that the government spent $106 million on legal costs for
the Department of Indian Affairs in 2012–13 but only $66 million
for the Canada Revenue Agency and $37 million for the RCMP.[40]
Thus, the single biggest legal cost for the federal government came
from fighting issues of First Nations rights. The cost dwarfs what
is spent going after tax frauds and crooks.

Cuthand pointed out that, when it came to court cases, the
federal government had a terrible track record of derailing First
Nations rights. Time and time again, courts have upheld the legal
rights of First Nations. So why does the government continue to
fight so hard against basic issues such as protecting children at
risk? Wrote Cuthand: "The federal government has adopted an
expensive, two-pronged legal strategy. First it hopes to overturn
the success of First Nation court victories. Second, it conducts a
scorched earth legal strategy that drags out cases and starves First
Nations organizations of funds. Sitting down for honest negotiations is simply not a part of the government's strategy."[41]

Thus, whether interfering with justice for the survivors of
St. Anne's Residential School or attempting to derail the human
rights case for children, the government appears to be determined
to use its endless financial resources to wage a "scorched earth"
campaign against the most vulnerable people in Canadian society.

THE DREAM IS LAUNCHED

Every day I struggle along with my classmates, knowing that we are not getting the [same] equal right[s] as any other Canadian child in this country. We especially struggle throughout the winter. . . . Sometimes we would have no running water because the water pipes tend to freeze during the winter. . . . Shannen had a dream, and that dream of hers was to see every child in this community have a good education, proper school and to have brighter futures. Shannen's dream could change not just Canada but this dream of hers could change the world, as she fought for what she believed in. And I too believe that Shannen's dream could change the world.
—CEDAR KOOSTACHIN[42]

Fourteen-year-old Chelsea Edwards was so nervous that she could hardly speak. She was at the CTV studio in Ottawa waiting to be interviewed on *Canada* AM as the spokesperson for the national launch of the Shannen's Dream campaign. It was seven in the morning, and the day ahead would be a whirlwind. There was a press conference on Parliament Hill with representatives from education, labour, and First Nations. Chelsea was the point person for this political kick-off, and she was scared to death. Her friend Shannen Koostachin had always done the talking. Chelsea had done the following. Now Shannen was gone, and it was her turn to start walking in her friend's moccasins.

The interview was a success. The media seemed to be smitten with the story of this Cree teenager carrying on her friend's fight for fairness. It was the first of many television and newspaper interviews for the shy new spokesperson for civil rights in Canada.

• • •

The Shannen's Dream campaign was officially launched on November 17, 2010, just five months after Shannen's death. The campaign had been planned through the late summer and early fall with a number of components. The first was to restart the enormously successful grassroots letter-writing campaign of students. This time the focus was not on a single school but on ending the systemic underfunding of First Nations education once and for all. The letter-writing campaign would complement a parliamentary push in the House of Commons.

In collaboration with the AFN's National Indian Education Council and provincial education leaders, the team worked on the language for a parliamentary motion containing the necessary steps for establishing equitable funding for First Nations students. This motion was a vision statement for making the dream of equitable education a reality.

In September 2010, I introduced Motion 571, the Shannen's Dream motion, in the House of Commons. A parliamentary motion does not contain commitments for spending, nor does it change specific legislation. It is a statement of principle debated and voted on in the House of Commons. Working within these constraints, the Shannen's Dream motion laid out the steps necessary to end the systemic underfunding of on-reserve education. It read thus:

That, in the opinion of the House, the government should:
(a) declare that all First Nation children have an equal right to high quality culturally relevant education;
(b) commit to provide the necessary financial and policy supports for First Nations education systems;
(c) provide funding that will put reserve schools on par with non-reserve provincial schools;
(d) develop transparent methodologies for school construction, operation, maintenance and replacement;

(e) work collaboratively with First Nation leaders to establish equitable norms and formulas for determining class sizes and for the funding of educational resources, staff salaries, special education services and indigenous language instruction; and,

(f) implement policies to make the First Nation education system, at a minimum, of equal quality to provincial school systems.[43]

The timing for a vote on this motion was left deliberately vague. There was no point bringing forward such a motion to have it defeated by a Conservative majority. But a motion on the parliamentary books would serve as a rallying point for a national public awareness campaign. Students or citizens could press their local MPs to state whether or not they supported the motion. As public support for the motion grew, we would judge the appropriate moment to bring it forward for debate and a vote.

To launch the campaign, a number of student leaders from Attawapiskat joined Chelsea Edwards and Cindy Blackstock at a gathering held at Elgin Street Public School in Ottawa. The students spoke eloquently of the effects that they had suffered from underfunded education in substandard facilities. Shannen's cousin, eleven-year-old Rob Koostachin, told the crowd that he was nervous coming all the way from Attawapiskat to speak his mind in Ottawa: "But when I thought of my cousin Shannen Koostachin, how proud she would be of me, my nervousness went away, and I said to myself, 'Shannen, give me the strength to walk in your moccasins and follow your footsteps to make your dream come true.'" He spoke of seeing his older cousins go to school down south, only to be put back into lower grades. He feared that he, too, would fall behind: "I am thinking, by the time I graduate from grade eight, I will be graduating from grade three level. This is not right, and it makes my heart sad." He spoke of his poor health from having been exposed to the chemicals in Attawapiskat:

I have asthma, heart problems, and eczema, a skin condition. . . . Any parent would not allow their kids to go to a mouldy school, but when you live up north where I am from, it's home, and that's all we have for education. . . . I have two eyes, two ears, two hands, two legs, one head, and one heart. We are no different from other children around the world. Our hearts all beat as one, like the beat of a drum.[44]

The presence of so many young Attawapiskat leaders showed the impact that the campaign had on inspiring local youth to stand up to injustice. Chelsea Edwards was the ideal voice for this campaign. She represented a generation of youth not only being denied their basic right to education but also being denied the chance to be teenagers. While she was dealing with national media in Ottawa, she was also struggling with the whirlwind of emotions and difficulties of leaving home at fourteen. That September she had flown out of Attawapiskat for school in Cochrane. She had cried the whole way on the plane. She had landed in a place where she didn't know how to get around and felt as if she were on her own. This is how she remembers her high school years: "I had nobody. I suddenly had to find my own way in the world. I had to look after myself."[45]

That first semester was too difficult emotionally for Chelsea, so her parents brought her back home. But being back in the community and attending local Father Vezina High School, she feared that she would never get the educational opportunities that she needed to succeed. From her home in Attawapiskat, she started searching for possible boarding houses in Timmins that she could move into in order to finish high school in the provincial system. Once she had lined up a possible place to stay, she begged her parents to let her leave home again, knowing that such a move would be a huge financial burden on them.

So, as Chelsea stood up to speak to the national media, she was coming to terms with the fact that, as a youth on a reserve, she had to give up the comfort of being a teenager in order to get an education. In her speech to the national media, she followed Serena Koostachin's lead by again comparing Shannen's Dream campaign to Rosa Parks's famous stand: "Perhaps you have heard the story of how Rosa Parks helped start the civil rights movement. Well, we are the children who have been sitting at the back of the school bus our whole lives. And we don't want to stay there anymore."[46]

A third element of this campaign was also vital—to tell the story of Shannen. There is a real need to have heroes and role models for First Nations youth, and Shannen's story resonates because it shows how one young person could make her voice heard across the country. The power of the Attawapiskat School campaign was that this story cut across racial and cultural lines. Young people of all backgrounds could look to Shannen as a potent symbol of hope and change.

Shannen Koostachin at her first high school pow-wow when she was in grade nine. This has become the iconic image of the young Indigenous leader. *Courtesy of the author.*

Clara Corbiere knew Shannen and reflected on why her story has such resonance: "People see a young girl who came from such isolation and deprivation and still had hope. This is what attracts people to her. They see the real strength and leadership in her willingness to stand up for the children."[47]

Shannen's story was told through a number of media. The First Nations Child and Family Caring Society created a poster that was sent to schools across the country. The symbol of the campaign was the blue forget-me-not, Shannen's favourite flower. A number of labour unions helped to cover the costs of promotional materials. An educational video company, Heartspeak, produced an eleven-minute documentary used in classrooms to tell the story. On top of this, internationally renowned filmmaker Alanis Obomsawin was working on a film about the political phenomenon of these youth activists.

Like the Attawapiskat School campaign, Shannen's Dream was spread through Facebook and YouTube. The photograph most widely shared among young people was of Shannen in her traditional regalia at her first high school powwow. It has been shared across cyberspace and retouched, redrawn, made into posters, and even recreated as a commemorative stained glass piece by Susana Rutherford, a professional artist from Prince Edward Island.[48]

Perhaps the photograph resonates with both Indigenous and non-Indigenous youth because it symbolizes power and pride. There is no hint of tragedy or injustice in the photo. It is the image of a girl who personified what all young people want to believe is true—that those with a dream can make a difference.

PART V
CANADA'S KATRINA MOMENT, 2011–12

The growth of the Shannen's Dream campaign was overshadowed in late 2011 when a housing crisis thrust Attawapiskat into international headlines. Footage of the shocking state of housing, which included families living in tents, shacks, and unheated trailers, presented a picture of a Canada that few knew existed. The crisis resulted in the intervention of the Red Cross and galvanized a national fundraising appeal. But the issues that should have been at the forefront of discussion   such as the dangerous conditions faced by people as winter descended—were quickly overshadowed by a politically generated media storm related to First Nations governance.

Rather than respond to the humanitarian crisis, the Harper government insinuated that the responsibility lay with band mismanagement of taxpayers' money. As such, Attawapiskat became a testing ground for Harper's increasingly combative relationship with Indigenous leaders. So, over the winter of 2011–12, the dire situation in the community took a back seat to a deeply polarizing culture war. This polarization helped to plant the seeds for the coming Idle No More movement.

THE 2011 HOUSING CRISIS

We are deeply ashamed that federal and provincial
officials are pointing fingers at each other and refuse to
take responsibility, particularly as children and elders of
Attawapiskat face life-threatening conditions as winter
approaches. As nurses, we are profoundly concerned
about the dangers of fire, freezing, infectious diseases,
skin conditions, and mental health challenges that arise
when people are force[d] to live in inhumane conditions.
—REGISTERED NURSES' ASSOCIATION OF ONTARIO[1]

John Duncan, the prime minister's newly appointed
Indian Affairs minister, had a straightforward task.
Empowered by a strong majority, the Conservative government was about to dramatically redefine Ottawa's
relationship with First Nations communities. Duncan
was the quarterback for the government's set piece of First Nations
legislation, Bill C-27, the First Nations Financial Transparency Act.
The legislation forced all bands to post online the financial data of
band salaries and staff remunerations. It also required the release
of financial data on band-based companies that had no connections with the federal government.

Accountability and transparency in spending public money are
important policy objectives. But given the Harper government's
meagre agenda for addressing the huge backlog of First Nations
issues related to housing, health, education, and so on, the obvious
question was whether this legislation should have been anywhere
near the top of the government's priorities. But in terms of political advantage, placing the spotlight on First Nations leaders for

their spending of "taxpayers' money" played well with the Conservative base and right-wing media pundits.

Shifting the focus to band accountability had the convenient benefit of directing attention away from the government's own problems with financial transparency. After all, the Harper government had shown no interest in being transparent when it came to the huge salaries of political insiders such as Nigel Wright and Bruce Carson.

Even as Duncan was calling for accountability from First Nations communities, Conservative minister Tony Clement was struggling to explain how $50 million of border infrastructure money had been diverted to his riding for an array of pet projects. The money had been spent on all manner of dubious projects, including building gazebos and lighthouses (in a forested area) and raising a sunken boat. Clement shrugged off the complete lack of documentation with the quip that the paperwork was "not perfect."[2] Rather than being held accountable for this spending boondoggle, Clement was promoted to president of the Treasury Board. This promotion gave him responsibility for holding all government departments to account for their spending and paperwork.

Such pork barrel spending offended the Conservatives' base, but Harper was adept at deflecting attention from such breaches by focusing attention on the Conservative government's triad of political bogeymen: "big union bosses," "radical environmentalists," and "elite (i.e., corrupt) chiefs."

Picking on chiefs was surprisingly easy. Few Canadians have ever been on a reserve, and popular imagery of First Nations life on a reserve is rarely positive or nuanced. To most people, reserve life is as foreign and unknowable as village life in Kandahar.

For Canada's small gene pool of right-wing media pundits, this unknowable reality has made for great press fodder. In their columns, the incredibly diverse realities of Canada's First Nations become a crude caricature of corruption and mendacity. Seen through the eyes of these opinion makers, the reserve is a black hole of entitlement draining tax dollars from hard-working (non-Indigenous) Canadians. Andy Thomsen, in a letter to the editor published in the *Penticton Western News*, provided a typical diatribe in which white resentment trumped the long succession of federal court rulings on Indigenous land and resource rights:

"It's time to tell [National Chief] Atleo and the other chiefs that the game is up—that all of their claims to land and resources are bogus. Those lands and resources have already been paid for by millions of Canadians who get up early in the morning and go to work to provide the means to support themselves and their families."[3] Lorne Gunter of Post Media told readers that the real problem with the reserve system was that the Department of Indian Affairs and white people in general were victims of reverse racism:

> Politicians and bureaucrats are worried about being labelled racist by Aboriginal leaders, so they won't call out the incompetence, nepotism, mismanagement and corruption.... [It's] not entirely the fault of civil servants. The model they implement is dictated by the Indian Act.... But most vocal First Nation chiefs don't want their absolute power diminished, so they resist every effort to repeal the Act; while most non-Aboriginal politicians are too timid to push through a repeal over the objections of the chiefs.[4]

A *National Post* editorial stated that the government should simply cut off funding to reserves: "No Canadian politicians will say it, but the only solution for [isolated reserves such as Attawapiskat] is to stop subsidizing their existence."[5] What would happen in isolated communities after funding was cut off was not addressed by the editorialist. But these calls to settle the "Indian Question" once and for all sold papers and kept conversations going around Tim Hortons tables across the country.

The Canadian Taxpayers Federation stoked this mood with its ongoing publicity campaign against the supposed financial excesses of First Nations leaders.[6] The Assembly of First Nations attempted to respond by pointing out that the average annual salary of a First Nations politician was $36,845.[7] Nonetheless, the Harper government picked up the campaign of the Taxpayers Federation and vowed to impose accountability on the chiefs.

As the lead man on the file, John Duncan didn't have the hard edge that marked a number of Conservative attack dogs, but the quiet MP from North Vancouver was a stalwart old Reformer, and the Reform base of the party was known for wanting to tackle the supposed sense of "entitlement" of First Nations communities. Duncan shrugged off complaints from First Nations leaders that they were being set up as straw men by the government's agenda. "We signalled very clearly where we were headed in the Speech from the Throne so none of this is a surprise. People have known that we were, as a government, going to take this kind of measure," he said.[8]

In terms of political influence, Duncan was many steps down on the caucus ladder from former Indian Affairs ministers Jim Prentice and Chuck Strahl. Perhaps the appointment of such a political non-entity was indicative of how far First Nations issues had dropped on the list of priorities for the prime minister.

Personally, I liked Duncan. I was hoping that, after the raucous relationship with Chuck, I could develop a less combative working relationship with the new top man at Indian Affairs (now renamed Aboriginal Affairs and Northern Development Canada).

And then, at the end of October 2011, three communities in James Bay declared states of emergency, and everyone's agenda went off the rails.

•••

Welcome to Attawapiskat. . . . Welcome to Shameful, Ontario. Shameful, because while children are peeing in buckets, while raw sewage is being dumped in ditches, two levels of government are bickering over who should deal with it.
—CHRISTINA BLIZZARD[9]

As the cold weather descended on James Bay, the communities of Kashechewan, Fort Albany, and Attawapiskat declared states of emergency because of the threats posed to homeless families in the region. The pressures of a rapidly growing population and inadequate housing had brought the communities to the breaking point. Within days of the declaration, the chiefs at Kashechewan and Fort Albany stood down because it was agreed that the situation in Attawapiskat was particularly dire and that attention should be focused there. Attawapiskat's crisis was compounded by many factors—some families had been left homeless in the 2009 sewage flood, while existing homes were filled to bursting with

Shack in Attawapiskat, one of many that had no running water, plumbing, or electricity, winter 2011. *Courtesy of the author.*

ever-increasing community numbers. The annual housing budget of $500,000 was in no way able to address the need for new homes, while existing substandard and mould-infested homes were in dire need of repairs.[10]

The housing situation in Attawapiskat was not an isolated phenomenon. It was part of a much larger crisis facing reserves across the country. The Assembly of First Nations identified a backlog of 80,000 homes needed, with 45 per cent of reserve families living in substandard or condemned housing.[11] The farther north one went, the worse the conditions tended to be. In some Treaty 9 communities, the vast majority of housing stock was substandard or condemned. Across Canada, there were communities such as Wasagamack, Red Sucker Lake, Kitcisakik, St. Theresa Point, Little Buffalo, Pikangikum, and Garden Hill where citizens lived without running water or indoor toilets.[12]

Oversight of the construction of homes on reserves was woefully inept. The auditor general blasted the department's failure to deal with remediation plans for the spread of mould, which had led to so many homes being condemned. A 2010 audit of Indian Affairs program spending on housing found that $272 million was spent annually; however, it was unable to track how the money was spent and discovered that the department failed to follow up on projects or keep paperwork to see if objectives were being met.[13]

In the case of Attawapiskat, plans had been put forward by the community to establish new subdivisions based on rent-to-own principles, but with hundreds of other communities also facing serious housing shortfalls these plans weren't moving ahead. The other problem was that Attawapiskat didn't even have the adequate land base to build a new subdivision since all of the land surrounding the reserve belonged to Ontario.

To add insult to injury, the provincial government received all the royalties from the $3 billion Victor Diamond Mine on the band's territory. When the mine opened in 2008, the Liberal provincial government boasted that it would provide a windfall to benefit students in southern Ontario as well as improving access to urban hospitals.[14] Attawapiskat, in their eyes, was a federal responsibility. And despite the riches being taken from Attawapiskat territory, the province just didn't see the urgency of sitting down with the federal government to transfer the badly needed land to band control.

By the late fall of 2011, there were 5 families living in tents, 19 families living in sheds without running water, 35 families living in houses needing major repairs, 128 families living in houses condemned because of black mould, and 118 families living with relatives (often 20 people in a small home). As well, the temporary construction trailers set up by De Beers two years before had become permanent homes to nearly 90 people—all of them living in depressingly small rooms and sharing one common kitchen and four toilets.

The state of emergency was declared on October 28, 2011, by Attawapiskat's new chief, Theresa Spence. I had known her through her work on council. She didn't strike me as a firebrand or overly political. She was worried that, as the arctic winter descended on the community, people in these makeshift quarters could die.

Chief Spence asked me to speak with Minister John Duncan about a plan to deal with the immediate crisis of families living in tents and sheds. I spoke to him the day after the state of emergency was declared, and I asked him to send his officials into

Attawapiskat to work with the community. He agreed, but then I never heard any more from him.

Days turned into weeks, and the temperature kept dropping. Officials from the regional office of Aboriginal Affairs spoke with the community about advancing some money to repair some of the condemned houses, but there was no offer to help get the families out of the tents and shacks.

In mid-November, Chief Spence and Grand Chief Stan Louttit became increasingly concerned as talks with the regional Aboriginal Affairs officials stalled.[15] They called on MPP Gilles Bisson, Dr. John Waddell of the Weeneebayko Health Authority, and me to come to the community to see the situation. I knew from past experience that nobody in the larger world would believe what was happening on the ground unless they had visual proof that the government couldn't deny. I brought with me a small digital video camera. As we toured the sheds, shacks, and construction trailers meeting residents, I filmed what we were witnessing.

We met Lisa-Kiokee Linklater, a young mother who lived in a tent with her husband and four young children. She had moved into the tent because there was no room left in a home that she had been sharing with twenty-seven people. The tent was heated by a small woodstove, and the family slept on two mattresses on the floor. She had recently purchased the main family mattress for $1,000, and in the short time that they had been living in the tent the mattress had become infested with mould. When one of the children became frustrated, she would say that she was going to "her room": a little couch at the edge of the mattresses.[16] This family wasn't destitute. Linklater's husband had a good job as a heavy equipment operator, but they had been living in the tent for two years because there was no housing available in the community.

Conditions were even bleaker for others, particularly the elderly and sick. On one street corner, there were fifteen people living in makeshift shacks with no running water or sewage. Electricity came from strung-up extension cords attached to other houses. Human waste was dumped into the ditches. The shacks were heated with half-cut oil drums fed with wood. A face cord of wood in Attawapiskat sells for $150 to $200 and might last little more than a week. With winters that last longer than six months, these heating costs are enormous. For those too poor to purchase

Young mother outside a tent that housed five people, Attawapiskat, November 2011. *Courtesy of the author.*

wood or too sick or old to cut their own in the territory, it made for dangerous conditions. One couple huddled in an unheated shed as the temperatures plunged. They lacked proper blankets, and the man, who was too sick to cut wood, was spitting up blood.

At the far end of town, many of the homeless were living in the De Beers construction trailers. Toddlers played in their long hallways, which looked like prison corridors. The image was appropriate: one young mother explained that the cells in the provincial jails were larger than the tiny room in which she was raising her children. The crowded families had to share the two sets of washrooms and one common kitchen. The possibility of a catastrophic fire in this rabbit's warren of rooms was a real concern.

I made a ten-minute YouTube video of what we witnessed. It was released along with an article in the *Huffington Post* entitled "What If They Declared an Emergency and No One Came?" As I noted in the article, "it's been three weeks since Attawapiskat First Nation took the extraordinary step of declaring a state of emergency. Since then, not a single federal or provincial official has even bothered to visit the community. No aid agencies have stepped forward. No disaster management teams have offered help."[17] The footage had an immediate impact on the Canadian public. The stark images shocked people and quickly went viral. Within days, the story was garnering national and international attention. The article was reposted 23,000 times on Facebook, and the video played on numerous news outlets both domestically and abroad. And still neither level of government moved. "In the three weeks since Chief Theresa Spence issued her frantic plea, they [the people of Attawapiskat] have been greeted with a sickening, baffling silence," wrote Bruce Urquhart in a syndicated column.[18]

At the provincial level, MPP Gilles Bisson called out the McGuinty government for not sending Emergency Measures Ontario (EMO) into the community to assess the situation. He noted that, when a tornado hit the town of Goderich, EMO had arrived in the community within twelve hours. "They were on the scene immediately and that's all we're asking them to do, their job," he said. "Their mandate isn't to fix the problem, but to make sure people are safe."[19]

Both Dr. John Waddell and Dr. Elizabeth Blackmore of the Weeneebayko Health Authority publicly warned that, as the temperatures plunged below minus twenty degrees, people could die. The Nurses' Association of Ontario urged both the federal government and the provincial government to take action. Its position was supported by the *Ottawa Citizen*'s editorial board: "Nurses shouldn't have to beg our governments to do the right thing to save lives.... Canada doled out millions of dollars for manicuring Ontario cottage country for the G8 summit last year when the world was watching. But, as a country and province, we acted slowly and inadequately where it counts, ... in a remote community with desperate needs."[20]

Rather than respond to the crisis in Attawapiskat, Minister John Duncan continued to push the government's accountability agenda. An editorial in the *Toronto Star* summed up his misplaced sense of priority: "No housing. No clean water. No schools. But Aboriginal Affairs Minister John Duncan found time last week to reintroduce legislation to force public disclosure of chiefs' salaries.... Minister, really? Transparency is a good thing ... but forging ahead with this in the face of true emergencies shows how badly misplaced the federal government's priorities are."[21]

Despite the lack of action from the government, ordinary citizens, church groups, and other volunteer organizations stepped up to help. My office received calls from across the country from people who were fundraising to send supplies to Attawapiskat. But where to send the donations, they wondered. Without an established NGO to step forward and help, little could be done.

Canadians might well have remembered the different responses to two international disasters in recent years and have drawn comparisons. The first was the failure of the Bush administration to respond to the Hurricane Katrina disaster. Many uncomfortable questions about race and class were raised in analyses of the slow reaction to the situation in New Orleans. Now Canadians were watching a similar slow-moving response to a disaster unfolding in their own country. The second scenario was that of the immense humanitarian response from citizens and NGOs to the recent earthquake in Haiti. Although the situation in Attawapiskat wasn't nearly as overwhelming as the catastrophe in Haiti, where were the NGOs to step in and help out this Haiti of the frigid north?

During this time, John Saunders, an emergency response planner with the Canadian Red Cross, was working behind the scenes with Chief Spence to get the EMO team into action. The EMO, however, didn't seem to see the urgency of the situation. As the issue dominated media and online commentaries, the provincial emergency agency stood on the sidelines claiming that it hadn't received proof that a state of emergency had been declared. Even after paperwork for the state of emergency declaration was refaxed to the EMO, provincial officials continued to stall. Saunders recalls a conference call with various government agencies about the crisis during which the EMO questioned the "value" of sending in emergency teams to assess the situation in Attawapiskat.[22]

Given the government stalling, the Red Cross decided to go in and assess the situation. Saunders said that he was warned by EMO officials about the Red Cross being "used" if it responded to the call for help: "At that time, EMO officials were concerned about [the] Red Cross being used as a political pawn. I suggested that we send in a joint team to do a joint assessment of the community before agreeing to do anything. When that offer failed, the Red Cross decided to send in our own team and do our own assessment."[23]

On November 25, 2011, the Red Cross launched a national fundraising drive to bring supplies to Attawapiskat. Money began to
flow in from concerned citizens across Canada. Students at Sacred
Heart School in Kirkland Lake, Ontario, started a fundraising
drive. Workers at Bruce Power raised $15,000.[24] Students at Car-
leton University led a bake sale. Similar projects were going on all
over Canada.

It was now a month since the state of emergency had been
declared, and temperatures were dropping into the minus thirties.
The Red Cross announced its plan to bring in sleeping bags, heaters, and insulation. It would work with the community to secure
safe accommodations for people.

Saunders had extensive experience in coordinating disaster relief. He had been at Ground Zero in the days following 9/11
and had worked in Haiti after the earthquake. However, he was
shocked by what he saw in Attawapiskat:

> Landing in Attawapiskat, I was surprised I was still in
> Canada. This was a real crisis. If nothing had been done,
> people definitely would have frozen to death that winter or
> burned to death trying to heat those tinderbox shacks. . . .
> I had seen abject poverty in other parts of the world, but I
> was impressed by how neat the community was and how
> well organized they were. There was a real pride of place.
> The problem was people were living in such run-down
> shitty housing. I was also impressed at how welcoming the
> people were.[25]

The Red Cross team immediately began working with local
residents on establishing priorities and addressing the most precarious threats: "I knew we could play a role because people were
going to die if something wasn't done. We planned to send in small
heating stoves, insulation, smoke detectors, building materials to
reinforce the shacks. We made sure the local healing centre was
up to snuff as short-term emergency housing."[26]

With the appearance of the Red Cross, national media outlets sent in journalists and television crews. The decision by the
Red Cross to respond to the crisis pushed the provincial Liberal

government to take action finally. It ordered the EMO to head north to work with the Red Cross and band council.

And as the first Red Cross plane touched down on a bitterly cold late afternoon, the prime minister stood in the House of Commons and spoke for the first time about the crisis. But Stephen Harper didn't speak about the threat posed to people living in tents; rather, he spoke about his concern for Canadian taxpayers, noting that the government had spent "some $90 million since coming to office just on Attawapiskat. That's over $50,000 for every man, woman and child in the community. Obviously, we're not very happy [with] the results." He vowed to take "action" to find out what had happened to the money.[27]

Within a day, Harper placed the band under third-party management, effectively deposing the new chief and her council. This meant that no funds could be spent by the band, even to deal with the emergency. All decision-making authority for spending was transferred to a financial manager based in Winnipeg. It was a government coup that in a single move had shifted the focus from a humanitarian issue to an issue of righting things for the ripped-off Canadian taxpayer. There was no non-Native community in the country where the response to a humanitarian crisis would be to strip the democratically elected officials of all authority and turn control over to someone living thousands of kilometres away. But this was Indian country, and the old colonial rules apparently still applied.

RISE OF THE TROLLS

I hope they didn't get used to the parade of media and
politicians up there in poor old Attawapiskat. . . . I hope
they didn't believe all the sorrowful head-shaking. . . .
I even hope they didn't buy the purported outpouring
of goodwill from Canadians in the rest of the country,
deeply moved by the terrible plight of the residents.
—CHRISTIE BLATCHFORD[28]

I guess this is the Native people's Katrina moment.
—ATTAWAPISKAT RESIDENT[29]

With a single statement, Prime Minister Harper
transformed the entire focus of the Attawapiskat
crisis. Reading through the media coverage of
the period reveals a dramatic cleavage between
how the story was portrayed before and after
Harper stood up to ask what had happened to the money. Prior
to November 29, 2011, media attention was focused on the crisis
and the lack of government action. Questions were asked about
the larger infrastructure crises plaguing northern reserves. The
human interest element was told in stories about people living in
tents as well as in coverage of average Canadians lining up to help.

But the prime minister shifted the storyline dramatically. Suddenly, there was little interest in finding out why the Red Cross had
to launch a humanitarian mission to a Canadian reserve community; instead, the concern was with what Attawapiskat had done
with the money, for $90 million was a huge figure. Overnight,

Attawapiskat became a testing ground for Harper's agenda to use First Nations issues to defend the beleaguered taxpayer.

It wasn't entirely a credible claim not to know how the money had been spent, for the band was legally obliged to provide the government with annual audited statements. Nonetheless, to the Canadian public, it was certainly reasonable to ask how it was possible to spend $90 million in a small community and still have such degraded housing conditions. Few knew about the long history of failed program management at Aboriginal Affairs. While in opposition, the Harper Conservatives had demanded accountability from the Liberal government over the $2 billion that had been spent by the Department of Indian Affairs on water treatment plants that had failed. The housing crisis could have been an opportunity for the prime minister to end this long-standing pattern of mismanagement that had repeatedly resulted in failed infrastructure on northern reserves. The prime minister could have turned to the many design experts who were stepping forward to offer advice on how to prevent such failures and their associated humanitarian catastrophes in the future.

But the Conservative government wasn't interested in advice. Now in power, Harper shifted the focus from the responsibility of government to the personal accountability of "every man, woman and child" in Attawapiskat to the taxpayer. His statement hung in the air like an accusation.

So where did the money go? At the time, the government threw a lot of numbers around, but if we stick with the prime minister's claim of $90 million it was based on the total federal program spending in Attawapiskat over the six years of the Conservative government. This broke down as roughly $15 to $17 million a year for education, health, infrastructure, and remedial projects for water, and it included the funds used to demolish J. R. Nakogee School.[30] The prime minister divided this amount ($15 million) by the 1,800 people living in the community, which gave him a per capita cost of $8,300 per person a year to cover programs. Harper then multiplied this per capita spending over the six years of the Conservative government to come up with the amount of $50,000—the price tag of responsibility that he placed on the individual residents of Attawapiskat.

In the coming weeks, some diligent bloggers and journalists did excellent work deconstructing Harper's math to show that, if one added up the health, infrastructure, and education spending on non-Native Canadians, the per capita amount would be much higher than the amount spent on residents of Attawapiskat. Blogger Lorraine Lund provided her own countermath exercise: divide the national federal budget of $280 billion per capita and the amount comes to $9,399 per person. For Ontario residents, if one divided the 2010 provincial budget of $123 billion per capita, it would add another $9,500 per person. If the comparison was with the residents of Toronto, one could add another $5,200 per person from municipal per capita spending for a total of $24,000 per Torontonian spent every year by the three levels of government.[31] This was a full three times higher than what was being denounced as extravagant for residents of Attawapiskat. Journalist Doug Cuthand noted that, in the previous ten years, the band's funding had remained virtually unchanged while the population had increased by 40 per cent.[32]

One could explain all of this in the media, but in the world of politics, once you're explaining, you're losing. No politician had ever put price tags on the heads of non-Indigenous people. But Harper was both an economist and a master of the black political arts. The decision to put a dollar figure on the individual residents of Attawapiskat was a game of vicious arithmetic. The public would not remember the breakdown of how program dollars were being spent, but it would remember $90 million. And it would certainly remember the image of every man, woman, and child being paid $50,000. In a single statement, the people at the centre of a housing crisis ceased being citizens and became an accountability problem.

David Krayden, writing in the *Ottawa Citizen*, presented the Harper government's imagery in a perfectly simplistic way: "Can you imagine if your community received an envelope of $90 million in taxpayer funding over the last five years?" Krayden conveniently left out the fact that the money had been annual funding for police, roads, the hospital, and education—just like in any other community. He then moved on to a broad generalization about reserves across Canada being beset by "corrupt leadership" and criminal activities, often resulting in "radical and violent responses to perceived grievances."[33]

Ezra Levant of Sun TV ratcheted the polemics up even higher. According to his arithmetic, every family of four in Attawapiskat received $70,000 tax free every year. To Levant, the proof of this high living was Attawapiskat's decision to build a "gorgeous" hockey arena and bring in a Zamboni to clean the ice.[34]

Bronwyn Eyre in the *Calgary Herald* echoed Levant's obsession with the community rink. She denounced the "palatial skating rink with its brand new Zamboni."[35] CTV also picked up on the luxurious hockey arena theme, with a reporter musing about why the community had been allowed to build the arena. Across Canada, the ice rink is a symbol of our commonalities. The image of children playing hockey in a rink is a positive image used to sell everything from gasoline to doughnuts and, above all, national unity. During the Attawapiskat crisis, however, the rink became a symbol of what was wrong and irresponsible about Indigenous people.

Contrary to media depictions, the Attawapiskat arena was hardly "palatial." It was a basic steel shed with a kitchen facility and a gymnasium that had been built through an extraordinary local fundraising campaign. It had also been partially paid for by the Attawapiskat Education Authority because there was no gym at the high school or for students in the portables. The Zamboni had been purchased through bake sales and bingos so that children and teens would be able to skate and have a positive outlet in the long winter months. Such committed volunteerism would have made a good counterpoint to the false image of a hapless community waiting for white people to send money. Unfortunately, the story of how the community fundraised to get the youth a Zamboni was largely ignored except by Indigenous filmmaker Alanis Obomsawin. Her film *People of the Kattawapiskak River* is a haunting exploration of the housing crisis through the eyes of the Cree.

Zamboni-gate was just one of a series of media "exposés" in the weeks following the prime minister's accusation. One journalist from a national newspaper called me after a visit to Attawapiskat to complain that the local people had refused to tell her what they had done with the money. I asked her if she understood that the money represented program dollars fixed into budgets for health, education, and so on. She didn't seem to get it. She had been sent by her editors to find out what had happened to the $90 million, and apparently the local people were refusing to tell her. She wanted to know what they were trying to hide. "They keep it hidden in a little gold pot under the Zamboni," I told her before hanging up.

This isn't to make light of the role of the media in trying to make sense of the crisis unfolding on the James Bay coast. The problem was that Harper's strategy of blaming the community had moved the focus off the dire situation facing the citizens. I spoke to media continually throughout this period. There were news outlets trying to cover the issue accurately, but there were numerous interviews during which not a single question was asked about the safety of the people at risk. Increasingly, I began to push back by pointing out the difference in how disasters in non-Indigenous communities were covered by media compared with the treatment being given to the Attawapiskat crisis:

> Questions about finances? Sure. But nobody ever stops in the Red River in the middle of a flood and says, "Hey, how come we're throwing this money at your communities that keep flooding?" No, they don't say that. All Canadians rally, all Canadians help out. But . . . when it's First Nation kids [at risk], it's like, "Hey, what did you do with our taxpayers' dollars?"[36]

The crisis didn't just happen. There had been over a dozen states of emergency declared in the region in the previous eight years. Many of them stemmed from chronic underfunding in basic infrastructure. Comparisons to the Kashechewan crisis of 2005 or the Attawapiskat housing crisis of 2009 could have helped to round out the picture. But such context was rarely provided.

In fact, Minister John Duncan played to the historical amnesia by portraying the issue as one in which the Conservatives were the victims of their own misplaced good-heartedness: "If the department [of Aboriginal Affairs] can be accused of anything," he stated, "it is extreme patience."[37]

● ● ●

In the days following Harper's statement, Chief Spence increasingly became a lightning rod in the opinion press over her refusal to let the government's third-party manager into the community. Right-wing media insinuated that she was trying to hide financial mismanagement. Peter Worthington denounced her defiance of the government as "chutzpah."[38] Spence stated that the imposition of a third-party manager had no legal authority and undermined on-the-ground efforts to address the crisis. By taking away spending power from the band and handing it to an office in Winnipeg, the government created numerous obstacles for the team on the ground attempting to alleviate the crisis.

Spence stated that the government could audit the books but that its first response should be to work with the community to resolve the crisis: "I'm not trying to create conflict here. We're supposed to be focusing on emergency measures.... It's like calling an ambulance because there's an emergency situation, and then they send in the police to arrest you."[39] Spence struggled to keep attention focused on the people in tents and unheated cabins: "People are dying slowly, but I don't think the government recognizes that or [they] don't care.... They only feel we're trying to embarrass them, but that's not the case. They must work with us. That's all we're asking."[40]

But media pundits, many of whom never went into the community, had little sympathy for the embattled chief. Some referred to her "reportedly large home."[41] Spence was living, in fact, in a second-hand police trailer.

In the world of these columnists, Attawapiskat ceased being a real place and quickly became an ugly caricature. An editorial in the *Orillia Packet and Times* described the crisis as another case of a Native community destroying their houses, backing up the sewage, and then looking to Ottawa for a handout. The editorial described the homes as "hovels" that "you wouldn't raise pigs in.... Obviously these people cannot look after themselves and end up in a drunken haze or they commit suicide." No one who has spent time among the Cree would recognize such a crude mischaracterization. But the editorial used the Attawapiskat housing crisis to launch a larger attack on First Nations people:

Whenever they had a problem, society tried to solve it with money. In an effort to help the natives, the churches set up schools to educate the native children and help them adjust. It had limited success, but in the end [the residential school system] has become a money pit for native activists who accused the churches of mistreatment of the children.[42]

Columnist Lorne Gunter described the situation in Attawapiskat as proof of misplaced white guilt. "Political correctness is the cause of the bleak conditions in Attawapiskat," he declared.[43] Tasha Kheiriddin picked up on the theme of political correctness gone wrong: "Children living in such squalor in non-native environments would be likely ... placed in foster care. ... The political incorrectness of jeopardizing the maintenance of their Aboriginal heritage means ... kids are still sniffing glue and hanging themselves, all in the name of maintaining connections to the land and Aboriginal traditions."[44]

Other articles mocked the community's call for help. In "One Thing about Attawapiskat: Where Has All the Money Gone?" Chris Brennan poked fun at the image of families living in unheated tents: "Living in a tent with no running water or bathroom amenities is about as close to a 'traditional' lifestyle as you can get."[45]

This nasty media commentary was buttressed by a new phenomenon—the rise of the digital troll. Deeply racist and hateful slurs have become the norm in the comments section of every major news site whenever an article about First Nations people is posted online. During the Attawapiskat crisis, people clearly saw the ugly face of the racist Canadian troll on Twitter and other online commentaries. "They get lots of money but much of it is stolen by chiefs and much of the rest goes for booze and big screen TVs," wrote one commentator. Another wrote that "I'm sorry but I do not have any sympathy for what is happening here, none whatsoever. ... All these stories about how the government did this and that, blah, blah, blah. Get over it, too bad so sad."[46]

International media attention, however, focused on Attawapiskat as an example of Harper's poor record with First Nations people. England's *Guardian* noted the government backlash

Makeshift housing in Attawapiskat, winter 2011. *Courtesy of Benjamin Dickerson Fox.*

against the community in an article entitled "Canada's First Nations: A Scandal Where Victims Are Blamed."[47]

James Anaya, the UN special rapporteur on Indigenous people, issued a statement of concern over the government's handling of the crisis. He pointed to the systemic underfunding that had led to the infrastructure crisis and stated that the United Nations would be monitoring the situation. John Duncan's media assistant Michelle Yao responded by saying that the UN concern was just a "publicity stunt."[48]

Across "Indian country," the treatment of the band council and the racist backlash in the media were a wake-up call. First Nations people saw Harper's treatment of Attawapiskat as a symbol of what the government does to communities that speak up. To many "grassroots" Indigenous people, Chief Spence became a symbol of resistance for refusing to give in to the third-party manager. A number of Indigenous artists became involved in public campaigns to support Attawapiskat. Blues guitarist Derek Miller organized fundraisers for the community. Tom Jackson flew to Attawapiskat to sing to the families as part of a special Christmas concert.

Non-Indigenous voices were also stepping forward. The band The Tragically Hip recorded a song called "Goodnight Attawapiskat" and later flew to Fort Albany for a special concert for James Bay people. In many ways, the government's response to the crisis sowed the seeds of the Idle No More uprising of the following year.

Canadian media commentators have spoken at length about the role of "new media" in the countries of the Middle East and North Africa during the "Arab Spring" and in other countries where people have been fighting oppression. But little attention has been paid to the fact that First Nations people in Canada don't see their reality reflected by the dailies or on the evening news. More and more Indigenous people look to Facebook and other social media platforms to pass on news and information that won't be filtered by white pundits. In the case of the Attawapiskat crisis, a younger generation of First Nations youth used new media to create alternative narratives.

One of them was Rose Paul Martin, a teenager in Attawapiskat. In the dark month of December 2011, she and her friends watched online depictions of the James Bay Cree with growing anger. Inspired by her cousin Shannen Koostachin's willingness to stand up and be heard, Rose set out to challenge these false perceptions. She obtained a camera and started documenting Cree life on Facebook. As she explained,

> the media that came to my community and told false stories made me the person who I am today. I was fourteen when I picked up a camera for the very first time and told myself that I should be telling my stories about Attawapiskat through my photos and tell the world what it's really like to live in my community and face the struggles we face every day.[49]

Rose started to write for the few online journals interested in on-the-ground perspectives of communities in the north. She was one of a number of young people from James Bay who responded to the crisis by acting as citizen reporters to counter the larger media narrative. They used digital cameras, Twitter, and Facebook to get their side of the story out.[50] In 2012, the organization Journalists for Human Rights went to a number of northern reserves to train a team of young "citizen journalists." Rose was one of the youth who underwent the training:

> The media that come and tell these false stories about my community—that will be the last time because I will train younger generations on how to get their voice out there and be heard. The Journalists for Human Rights encouraged me to have a voice of my own and speak the truth of what we go through on a daily basis.[51]

Rose is now in college studying journalism and working with First Nations youth in northern Quebec on developing grassroots journalism.

CHRISTMAS IN ATTAWAPISKAT

Stay strong. We are praying for you and praying for
Mr. Harper. Why pray for Mr. Harper? We pray for
Mr. Harper because we refuse to be like him.
—FACEBOOK MESSAGE TO THE AUTHOR FROM
ATTAWAPISKAT RESIDENT, DECEMBER 1, 2011

Stephen Harper's attack on the leadership in Attawapiskat was a public example of the politics of confrontation becoming the new norm in Ottawa. It was a dramatic break from the traditional crisis management
strategy of Indian Affairs of getting issues out of the
media spotlight by saying as little as possible.

Harper's political instinct was to use the Attawapiskat crisis to
push the "accountability" agenda. But in doing so, Harper made
a number of miscalculations. First was that he relied on his minister, John Duncan, to carry through on the mission. Second was
that nobody expected Chief Spence to stand up to the government
on the imposition of the third-party manager. Third was that
Christmas was coming. It was getting very cold. By mid-Decem-
ber, with the situation at a standoff, the government was beginning to look downright mean. Nobody wanted to see children living in tents as Christmas approached. That the government's only
response to the crisis was to send in a financial auditor just seemed
cold blooded. By the second week of December, media coverage
had shifted away from the question of finances and become more
focused on the steps needed to bring about a resolution.

The media gave extensive coverage to NDP interim leader
Nycole Turmel when she visited Attawapiskat on a bitterly cold

day. Turmel brought a sense of compassion sorely lacking on the Conservative side. In the weeks after her visit, interim Liberal leader Bob Rae also visited the community. But still no Conservatives came to it. Yet, as the crisis dragged on, the government's adversarial campaign appeared to be running out of steam.

Throughout the crisis, there continued to be an enormous outpouring of support from many ordinary Canadians. As the Harper government struggled to maintain control of the media "narrative," ordinary citizens stepped up to the plate to help the community. Students in Toronto's Regent Park region organized a Christmas toy drive. Church groups and other organizations did similar community fundraising. The Red Cross initiative quickly reached the $300,000 goal. John Saunders said that the response was overwhelming. "I was impressed at how quick Canadians were to respond," he said. "Other First Nations were there with help from the beginning, but all over Canada Canadians responded, and within a couple of weeks we had all the donations we needed with over $330,000 collected. We had to ask people to stop donating."[52]

Truck driver Michael Clark volunteered to drive an eighteen-wheeler loaded with 25,000 pounds of supplies to the Red Cross loading bay in Timmins. Clark was a volunteer with the evangelical aid organization True North Aid, which had been delivering supplies to far northern First Nations. He picked up supplies from grassroots groups in Ottawa, Kanata, Bowmanville, Peterborough, Mississauga, and Toronto. The result was twenty-four skids of supplies to be transported to Attawapiskat. "We had food and diapers on about four skids and the rest was winter wear and electric heaters. . . . If you get to know [the people of James Bay], you'll fall in love with them. They deserve better than what they have. We [True North Aid] go way beyond the politics. If people need help, we will deliver the help they need," Clark told the press.[53]

Heather Cranny was one of a number of Red Cross workers who helped to move the supplies to James Bay:

> Working for the Red Cross allows my mothering instincts to come through. When I hear stories from our volunteers in Attawapiskat, I know their hearts are full. It's stressful

what they've seen. I feel that when I go to bed at night, maybe one more child is warm tonight and that one more mother is going to sleep a little better because they know their child will be warmer than they were last night.[54]

The problem for the Red Cross relief effort was that the Conservatives' decision to depose the band council had made the situation on the ground increasingly complicated and politically volatile. Saunders said that the Red Cross had to deal with the interference of government officials more interested in managing the "message box" of the crisis response:

> The imposition of the third-party manager caused us to become bogged down in a quagmire of politics. We were there to ensure people were warm. Instead, the Red Cross was being asked to explain why people had been given all this money. It added a level of complexity.... Instead of doing what we thought was necessary, we had to work with the Government Operations Centre, individuals from AANDC [Aboriginal Affairs and Northern Development Canada], and the third-party manager. Most of AANDC's interest was that the Red Cross toed the government line and that we weren't pointing the finger at the government.[55]

But the Conservative government's brass knuckles approach wasn't winning over Canadians. The Prime Minister's Office was inundated with letters and emails. Correspondence obtained through Access to Information legislation makes for fascinating reading. Among the letters were certainly some that supported the Harper government's strategy of blame: "I respectfully ask for my $90 plus million dollars to be returned to Canadian Taxpayers. I could use a little taxpayer's money to fix up my house," wrote one person from Sioux Lookout on December 6, 2011.[56]

Striking, however, is the number of letters calling on the prime minister to stop beating up a poor community. As one email sent on December 7 put it, "just putting in my two cents worth: Let's help them, and sort out the responsibility mess later, shall we? There are children involved."[57] And many of the writers expressed their shame at the government's handling of the situation. Many Canadians might not have known the history of the issues at James Bay, but they recognized heartlessness when they saw it. Of particular interest in the letters to the government were messages from long-time Conservatives offended by Harper's position. "I am a white, middle class Canadian of Protestant decent [sic], and conservative voting. It disgusts me that the gov I voted for is letting this happen," wrote one writer on November 15.[58]

• • •

Harper's iron-fist approach was undermined when it was leaked that the third-party manager, Jacques Marion, was being paid $1,300 a day for his services.[59] That was much higher than the prime minister's salary. Isn't this the kind of spending that should have drawn the ire of the Canadian Taxpayers Federation?

Marion's salary was being taken from the band's already limited finances. This led to an obvious question: wouldn't such an amount of money be better spent on housing? As the media turned their attention to the long-standing use by Aboriginal Affairs of third-party managers to deal with "obstructive" or "financially incompetent" reserves, the picture that emerged wasn't pretty.

The department had a long-standing policy of imposing outside financial management on bands that had become too debt-ridden or politically unstable. Such a move immediately stripped the band council of any decision-making authority for expenses. As well, capital projects were halted until the debt was paid down. And, for an impoverished community, the cost for an outside manager could run anywhere from $200,000 to $400,000 a year.

One would expect that, given their high salaries, third-party managers would establish remedial financial plans and focus on capacity building with troubled bands to restore financial stability. This would be a reasonable response to the extreme circumstances of some bands, but the record of third-party management had been less than stellar. Many of the problems with the system stemmed, ironically enough, from the lack of accountability measures placed on these managers by AANDC.

On December 15, 2011, the Canadian Press did an exposé of the failures of the third-party management system. It pointed to the Lake St. Martin reserve in Manitoba that went into debt from flooding, snake infestations, and evacuations. Following the government's decision to impose a third-party manager, the band's deficit actually increased.[60]

Barriere Lake, Quebec, was also placed under third-party management because of an internal political split in the community. Soon after, the band found itself in difficulty trying to pay the bills for its school. Principal Alec Wright was forced to cancel gym classes for three weeks because the door locks were broken, and he couldn't get them fixed without authorization from the third-party manager in Manitoba, who had to sign the necessary cheques in person.[61] According to the Canadian Press article, the manager made two trips from Winnipeg to Barriere Lake: one to deal with the quote for the gym door, the other to write the cheque for the repair. In addition to such issues, the Barriere Lake Band Council was concerned about being blamed for a series of bounced cheques apparently written by the third-party manager.[62]

But Attawapiskat wasn't in a financial crisis. Its books were audited and posted online. Ordinary Canadians wondered why a financial manager was sent in to deal with what, everyone had agreed, was a life-and-death emergency? One letter to the prime minister is particularly telling about how the third-party manager's fee was playing among the Conservative base. "Attawapiskat to pay 3rd-party manager $1,300 a day. I have been … a strong supporter of your [sic] and your government, but this is bordering on the ridiculous and obscene. At the very best the optics are horrible," wrote a party supporter from Moncton.[63]

With Christmas approaching, the government sensed the shifting public mood, and John Duncan struggled to present the third-party manager in another light. In a letter to Chief Spence, he stated that the only goal of the third-party manager was to ensure the safety of the residents: "I am reiterating my concern about the health and safety needs in your community. I continue to encourage you to work with my officials. … Our goal is to ensure all residents have access to safe, warm shelter."[64] He then offered to provide the community with fifteen modular homes to be delivered once the ice road had frozen sufficiently.

Spence wrote back to Duncan thanking him for the help but stating that fifteen homes weren't enough to get people out of tents and shacks. The community needed twenty-two modular homes. She reiterated her refusal to accept the costs of the third-party manager: "My community will not consider third-party managers nor pay for them out of our already depressed ... budget. ... My council does not lack the capacity. What we lack are funds to accomplish the above."[65]

Duncan was hammered by the media for his handling of the crisis. When pressed about who would pay for the houses and third-party manager, he responded in language completely at odds with that used by the prime minister just ten days before. No longer was the government demanding to know what had happened to taxpayers' money; now, Duncan declared, the third-party manager had been put in place to ensure that everyone stayed warm: "Our first concern is for the health and safety of the community. We want to make sure they have safe, warm, dry shelter. ... This is an emergency-management response. We will worry about who's paying for this afterwards."[66]

Bob Fife, a respected CTV journalist, summed up the feeling among the Ottawa media that Duncan had botched the government's response to the Attawapiskat housing crisis:

> He is probably one of the weakest Indian Affairs ministers in recent memory. ... [John Duncan's] performance has been very shoddy, very poor. ... When the reporters kept questioning him, his press secretary ... hauled him away, as if Mr. Duncan was a blabbering idiot. ... Mr. Harper has got a problem on his hands and he's got a very, very weak minister in charge of a very important portfolio that involves human lives.[67]

On February 1, 2012, I challenged Minister Duncan on news that the money needed to prepare the sites for the modular homes had not been provided by the third-party manager. Crews from De Beers as well as local volunteers were on the ground ready to move the trailers into the community, but the homes were held up in Moosonee awaiting the disbursement of funds. Duncan tried to blame the band for not cooperating with the third-party manager, but the government was losing credibility.[68] Harper's response to the Attawapiskat crisis had been ham-fisted and ruthless. It was now beginning to look incompetent.

Commentator Chantal Hébert called Harper's handling of the crisis the "low point" in the first parliamentary session of his majority government and yet another example of the kinds of decisions that have given him and his government "a Jekyll-and-Hyde reputation." According to Hébert, "spinning a simplistic message that inevitably tapped into a stubborn vein of prejudice against Canada's Aboriginal communities was ... beneath the dignity of the office of a responsible prime minister."[69]

FROM HAWAII TO IDLE NO MORE

The people of Attawapiskat wanted dignified
housing. They wanted a place they could call
home. This is what appealed to ordinary Canadians. How could this be happening in our
country? Canadians rallied to help other Canadians. This wasn't us versus them. Canadians
responded to help their neighbours.
—JOHN SAUNDERS[70]

The decision to depose the chief and council of Attawapiskat in the midst of a housing crisis burned whatever goodwill Prime Minister Harper had established
with First Nations across Canada. At a meeting of the
national chiefs in Ottawa in December 2011, a number
of leaders marched on Parliament Hill. Some weren't content to
merely protest. They wanted to storm the building for a full-out
confrontation.

Prime Minister Harper had an opportunity to reset the agenda
when he agreed to meet with the national chiefs in January 2012.
National Chief Shawn Atleo told the media that this was an opportunity to move forward from the Attawapiskat debacle:

Attawapiskat is the first time we've had YouTube bring the
kind of stark images that you would expect somewhere
else in the world. Those are images that cut through ...
a lot of the conversation. It really touches people's hearts.
And then the questions start to emerge. It's really encouraging that so many Canadians are saying, "We need to

seize this moment." It feels like there is a raising of con-sciousness and I'm hopeful that maybe this is the tipping point that pushes us over the edge towards real change.[71]

Chief Derek Nepinak, head of the Assembly of Manitoba Chiefs, was less hopeful about the summit. He warned the gov-ernment that a new militancy was emerging: "Our young people are fed up with the way things are. We've made several attempts to deal with this through diplomatic means and political means, but we're reaching a point where the winds have shifted. People are frustrated. If diplomacy fails, we can't speak for what happens."[72]

Grand Chief Stan Beardy of Nishnawbe Aski Nation agreed: "We're very, very patient people. Being nice is not helping me today. I think I need to stand up and say it's time." He warned of widespread unrest if Harper failed to come to the table with an agenda for change.[73]

Stewart Phillip, grand chief of the Union of BC Indian Chiefs, warned of an "Arab Spring" if First Nations did not see results. "Otherwise," he predicted, "an Aboriginal uprising is inevitable."[74]

The national summit was scheduled for January 24, 2012. One of the issues at the top of the agenda was the need to deliver on education, an obvious benefit for all of Canadian society. Many observers saw this national summit as a chance for Harper to dial down the tension and set a new course with First Nations commu-nities. Coming through with a deal on education would have gone a long way toward achieving this goal.

But Harper didn't deliver on education or any other issue that day.

He left soon after the meeting began to catch a plane to attend a meeting of economic leaders in Davos, Switzerland. After he was gone, his staff released a statement on his willingness to work on employ-ment opportunities in the booming oil and gas and mining sectors.[75]

The chiefs who had come to Ottawa hoping for a historic break-through had nothing to show for their efforts. Manitoba Grand Chief David Harper stated his frustration: "My children, in my communities today as we speak, are getting water from chiselling ice from the rivers and the lakes. Still today, there are 1,000 homes that require indoor plumbing."[76]

The *Montreal Gazette* condemned Harper's indifference at a his-toric moment:

> It must have occurred to Prime Minister Stephen Harper that it would be bad optics, both at home and abroad, for him to take off halfway through Tuesday's Crown–First Nations summit in Ottawa for the World Economic Forum in Davos. In light of the pitiful state of many Aboriginal communities in Canada, highlighted by the widely publicized housing crisis in ... Attawapiskat, it would have been perceived as a shameful slight, not just by the 400 chiefs ... , but also by informed participants at the Davos schmoozefest.[77]

Anyone close to First Nations communities was aware of the growing grassroots anger. To many Indigenous people, regardless of where they lived in Canada, Attawapiskat touched them personally. *Wawatay News* director Brent Wesley summed up the feeling in a piece for the *Toronto Star*: "Lazy. Incompetent. Dead weight. Basically, a burden on the taxpayers. Harsh descriptives for anyone to swallow, yet it's par for the course for First Nations in this country. Especially when a major issue hits mainstream news like the state of emergency in Attawapiskat."[78]

But Harper's cheerleaders in the bully press weren't interested in what people in Little Buffalo, Serpent River, or Attawapiskat thought. Quebecor Media released an editorial calling First Nations threats of action "tiresome": "Why not shut it [Attawapiskat] down? It's a lost cause.... It's time for all First Nations to face the music.... And it's time for the chiefs to hear the same tune, and give their veiled and tiresome threats a rest."[79]

When, ten months later, grassroots First Nations people across the country began shutting down roads as part of the spontaneous Idle No More protests, the same pundits expressed their incredulity that so many Indigenous people across the country were rising up. The flashpoint for Idle No More was the government's massive omnibus legislation, Bill C-45, that stripped environmental protection for Canada's lakes and rivers.[80] But the Harper government's adversarial response to Attawapiskat had helped to light the fuse.

• • •

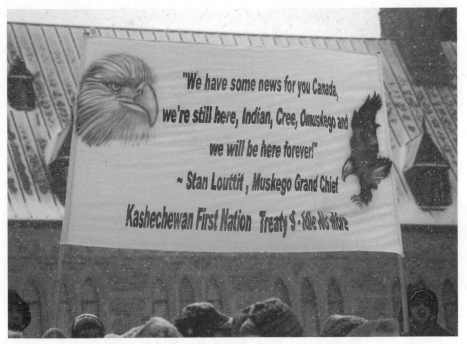

Cree banner waving during Idle No More demonstration on Parliament Hill, winter 2011–12. The Harper government's treatment of the Attawapiskat housing crisis created a growing sense of militancy among First Nations people. *Courtesy of Janet Doherty.*

By the early spring of 2012, the Attawapiskat issue was receding from media attention. The Red Cross had finished its work, and twenty-two modular homes had been moved into the community. Nonetheless, the standoff in Attawapiskat continued because the third-party manager refused to release funds to pay for band employees. The community was owed $168,683, funds that had not been released since early December.[81] Having taken control of band finances for four months, the government had not found any evidence of financial mismanagement in the community.[82]

In late March, I began to get phone calls from Attawapiskat residents who informed me that their young people were facing eviction from college courses in Timmins and elsewhere because the funds for education had not been paid. These students were far from home without money for food or rent. One student had been kicked out of residence and had no place to live.[83] The parents said that, when they phoned the third-party manager to find out why the money had not been allocated, they were informed that he was vacationing in Hawaii. At this time, the school breakfast program, which provided nourishment to the children, was also cut off because there were no funds to pay for the food.

I phoned and wrote to the third-party manager but never heard back. I then wrote an email to Aboriginal Affairs official Yves Chenier to find out if the third-party manager in charge of dealing with a national crisis was indeed on vacation in Hawaii. The email was straightforward:

> Mr. Chenier,
>
> I am sure that you will agree that it is unacceptable that Attawapiskat students are unable to follow through with their post-secondary studies because basic education funds ... have not been supplied by the Third Party manager. ... I have emailed and called Mr. Marion. He appears to be unavailable. I have been informed that [he] is on vacation. ... These students have a right to education that should not be arbitrarily interfered with. ... What steps will you put in place to ensure that their education will not be interfered with in the coming months? I look forward to hearing from you at your earliest convenience.[84]

Chenier contacted his regional superior at Aboriginal Affairs, Leigh Jessen. She forwarded the email on to her colleague, Joseph Young, stating, "read what nugget that mr angus sent to yves."[85] Rather than respond to a legitimate inquiry about why young people were being kicked out of college programs because of withheld funds, the AANDC circled the wagons. Jessen told Chenier not to respond. "He [Angus] would only use your response against you/ us etc. ... Let's see what comes from H.Q. So hang tight."[86]

But now questions about whether the $1,300-a-day manager was vacationing in Hawaii began breaking in the media. The next day the government removed the third-party manager, declaring his work in addressing the "urgent health and safety needs" of Attawapiskat to have been a success.[87] Nonetheless, the community continued with its court case against the federal government over the legality of deposing the band council during the emergency.

On August 1, 2012, Justice Michael Phelan of the Federal Court rendered a ruling that denounced the government's response to the crisis as "unreasonable":

> This judicial review confirms, if such confirmation were needed, that decisions made in the glare of publicity and amidst politically charged debate do not always lead to reasonable resolution of the relevant issue.... The decision to appoint [the third party] did not respond in a reasonable way to the root of the problems at Attawapiskat nor to the remedies available upon default under the Comprehensive Funding Agreement.[88]

The government expressed its dismay with the decision. The next day the Conservatives got their payback when Minister John Duncan torpedoed a plan to have thirty new houses built in Attawapiskat. The plan for alleviating the housing crisis with a long-term solution had been worked out by the band council in a financial agreement with the Canada Mortgage and Housing Corporation (CMHC). Under the plan, CMHC would provide the financing for thirty new houses that would be paid for through rent-to-own agreements with the residents. CMHC wouldn't have agreed to the deal if the band wasn't considered financially trustworthy, but under the constraints of the Indian Act the community could not move forward without the minister signing off, even though the department wasn't bringing any money to the table. In the tit-for-tat war with this impoverished community, the government killed the project, claiming that Attawapiskat had not established the "necessary capacity" to receive government support.[89]

Within a year, Chief Theresa Spence was back in the headlines, this time in a high-stakes political showdown with Stephen Harper. On December 11, 2012, she declared a hunger strike to force another national summit with First Nations leaders to address the issues that the prime minister had ignored at the summit during the housing crisis. The burgeoning Idle No More movement hit its peak through the tense winter of 2012–13, and her hunger strike was a catalyst for militant First Nations action across the country.

The government responded to Spence's stand by leaking an audit of Attawapiskat finances. Even though the audit didn't make any allegation of fraud, questions about the lack of paperwork only served to inflame the situation.[90]

Spence's hunger strike was part of the growing polarization of First Nations relationships in Harper's Canada. Spence was ridiculed in the opinion pages but regarded as a folk hero by many First Nations people. Her role as a radical leader was a far cry from where she had been just over a year before when, as a new chief, she had asked the government for help to alleviate a housing crisis.

A quotation from Spence from the dark days of the housing crisis is worth noting: "When I declared a state of emergency last September, it wasn't my intention to cause embarrassment to Canada; I didn't plan this kind of exposure. I just wanted to help my community."[91]

PART VI
THE FUTURE IS NOW, 2012–15

The Shannen's Dream motion was brought forward for debate in Parliament while the Attawapiskat housing crisis was at its peak. The government was under increasing pressure to move forward on the education file. The unanimous support in Parliament for the Shannen's Dream initiative was a historic milestone in the fight for equitable Indigenous education rights.

However, action on resolving the issue of education equity has remained elusive. The fight over education reform has stalled as Aboriginal Affairs and First Nations communities argue about who will be in the driver's seat. But a deeper question remains: what will it take for the federal government to begin moving forward on a relationship of respect and reconciliation?

THE UNITED NATIONS

It's not fun when you are crowded in a classroom and
it's not fair that mice eat the snacks. It's not fun when
cold winds are in the school, it's not fun at all!
—ANGELIQUE, LETTER TO THE UNITED NATIONS[1]

Stephen Harper skipped out of the national summit
with Indigenous leaders to fly to Switzerland on January 24, 2011. Ten days later sixteen-year-old Chelsea
Edwards followed him. Harper had flown to a meeting of the über rich in Davos. Chelsea flew to Geneva
to meet representatives of the UN Committee on the Rights of the
Child. She was part of a group of Indigenous youth who went there
to challenge Canada's failure to live up to the Convention on the
Rights of the Child (CRC).

The meeting had been requested in 2008 by Shannen
Koostachin and a small group of grade eight students in Attawapiskat. "This systemic discrimination [faced by First Nations stu-
dents] is a breach of the key clauses of the UN Declaration of the
Rights of the Child which Canada is a signatory to," they wrote at
the time.[2] Unfortunately, Shannen didn't live long enough to follow through on her promise to go to the United Nations.

So the task fell to her younger friend to meet with the UN representatives. Leading a delegation to the United Nations was a huge
step for Chelsea. But the timid youngster who wanted to walk in
the big footsteps of her friend wasn't quite so timid anymore. To
get through high school, Chelsea was now living in Timmins, 400
kilometres from her family. Throughout grade ten and eleven,
she had moved from boarding house to boarding house in order

to find a safe and supportive environment for her education. She often did her homework at the local Tim Hortons at night. It was a lonely world for an adolescent:

> I've lived in eight boarding homes. I've lived in Cochrane, I've lived in Timmins, South Porcupine.... My parents often had a hard time supporting me financially.... It was really difficult. I had to leave half of myself back at home— my identity, my language, my family, my friends.... I cried almost every night.... I was so mad at the world because how can this happen in a country like Canada? Why should I have to move away from my family?... I was just so fortunate to have that opportunity to go to school, but at the same time I was very angry and bitter about it. But there was no way that I would learn anything if I were to stay bitter. And from then on I became passionate about First Nations education, and I just knew that no one should ever have to go through what I had to go through.[3]

Chelsea really wanted the United Nations to understand what such conditions meant for the social and educational well-being of Indigenous youth:

> It sucks having to walk portable to portable when it's –40 degrees, and you have the ... wind blowing in your face. I basically wore my jacket inside the portable during winter. You could feel the draft coming in. You can often smell this, ugh, you can smell something in there. It was disgusting. I didn't want this to go on any further.[4]

Chelsea was also able to articulate the emotional price of having been forced to leave her home, family, and culture at such a young age. "I lost half my childhood. I never got to live as a teenager. I had lots of pressures and responsibilities I shouldn't have had," she said.[5] So she saw herself as an ambassador for other First Nations children who wouldn't have opportunities to tell their stories of inequity to the international community.

The UN meeting was coordinated by a group of human rights advocates—Cindy Blackstock, KAIROS (Canadian Ecumenical

Justice Initiatives), and Office of the Provincial Advocate for Children and Youth. Irwin Elman, the provincial child advocate, was an independent ombudsman for children's rights in Ontario. He monitored programs for compliance with the CRC. He had become deeply involved in the Shannen's Dream movement and the fight for First Nations youth equity.

The team included Indigenous youth from across the country. In addition to Chelsea Edwards from Attawapiskat, fellow delegates included Kendall White, seventeen, of Temagami First Nation; John-Paul Chalykoff, twenty-four, of Michipicoten First Nation; Madelynn Slade, twenty-two, of the Michel Cree in Alberta; Helen Knott, twenty-four, of Prophet River First Nation in British Columbia; and Collin Starblanket, fifteen, of Star Blanket First Nation in Saskatchewan. All of them were young leaders engaged in the fight for First Nations education rights.

The focus of the meeting was whether or not Canada had met the international obligations that it had undertaken upon signing the convention in 1990. Article 4 of the convention requires signatories to take "all appropriate legislative, administrative, and other measures" for the realization of the rights of children.[6] On the Department of Justice website, Canada's commitment to these principles is stated clearly: "Children ... deserve special protection because of their particular vulnerability. This is the modern concept of the child on which the Convention on the Rights of the Child (CRC) is based. ... The best interests of the child shall be a primary consideration in all actions concerning children."[7] The website is emphatic in stating that the obligations to protect the rights of children cannot be undermined by domestic laws or considerations. This is an inspiring statement by the government, as was its commitment to abide by the UN Declaration on the Rights of Indigenous Peoples. Yet, when it came to implementing these principles in the area of First Nations equity, the Department of Justice took a very different position. In its legal brief to the Human Rights Tribunal, the department shrugged off the legal and moral obligations that had been signed at the international level:

> The Declaration is not a legally binding instrument. It was adopted by a non-legally binding resolution of the United Nations General Assembly. As a result of this status, it does

not impose any international or domestic legal obligations upon Canada. As Canada noted in its public statement of support, the Declaration does not change Canadian laws. It represents an expression of political, not legal, commitment.... The same situation applies here with respect to child welfare services.[8]

The youth delegation planned to challenge Canada's doublespeak on rights by presenting the UN committee with a report entitled *Our Dreams Matter Too*, which included handwritten letters from Indigenous and non-Indigenous students across the country. Prior to leaving for Geneva, the delegation released the report to a gymnasium full of Shannen's Dream primary school activists at Pierre Elliott Trudeau School in Gatineau, Quebec. Some of these students, as well as others from across Canada, later followed the youth delegation's progress in Switzerland online and through Skype. In Geneva, the UN committee was given a message from Shannen:

> Shannen wanted you to know that First Nations children across Canada have dreams of becoming doctors, teachers, grass dancers, engineers, cooks, producers, and other things.... She also wanted to let you know that the Government of Canada provides less funding for elementary and secondary schools on reserve than for schools off reserve. This makes achieving our dreams very difficult.... The discrimination and denial of our rights continues.[9]

The students formally asked the United Nations to rule against Canada for failing in its obligation to live up to the convention:

> With this document, First Nations children and youth are fulfilling Shannen's dream of submitting an alternate report to the UNCRC [United Nations Committee on the Rights of the Child] in hopes that the Committee will order an Article 45 review on Canada's implementation of the United Nations Convention on the Rights of the Child for First Nations children and youth across Canada. The Article 45 review should explore all areas of inequity in

From nervous adolescent to spokeswoman for Indigenous youth rights, Chelsea Edwards speaks with national media. *Courtesy of Janet Doherty.*

government service delivery as the problems in educa-tion are replicated in child welfare and health services on reserves.[10]

Prior to the meeting with the UN delegates, Chelsea had her usual case of nerves. But it cleared up when she walked into the boardroom:

> At the United Nations, I was really nervous before going into the building, but when I got there I felt very calm. We sat at the table with the UN delegates, and I told my story. I told them that we had a national campaign, but there were still no schools and no commitment from the government. People thought I would be the one crying when I spoke, but I looked to the UN delegates and saw that they were the ones crying.[11]

In a Facebook message to her friends back home, Chelsea sounded like a young woman who had taken on the world and won: "Watch out Harper and Duncan. You're out of excuses now that they've heard our voices."[12]

Given the long history of Canada's resistance to First Nations equity, Chelsea's Facebook message might seem to have been tinged with naive youthful exuberance. But the government really was running out of excuses. Even as the Indigenous youth delegates were landing back in Canada, there was increasing pressure on Prime Minister Harper to address the education crisis.

On February 9, 2012, a government-appointed panel presented an in-depth report calling for a total overhaul of the delivery of First Nations education. The report, *Nurturing the Learning Spirit of First Nation Students*, cited the example of Shannen Koostachin and warned the Harper government that the clock was ticking. The panel's language echoed the message used by Chelsea and her team in Geneva:

> Childhood lasts only 988 weeks, and school years pass by even more quickly. It is, therefore, critical that the Government of Canada and First Nation leaders move forward together to change a system that has consigned so many First Nation students to an education that poorly prepares them to take full advantage of the education and career opportunities that are readily available to other students across the country. Access to quality education is the right of every child in Canada.

The report outlined an action plan for creating a "child-centred, quality First Nation education system" for Canada's Indigenous children.[13] The report cost the government $3.1 million and offered Minister Duncan the opportunity to rebuild bridges that the prime minister had burned by skipping out of the national chiefs' meeting just weeks before.

But Duncan wrote off the report's timelines as merely "aspirational." He said that his government's priority was to remain focused on the economy.[14] He was overlooking the fact, however, that addressing the crisis in First Nations education *was* about the economy. The social costs of low graduation rates have created a serious and completely unnecessary drag on the economy. The report pointed out that the 40 per cent failure rate of First

Nations students to graduate from high school has significant costs. For each successive group of fifteen- to nineteen-year-olds who fail to graduate, the estimated cost to the economy is $887 million because of higher levels of unemployment, the need for social assistance, and anti-social and criminal behaviour that often requires involvement of the justice system.[15]

And by failing to develop relationships with First Nations, the Harper government was missing out on the potential boom from a growing Indigenous economy. A TD Economics report identified the value of the First Nations economy as $24 billion, expected to reach $32 billion by 2016.[16] Right-wing pundits continually framed First Nations issues as a drain on taxpayers when, in fact, Indigenous communities were presenting a major growth opportunity.

• • •

On Valentine's Day, 2012, young people across Canada held marches and protests calling on the government to pass the Shannen's Dream motion. Students from Pierre Elliott Trudeau School in Gatineau and Lady Evelyn School in Ottawa launched a book of poems and pictures called *Children Have Power! Voices of Children Standing in Solidarity with First Nations Children.* Students from the Kitigan Zibi Algonquin reserve in Quebec led a march on Parliament Hill in which the youth called for political action.

The rally included speeches by numerous students. A grade five student named Elliot summed up the inanity of the federal government's position: "Why should Aboriginal children have equal access to health and education? The answer to that question is so obvious that I don't even understand why we need to be raising this issue."[17] Two days later the New Democratic Party brought forward the Shannen's Dream motion for a debate as an opposition day motion that would force a government vote on the matter.

It was now two years since the motion had first been introduced in the House of Commons. Given the Harper government's open hostility to voting for opposition motions and bills, there had been little sense in bringing this motion forward earlier only to see it defeated. But with tension still high over the government's handling of the Attawapiskat crisis, and with mounting pressure from various political voices to deal with the education inequities,

Serena Koostachin with her new baby, Shannen, cutting a cake on Parliament Hill to celebrate the success of the Shannen's Dream motion, February 27, 2012. NDP interim leader Nycole Turmel and Charlie Angus watch as young Shannen's Dream activists celebrate. *Courtesy of Janet Doherty.*

the Harper government was boxed into a corner. The prime minister's relationship with First Nations leaders was becoming toxic, and it could have been politically damaging to openly oppose the principle of equity for First Nations education.

In the House of Commons, I spoke about the significance of the vote and the fact that we were voting on a motion rooted in the activism of young people:

> This is a historic moment in Parliament and for Canada. This is the first motion that has been driven by children. The reason we are debating this issue is because children across the country have recognized their brothers and sisters have been denied basic education rights. This is about putting children first. I cannot think of another instance where school children in New Brunswick, Nova Scotia, Ontario, and across western Canada could tell every member in Parliament about what Shannen's Dream means. They know it, they have been living it, and they

have been inspired by the story of Shannen Koostachin. This is a historic opportunity.[18]

The vote came down on February 27, 2012. The public gallery of the House of Commons included First Nations education leaders and many grade school students from the Ottawa region. Shannen's parents were in the House of Commons visitors' gallery along with their daughter Serena, who had brought her new baby, Shannen. Chelsea Edwards sat with them. As the motion was read out, the members of each party rose one by one to vote.

"Serena and I were sitting side-by-side with baby Shannen, and we thought they were just taking attendance," Chelsea recalled. "After everyone sat down, we were like 'OK, good, everyone's here, let's get it started.' And they looked at us and started clapping." As the Attawapiskat group looked down on the politicians, they noticed that the MPs were giving them a standing ovation. Chelsea recalled their amazement: "We looked at each other and were like, 'Did we win?'"[19]

• • •

The vote was a moment almost unprecedented in the life of the Harper majority government—a unanimous vote of support by the House of Commons. For the first time in Canadian history, the Parliament of Canada acknowledged the obligation to ensure equitable education standards for children on reserves. Although the motion was non-binding, it was a milestone that Stephen Harper and every member of his government had stood in the House to support the principle of closing the funding gap and recognizing "that all First Nation children have an equal right to high-quality, culturally-relevant education."[20]

At a celebratory event afterward, the Koostachin family thanked the assembled politicians and young people. Andrew Koostachin stood at the microphone in the large parliamentary hall and reflected on the life of his late daughter:

I was given a girl, a very special girl with a special gift. I was told she had this gift to move people with words, and I was honoured to be her father. She believed in God, she believed in people. She believed God lived in every one of us. She believed she could change people. When she made that speech here four years ago, when she was told there would be no funding for Attawapiskat to get a new school, she stood up to that, and she said, "We're not going to give up." That made a believer out of me. As a father, I always thought that I would be the teacher for her, but she taught me a lot of things. . . . She started reaching out to the young people. When the young people speak, they have power. Dreams *can* come true.[21]

THE ROGUE CHIEFS

[Shannen] Koostachin passed away two years ago in
an automobile accident, at 15 years old. But she was on
the mind of everyone in the education strategy session
during the second day of the 32nd Annual Assembly of
First Nations general assembly yesterday in Moncton.
—LAURA BROWN[22]

Long before Shannen Koostachin spoke up for her classmates, there were educators who had been working out
the nuts and bolts of making quality First Nations education a reality. In Quebec, the 1975 James Bay Agreement
established the Cree School Board, giving the James Bay
Cree of that province authority over curricula, the school calendar,
and the language of instruction for their children. In Nova Scotia,
the Mi'kmaq Education Act had been in place since 1999, ensuring
the Mi'kmaq had the power of law to design and deliver culturally
appropriate education programs. In British Columbia, Indigenous
Enhancement Agreements had been put in place to ensure quality
and culturally based education in local school districts.

But in other parts of the country, attempts to establish new
education systems were bogged down in frustratingly slow negotiations with the federal government. In NAN territory, the communities had been negotiating for seventeen years for a regional
education agreement. Deputy Grand Chief Alvin Fiddler of the
Nishnawbe Aski Nation was frustrated by the government's lack
of urgency on the issue: "We have spent years in a process with no
sign posts or markers. It hasn't been fruitful for our communities.
The consultants get paid. The lawyers get paid, but our children

haven't seen the results. We are very frustrated by the inaction and dragging it out. There is no light at the end of the tunnel."[23]

The implications of such foot dragging have been glaring. A 2014 report by Aboriginal Affairs revealed that the literacy and numeracy scores for First Nations students in Ontario were dismal.[24] First Nations schools in Atlantic Canada had a 65 per cent literacy rate for males and a 70 per cent literacy rate for females, but in Ontario the numbers were a mere 21 per cent and 32 per cent respectively. This put the literacy rate for First Nations students in Ontario below that of nearly every other country in the world outside sub-Saharan Africa. Numeracy rates in Ontario were even more abysmal: only 18 per cent of males and 20 per cent of females could meet provincial standards for mathematics.

First Nations youth protesting for equal education rights on Parliament Hill. *Courtesy of Janet Doherty.*

Aboriginal Affairs presented these dismal numbers as part of its "Strong Schools, Successful Students Initiative."[25] But rather than look into the cause of these terrible results, AANDC announced that it was cancelling a planned performance audit of schools under its authority. Nonetheless, the dismal numbers served as more proof of the desperate need for education reform.

What the disparity in literacy scores across the country also showed was that overhauling the broken education system at the federal level wasn't a simple task. Given the immense differences among various First Nations communities, the delivery of equitable education would pose numerous challenges. There were many education experts, however, who had spent decades putting thoughts together on how to make reform workable.

Karihwakeron, former education director of the Assembly of First Nations, said that the overhaul of education had to be flexible given the huge disparities facing First Nations communities across Canada:

> Aggregation of educational services is required, but the difficulty is there is so much diversity across the country. Larger First Nations are pretty much self-contained education systems. They can purchase the services they are lacking. Smaller communities could benefit from an aggregation of services, but it doesn't have to be the same model everywhere. In small communities in the south, there can be good relations with the provincial systems. In more remote communities, there needs to be different access to services.

To Karihwakeron, the solution lies in putting the needs of children ahead of the interests of the bureaucracy. "Aggregate development can happen [among smaller and isolated communities]," he said. "It is about empowering. You can't give a narrow set of options that simply benefit the department."[26]

To Bill Blake, it is essential to ensure that the money flows to an education authority legally separate from the local band council:

> The reason we have such [a] high quality of education in Ontario [off reserve] is because the school boards are separate from the municipal councils. If the municipal councils could control education funding, education would die. There are always more votes to be had in fixing roads than in providing school resources. The same situation exists on reserves. The money should go totally to education and to a separate education authority.[27]

John B. Nakogee believes that the bottom line for success is closing the funding gap between federal and provincial school systems:

> Attawapiskat has the potential to make education move forward, but we need the funding that meets the needs of children. We need cultural teaching in our schools, but our students also have to be taught in a way that is

comparable to the provincial standard. This means having special support teachers who can travel between the
various communities to provide in-service support.[28]

Today isolated communities can benefit from online, digital,
and video conferencing opportunities with larger education systems. In the Treaty 9 region, colleges and universities are con-
necting with isolated reserves to offer online long-distance education. Additionally, some provincial school boards have expressed
interest in working on curricula and e-learning. The digital age
offers huge potential for overcoming distance through innovative
learning strategies. But the implementation of such innovation is
dependent on federal bureaucrats' recognition of the need to work
with the larger education community.

The passage of the Shannen's Dream motion gave the federal
government the instructions that it needed to close the funding
gap and establish credible Indigenous-centred education.

But this historic leap toward equity was dependent on goodwill and a willingness to put students first. Stephen Harper had
demonstrated goodwill during the residential schools apology of
2008, but failure to implement the principles outlined in the historic Shannen's Dream motion was glaring.

In December 2012, several months after the unanimous vote
in the House of Commons, Minister John Duncan announced a
national consultation process for creating a new First Nations Education Act. But Duncan was on his way out. The man who would
carry the ball on education reform was the new Aboriginal Affairs
minister, Bernard Valcourt, an MP with an even lower profile in
the Conservative caucus than Duncan had when he was chosen.

Valcourt was also more combative than Duncan. In taking control of the file, he claimed that there was no funding gap between
First Nations schools and those in provincial systems. In fact,
according to Valcourt, First Nations students received more funding than their provincial counterparts. Where the AFN put per
pupil spending at just over $7,000, Valcourt claimed that it was
more like $14,000.[29]

In October 2013, Valcourt presented the government's first
attempt at a deal. It included more than a billion dollars in top-up
funding for First Nations schools. Although the number sounded

impressive, First Nations educators saw it simply as the replacement for a huge shortfall that had grown over the previous seventeen years as a result of Paul Martin's 2 per cent annual cap on First Nations education funding.

In response to Valcourt's offer, respected economist Don Drummond pointed out that the compounded effect of the 2 per cent cap on funding (while communities grew at more than double this rate) had left the system seriously underfunded compared with the early 1990s. When the cap was first imposed in 1996, First Nations were told that it would be temporary, but instead it had become a permanent impediment to equitable funding. Drummond warned the AFN that it would be "silly" to agree to Valcourt's deal since future funding had not been clarified—it would be like signing up for a second round "with somebody who tricked you 17 years ago."[30]

The offer was immediately panned by the Assembly of First Nations. It insisted that the government agree to five principles before any deal could be reached:

1. Recognize First Nations jurisdiction, including treaty rights.
2. Guarantee stable and equitable funding.
3. Recognize the right of First Nations to establish cultural and language teaching.
4. Establish reciprocal accountability through mechanisms that involve parents, the community, and First Nations, with no arbitrary control by the federal government.
5. Commit to meaningful dialogue to guarantee the implementation of quality First Nations education.[31]

A mere four months after these conditions were sent to the government, Stephen Harper announced that the government had finalized legislation reform in the form of Bill C-33, the First Nations Control of First Nations Education Act (FNCFNEA).[32] This announcement stunned Indigenous education experts since they had not been consulted on its development.

One of those surprised by the statement was Chief Gilbert Whiteduck of the Kitigan Zibi reserve. He had spent years working on the education portfolio at the Assembly of First Nations. He had spoken with Chief Shawn Atleo on February 1, 2014, and was assured that there was no deal in the works with the federal government.[33] Less than a week later Atleo joined Harper on stage at the Kainai High School in southwestern Alberta to announce the new Education Act. If everything went according to plan, Bill C-33 could have been a defining moment for the Harper government.

Harper and Atleo were joined by representatives of the Truth and Reconciliation Commission. It wasn't surprising that the prime minister drew on the symbolism of the residential school apology as he stood with the commission delegates.

George Lafond, of the Treaty Commission Office in Saskatchewan, said that the new Education Act was supposed to show a commitment to follow through on the meaning of the apology: "With the Truth and Reconciliation panel sitting there, it buttressed the argument that this was an attempt to show that reconciliation could be made between a government and its peoples." Lafond had played a role in trying to get both sides to agree to a package of education reform. He said that the Harper government saw moving forward with education reform as proof that they were serious about making good on the residential school apology: "One of the biggest criticisms was, OK, it's one thing to say we're sorry and seek reconciliation for the past. Where's the actual action? Where's the talk and where's the walk?"[34]

But an increasingly politicized grassroots base didn't see the symbolism of the prime minister standing with the Truth and Reconciliation commissioners. They saw the symbolism of National Chief Shawn Atleo sitting on stage with a prime minister who was a lightning rod for a new generation of First Nations political activism.

Ever since the Idle No More protests, Atleo had been steadily losing ground among chiefs, particularly those in western Canada and Ontario. They were feeling the heat from an increasingly restless base with a large youth population. The Harper government's imperious attitude put Indigenous leaders in an increasingly difficult position with their frustrated communities. Atleo, who had built his tenure on conciliation and negotiation with the government, was out of sync with the polarized climate.

To many First Nations people, Harper simply couldn't be trusted. The lack of involvement of First Nations education experts in crafting the bill only added to the suspicion. Within

Underfunded classrooms: students wear winter coats to keep warm in Kashechewan portable school, winter 2013. *Courtesy of the author.*

the bill itself were laudable elements, such as increased funding of $1.9 billion; however, the bill raised numerous concerns with its one-size-fits-all approach and continued control by the minister of Aboriginal Affairs.

To ensure credible oversight of this new education system, the government could have worked with the numerous education planning councils in place across the country. Instead, the minister announced a nine-person Joint Council of Education Professionals (s. 10 of the act) mandated to oversee accountability and education outcomes. Control of this council would remain with the minister since the government gave itself the power to appoint four members plus the chair. The minister would also have the authority to remove anyone from the panel.

The act stipulated that local school authorities were obligated to hire a principal, an education director, and a school inspector. Such oversight in isolated communities would be especially onerous, particularly when local schools didn't have adequate funding to hire special education teachers.

Under the act, the minister could arbitrarily revoke the powers of a local education authority or administrative body (s. 27.3) and impose temporary administrators (s. 40.4).[35] The removal of such an authority could be necessary at times; however, First Nations people had long and bitter memories of the arbitrary control of the department. That the minister gave himself a liability-free clause (s. 46.1) to protect the government from the fallout of any decision related to suspensions of education authorities or impositions of temporary administrators only fuelled the suspicion.

These arbitrary stipulations ignored the numerous agreements and accountability mechanisms that frustrated First Nations had been attempting to negotiate for years. Given the historic importance of this legislation, such issues could have been negotiated if both sides were willing to give a little bit. But this wasn't going to happen. The Conservatives took a hard line because they had already secured Atleo's signature on the agreement. Atleo had apparently agreed to support the bill following a "contentious phone conversation" with the prime minister on January 31, 2014.[36] As far as the government was concerned, there was nothing to negotiate.

The hard-core opponents of Atleo trashed the agreement. Pam Palmater, a political opponent, savaged the Education Act as yet another example of his sellout of the grassroots:

> What makes this deal so historic? Well, it's the deal that no First Nation asked for and it's one that Atleo had no power to make. It's historic because not only will Atleo go down in history as the worst National Chief, but he has taken the AFN down with him. For the most part, many Regional Chiefs sat by and watched him do it. Now, the AFN thinks that by analyzing its own deal, this will help make the bitter taste of assimilation wash down more easily. They are wrong.[37]

The splinters in the AFN ranks over the legislation revealed the deepening political fault lines that had first come to public attention during the tense Idle No More days. Manitoba, Ontario, and Quebec chiefs denounced the legislation. Others wanted to tone down the political fight and stay focused on the educational opportunities that might be attained if the chiefs remained at the negotiating table. But the Conservatives had Atleo's signature on the agreement. They told the chiefs that they could take it or leave it. The chiefs rejected it, and on May 5, 2014, Shawn Atleo resigned as national chief.

Grand Chief Doug Kelly of the Sto:lo Tribal Council in British Columbia said that he was "disheartened and deeply troubled" by the chiefs who were calling for the scrapping of the legislation: "Are they prepared to say that they are proud of their accomplishment where they cost our schools $1.9 billion in terms of funding?" he asked.[38]

On May 14, 2014, the Confederacy of Nations, which represented communities from Ontario, Quebec, Manitoba, Saskatchewan, Alberta, and the Northwest Territories, called on Valcourt to begin immediate negotiations on legislation that would respect First Nations rights to quality education and include the transfer of funding to schools.

But this wasn't about to happen. Frustrated First Nations leaders of the confederacy met to find a way to bring the government back to the table. Some chiefs suggested economic boycotts if the government refused to negotiate.

Speaking in the House of Commons, Valcourt used the musings about an economic boycott to denounce the national leaders as "rogue chiefs": "I think that members of the House will agree that we should ask members to condemn in the strongest terms the rogue chiefs who are threatening the security of Canadians, their families, and taxpayers."[39]

It wasn't about the children anymore. It wasn't about following through on the commitments made during the residential school apology. The Harper government had been challenged on what could have been a signature piece of legislation. The government's instinct was to show its fangs. Rather than honour the promise to establish "child-centred" learning, the government retreated to right-wing talking points that painted a picture of bad chiefs and threatened taxpayers. In the fight among politicians, the children lost again.

SHANNEN'S TEAM

Changes in human rights don't happen in a shuffle. It takes a leap. It takes a commitment. But we're always being told we have to be practical in our expectations. Kids don't believe that nonsense. They measure progress in terms of what is good for children.
—CINDY BLACKSTOCK[40]

A s Bernard Valcourt was clanging swords with increasingly frustrated Indigenous leaders, the children were marching. Across the country, young people joined the annual Our Dreams Matter Too march on June 11, 2014, the sixth anniversary of the residential school apology. Many of the young marchers who carried signs and wrote letters to the prime minister weren't even old enough to remember the apology. But they remembered Shannen and her call for fairness. Across the country, over 4,000 young people marched in protest over continuing inequity.

Marchers in the Tyendinaga Mohawk Territory walked through pouring rain to deliver 400 letters to the Desoronto Post Office to be sent to the prime minister. In Saskatchewan, young people marched in Saskatoon, Prince Albert, and Regina, and at the Montreal Lake Cree First Nation 200 young people marched with homemade posters calling for education equity. At the Samson Cree First Nation in Alberta, students from Nipisihkopahk Elementary School marched to the local post office with their letters. These letters joined hundreds being sent from Nanaimo, Toronto, and Georgian Bay. In suburban Oakville at the outskirts of Toronto, marchers were joined by local city councillors and MPPs.

Students from Notre Dame High School in Brampton, Ontario, marching for Shannen's Dream. *Courtesy of Judy Vella.*

In Chateauguay, Quebec, 350 young people marched. In Ottawa, the march to Parliament Hill had to be cancelled because of a thunderstorm threat, so nearly 500 students gathered at a rally at Fisher Park Public School.

The Our Dreams Matter Too walk in June had become an annual event promoted by the First Nations Child and Family Caring Society. Blackstock's agency also promotes the Have a Heart Day, when young people hold rallies on Valentine's Day to send messages to the prime minister about the need to ensure equity in education for First Nations students.

"The success of the Our Dreams Matter [Too] campaign is that it isn't tokenism," explained Blackstock. "The marches take the adults out of the mix and create a space where young people are given the opportunity to have the conversations with the power brokers. You as a child have a right to be heard. You as a child have a right to write a letter to the prime minister and tell him what you think."[41]

These marches demonstrate only some of the ways that Shannen Koostachin's story continues to resonate with young people. Some students learn the story and then organize fundraising projects for northern First Nations. Other schools have started pen pal clubs or friendship links with isolated communities. In the James Bay region, students in Fort Albany, Moose Factory, Kashechewan, and Attawapiskat are developing relationships with urban students in the south.

Brenda Stewart, who helps to coordinate an outreach link between students of Our Lady of Fatima School in Toronto and the primary school in Attawapiskat, said that these efforts are about creating reconciliation: "When I tell the story of Attawapiskat to my students, they are amazed that such conditions exist in Canada. I say, 'Now you know, and when you grow up you can make a difference so things can change. You have this power.' This is what reconciliation is all about."⁴²

Why does this story continue to resonate so deeply with Canadian youth? During the Our Dreams Matter Too rally in Ottawa in June 2014, I met a grade six student from Featherstone Public School in the city's suburbs. She was a first-generation Canadian, and her face was framed by a purple hijab. She caught my attention because she was carrying a large sign on which she had written the words that Shannen had written in a letter to the International Children's Peace Prize committee back in 2010: "I would tell the children to ignore people who are putting you down. Get up and tell them what you want . . . what you need! NEVER give up hope. Get up; pick up your books and GO TO SCHOOL (just not in portables)."

I was fascinated to know why a first-generation immigrant child in suburban Ottawa was inspired by a young Cree girl from an isolated reserve. At the rally, I asked her what moved her about Shannen's story. A few days later I received her email response inviting me to her school's Shannen's Dream Club's pizza and pop party: "We started reflecting on the question you asked about why Shannen has inspired so many children. If you come visit our school we will spend some time discussing our ideas and answers revolving around that question."⁴³

Impressed by the articulate directness of the invitation, I accepted. The vast majority of the students involved in this club were the children of Muslim immigrants from the Middle East or North Africa. Shannen, they told me, was their heroine. She was a role model for being a culturally proud and assertive young woman. They had established their school club to fight for the rights of First Nations students to have access to quality education.

What did they think of the government of Canada for leaving children in such a situation? One determined little girl was ready with an answer. She thought that the government needed to be scolded. "Didn't their parents raise them right to know the difference between right and wrong?" she queried.

Like Shannen, these young people see an injustice and know that it should be fixed. They see adults who have the ability to right the wrong and wonder what happened to their moral courage. Didn't their parents raise them right? They identify with Shannen because she wasn't afraid to confront adults over their responsibility to make the world fair for children.

Cindy Blackstock isn't surprised that youth feel this personal connection to the Shannen Koostachin story. As she stated, "children may not be experts in law and process, but they are experts in fairness and love. They understand what a broken promise means. They know when something isn't right, and they want it to be fixed."[44]

Part of the success of the Attawapiskat School campaign lay in the fact that a young girl could tell a story of terrible inequity in a way that resonated with other young people. When Shannen spoke of "comfy" schools, she used language that resonated with other children. Her challenge to adults was direct and cut through the political jargon and the spin. The campaign refocused the question about the obligation of the federal government regarding treaty people. Was the role of department officials to protect failed policies and the reputations of ministers, or was it to ensure that First Nations children have inalienable rights that must be protected in law?

So what is the lasting political influence of this movement? It remains to be seen. So far Attawapiskat is the only First Nations community that has used this level of public engagement to push for action on a school. Nonetheless, labour activist Terry Downey believes that there is incredible power in the story of a First Nations girl who could inspire youth across racial and cultural lines. She

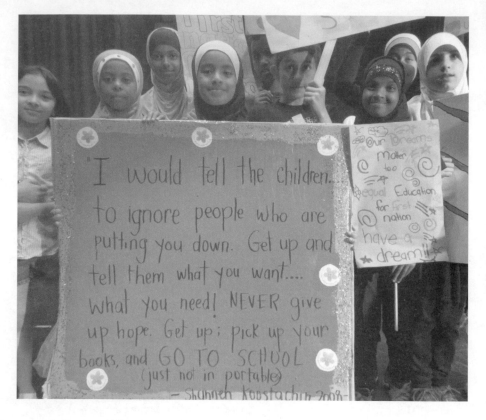

Members of the Shannen's Dream Club at Featherstone Public School in Ottawa, June 2014. *Courtesy of the author.*

sees it as a story that symbolizes hope: "Young people gravitate to the story of Shannen. White kids of privilege heard from some-one their age, and they wanted to help. They wanted to right a wrong. Among the diverse community, young Muslim women for example, they made a connection to Shannen because they had come from countries with similar issues." Downey believes that the movement has powerful potential to effect change: "Seeing all these young people come to Parliament Hill with their signs blew me away. These young people spoke out in a way that transcended their own reality and became a political force."[45]

To Chelsea Edwards, who has gone on to speak about youth rights in forums across Canada and in Europe, the movement is about Indigenous youth finding their rightful place in Canada:

Canada should be a place where we are proud of who we are, but I was ashamed of who I was because of my ethnicity. I had no confidence when I started this campaign, but I knew it was the right thing to do. It is about being proud and having what every other child takes for granted. This is what Shannen dreamed was possible.[46]

CONCLUSION

The hearts of little children are pure and
therefore the Great Spirit may show them
many things that other people miss.
—POSTER IN CLASSROOM AT THE NEWLY
OPENED SCHOOL IN ATTAWAPISKAT

On a bright blue and crisp September day in 2014, I
saw a possible future for the children of Treaty 9
territory. I sensed it as soon as I walked through
the doors of the beautiful new elementary school
in Attawapiskat. Walking into the building, I heard
laughter in the hallways. It was the unmistakable sound of joy
and delight in children. The school was a flurry of activity as children and teachers were still acclimatizing themselves to life in
their brand new facility complete with brightly lit classrooms, a
library, a music room, and a home economics department. By far
the greatest excitement, however, was in the gymnasium, where
the final dress rehearsal for the school's first play was under way.

Children with painted noses and outlandish costumes peeked
out from behind the stage curtains as a teacher attempted to shush
them. Jackie Hookimaw-Witt was the director of the production.
She pointed out that, for students who had never been on a real
stage before, this dress rehearsal was like being on Broadway. The
little Broadway stars came on stage dressed as otters, bears, and
turtles. Water nymphs danced across the imaginary waters as
graceful powwow dancers circled the centre of the stage.

The play told the legends of the people who live along the
mighty Attawapiskat River and of the guardian angels who keep

them connected to the land and their spirituality. We learned that the guardians had called forth a child to speak up for the community and that the result was this beautiful school. And now this child resides with the guardian angels. She watches over the young people, making sure that they will grow up strong and confident.

Sitting in the back of the gymnasium listening to the children singing, I couldn't help but think of the girl whom these youngsters were invoking from the stage. I remembered Shannen Koostachin standing outside the portables on a bitterly cold day when she assured me that one day there would be a better future for the students' little brothers and sisters. Until that moment, as a politician, former school board trustee, and parent, I had looked upon schools as simply one part of the basic infrastructure of Canadian communities. Shannen had taught me, however, that building a school isn't just an investment in infrastructure but also a project of hope. It is a commitment to the future. She had been right. I could see this hope manifested in a beautiful building in which spirited children played in an environment free from mice, toxins, and almost certain failure.

But this beautiful school didn't just happen, and if young people like Shannen hadn't stood up it never would have happened. The fight for a new school had lasted fourteen long years and required the outraged energy of young people across Canada to win it.

Without this campaign of organized resistance, the youngsters of Attawapiskat would have been in the same situation as their cousins in Kashechewan, who, that September, were preparing for yet another year without proper supplies in broken-down portables. A teacher in the community had emailed me asking if I could help to get the students pencils, papers, and one-inch binders. "We have such good students here," she wrote. "We just don't have the resources to help them."[1]

This call for help came as I was being pressed by students at Boxwood Public School in Markham on how they could help to carry on Shannen's Dream. When they learned about the situation facing Kashechewan students, they, along with youngsters at Markham's Wismer Public School, began a campaign to send backpacks filled with school supplies to the students. Grade six student Arvind Arulraj told media that this wasn't an act of charity—it was an act of solidarity. He said that the Markham students

Students practising for the first play performed on the stage of the new Kattawapiskak Elementary School, October 2014. *Courtesy of Jackie Hookimaw-Witt.*

had taken action in order "to make allies with the kids in Kashechewan" and that this wasn't just a cause *du jour.* "We just don't want to do something good and get it over with," Arvind added. Each backpack was sent with a handwritten letter with messages such as "We've got your back" and "We are on your side."[2] This peer-to-peer act of solidarity is fundamental to the vision of Shannen's Dream. As grade five student Hasna from Boxwood Public School stated in her class project about Shannen, these actions were about being a "part of the change."

Aboriginal Affairs remains very aware of what this continuing momentum might mean. In an internal document on the conditions faced by students in Kashechewan, bureaucrats noted that the substandard school facilities could become politically problematic if the situation became known to the public. The report declared that a potential Shannen's Dream campaign for this community could "bring attention to the conditions of education facilities." However, Aboriginal Affairs believed that if there wasn't such an uprising of young people the department could continue to keep the children in substandard facilities for generations. In fact, it stated that the broken-down portables could "serve the community's needs for 40 plus years."[3]

So there you have it. The children in Attawapiskat were celebrating a new school because their community had fought relentlessly for one in a public awareness campaign. But other communities in equally dire circumstances might never see proper schools unless they also mobilize to shame the government into action. It shouldn't have to be this way. What will it take for Canada to finally recognize its obligation to First Nations children?

Many incredible people have come through on-reserve schools and made their marks in politics, health, and the arts. But far too many innocent youngsters have been needlessly ground up in a bureaucratic meat grinder. There isn't anything accidental about such a waste of potential and life. If you look for the pattern, you'll see it repeated again and again throughout the history of this country's relations with its First Nations people.

Consider this: following the famines on the western plains in the 1880s, as the Cree and Assiniboine people were being forced onto reserves, the government told them that their future lay in farming. With the bison gone and a flood of immigrants competing for the land, the people who signed the treaties saw little choice but to make this transition. But the Department of Indian Affairs established a framework that made success nearly impossible. First Nations people were often forced to settle on poor land, and government policy made it illegal for Indian people to use anything other than hand tools, whereas their neighbouring white farmers were able to purchase the latest technology in farm machinery.[4] And, when First Nations farmers were able to produce crops, their movements were restricted, and they weren't able to market them as their white neighbours could. The results were obvious: the farms failed, and the people went hungry. The blame for this colossal failure of development wasn't laid at the door of the federal government but on the Indian people themselves for being fundamentally less productive than their white neighbours. In short, they took the blame for a deliberately detrimental policy because the white public saw them as lazy—a slur that continued to echo through the years.

What was done with agriculture in the nineteenth century is being done with education in the twenty-first century. Indigenous youth are told that their future lies in education, yet the government has systematically failed to provide the tools that they require to succeed: proper libraries, science labs, textbooks, and so on. And this parsimony extends to the most marginal and needy—insisting that heavily handicapped Indigenous children can make do with a push wheelchair when non-Indigenous children in similar circumstances would be given a motorized wheelchair.

Year after year, government experts scratch their heads about the education gap and then carry on as they have always done. But underneath it all is the pattern laid out by John A. Macdonald, Edgar Dewdney, Duncan Campbell Scott, and successive governments into this century. A century ago Peter Henderson Bryce exposed this pattern as a national crime. A hundred years later the criminal failure to protect and nurture children continues.

In earlier times, it was believed that the "Indian Question" could be settled by the gradual disappearance of Indigenous identity through forced residency on reserves, controlled under the Indian Act, and indoctrination of children in residential schools. The government tried to force people off the land and onto reserves. In the twenty-first century, the desire seems to be to get people out of reserves. The government seems to believe that, if reserves are reduced to places of increasingly degraded opportunities, people will inevitably get discouraged and move to cities to become absorbed into the broader cultural mosaic.

But this hasn't happened. Even as urban Indigenous populations have grown, cultural identity and connectedness to the land show a remarkable durability. And treaty rights haven't withered either. In fact, they have only been further defined by numerous court decisions. To move ahead as a nation, Canada must recognize this reality. The people who handed over such immense geography and wealth are still there on the land, and they aren't leaving. They are waiting for the other partner of the treaty—the Canadian people—to hold up their end.

Would building First Nations schools and protecting the interests of Indigenous youth be enough to address the historical breach between Indigenous and non-Indigenous people in Canada? No, perhaps not. But it would be a damned good start.

What I have come to understand from the treaties is that First Nations and non–First Nations people are bound together in a relationship. This is Canada's primary relationship. Duncan Campbell Scott said that it will last "so long as the grass grows and the water runs." For many decades now, it has been a dysfunctional and at times hostile relationship. None of us can change what happened before. But we all have the power to decide what kind of relationship will exist in the future.

This is perhaps another reason why I think so much of Shannen. She was a young woman who refused to have her dreams limited by the system. She believed that the Canadian people were better than the miserly limitations imposed by the federal government. She believed that, by reaching out to Canadians, reconciliation and change are possible. I believe that too.

Shannen taught me to see the issues of First Nations inequity through the eyes of a child. She knew that children have only one childhood—once it's gone, it can never be brought back again. This realization was the driving force behind everything that she did in fighting for the younger brothers and sisters coming in her wake. Shannen had a burning urgency because she saw the issue from the perspective of a disappearing childhood.

Ottawa students creating a banner entitled "Why Does Shannen Inspire?" *Courtesy of Janet Doherty.*

Students across Canada have instinctively understood this urgency. And we can learn from them that children can't wait. Canada will never be the country that it was meant to be until it recognizes the obligation to ensure that all children of the treaty—Indigenous and non-Indigenous—can live in a country where their dreams and hopes are nurtured and protected. This was Shannen's dream, and with goodwill we can get there.

NOTES

INTRODUCTION

1 Linda Goyette, "Still Waiting in Attawapiskat," *Canadian Geographic,* December 2010, www.canadiangeographic.ca/magazine/dec10/attawapiskat.asp.
2 Shannen Koostachin, "Education Is a Human Right," speaking at the Education Is a Human Right Conference, Ontario Institute for Studies in Education, Toronto, November 26, 2008, www.youtube.com/watch?v=shX-KTTKsZto.
3 *Hi-Ho Mistahey!,* dir. Alanis Obomsawin, National Film Board, 2013.
4 "New DC Comics Superhero Inspired by Young Cree Activist," CBC News, October 30, 2013, www.cbc.ca/news/canada/sudbury/new-dc-comics-super-hero-inspired-by-young-cree-activist-1.2288680.
5 The department overseeing Indigenous issues in Canada has undergone many name changes over the decades, most recently Aboriginal Affairs and Northern Development Canada (AANDC). It has also been known as the Department of Indian Affairs and Northern Development (DIAND) and Indian and Northern Affairs Canada (INAC). For the sake of simplicity, I have opted for the Department of Indian Affairs or simply the department unless the name is used in a specific period of time regarding a specific set of incidents.

PART I: THE SHADOW OF ST. ANNE'S

DUNCAN CAMPBELL SCOTT COMES TO JAMES BAY

1 Duncan Campbell Scott, Samuel Stewart, and Daniel McMartin, "The James Bay Treaty—Treaty No. 9. Report to Superintendent of Indian Affairs," November 6, 1905, n. pag., www.aadnc-aandc.gc.ca/eng/1100100028863/110010 0028864.
2 Duncan Campbell Scott, "The Last of the Indian Treaties," *Scribners,* November 1906, 578, www.unz.org/Pub/Scribners-1906nov-00573.
3 Scott, Stewart, and McMartin, "The James Bay Treaty," n. pag.
4 Scott, "The Last of the Indian Treaties," 581.
5 Scott, Stewart, and McMartin, "The James Bay Treaty," n. pag.
6 Unlike the Plains First Nations, structured as "tribes," the boreal Indigenous peoples are smaller, family-based hunting groups more accurately known as "bands." See John Long, *Treaty No. 9: Making the Agreement to Share the Land in Far Northern Ontario* (Montreal: McGill-Queen's University Press, 2010), 33.

7   James Morrison, *Treaty Research Report—Treaty 9 (1905–06) for Treaties and Historical Research Centre*, 1986, www.aadnc-aandc.gc.ca/eng/1100100028859 /1100100028861.

8   The railways were dramatically changing the traditional economic centres in the isolated north. The HBC posts had been set up along the rivers, which, until then, had been the key transportation routes for trade. Many of the fledgling reserves were being set up near these posts, even though the railway depots were quickly consigning these traditional centres to economic isolation and irrelevance.

9   Long, *Treaty No. 9*, 41.

10 Morrison, *Treaty Research Report*.

11 Scott, Stewart, and McMartin, "The James Bay Treaty," n. pag.

12 Ibid.

13 Ibid.

14 Morrison, *Treaty Research Report*.

15 R. L. McDougall, ed., *The Poet and the Critic: A Literary Correspondence between D. C. Scott and E. K. Brown* (Ottawa: Carleton University Press, 1983), 1.

16 Scott, "The Last of the Indian Treaties," 573.

17 Duncan Campbell Scott, "Powassan's Drum," in *Powassan's Drum: Poems of Duncan Campbell Scott*, ed. Raymond Souster and Douglas Lochhead (Ottawa: Tecumseh Press, 1985), 12.

18 Scott, Stewart, and McMartin, "The James Bay Treaty," n. pag.

19 Mark Abley, *Conversations with a Dead Man: The Legacy of Duncan Campbell Scott* (Madeira Park, BC: Douglas and McIntyre, 2013), 209.

20 Duncan Campbell Scott, "Circular," Department of Indian Affairs, December 15, 1921.

21 Edmund Metatawabin, *Up Ghost River: A Chief's Journey through the Turbulent Waters of Native History* (Toronto: Alfred A. Knopf, 2014), 128.

22 Edwin Killorin Brown, "Duncan Campbell Scott: A Memoir," in *Responses and Evaluations: Essays on Canada*, ed. David Staines (Toronto: McClelland and Stewart, 1977), 134.

23 Long, *Treaty No. 9*, xv.

THE MISSION SCHOOL

24 Department of Indian Affairs, "Annual Report of the Department of Indian Affairs," 1907, Library and Archives Canada (hereafter LAC), RG 10, Vol. 3093, File 289, 590.

25 LAC, RG 10, Vol. 6810, File 470-2-3, Vol. 7, 55 (L-3) and 63 (N-3).

26 John S. Milloy, *A National Crime: The Canadian Government and the Residential School System 1879–1986* (Winnipeg: University of Manitoba Press, 1999), 62–63.

27 Jerry Paquette and Gérald Fallon, *First Nations Education Policy in Canada: Progress or Gridlock?* (Toronto: University of Toronto Press, 2010), 7, citing Milloy, *A National Crime*.

28 Robert Choquette, *The Oblate Assault on Canada's Northwest* (Ottawa: University of Ottawa Press, 1995), 1.

29 Scott, Stewart, and McMartin, "The James Bay Treaty."

30 Department of Indian Affairs, "Annual Report of the Department of Indian Affairs," 1907, LAC, RG 10, Vol. 3093, File 289, 950.

31 Ibid.

32 Ibid. ˙

33 In 1907, Scott's own daughter Elizabeth died in a boarding school in England from a fever.

34 Peter Henderson Bryce, *Report on the Indian Schools of Manitoba and the Northwest Territories* (Ottawa: Government Printing Bureau, 1907).

35 Megan Sproule-Jones, "Crusading for the Forgotten: Dr. Peter Bryce, Public Health, and Prairie Native Residential Schools," *Canadian Bulletin of Medical History/Bulletin canadien d'histoire de la médicine* 13 (1996): 199–224.

36 Dean Neu and Richard Therrien, *Accounting for Genocide: Canada's Bureaucratic Assault on Aboriginal People* (Black Point, NS: Fernwood Publishing, 2003), 104.

37 James Daschuk, *Clearing the Plains: Disease, Politics of Starvation, and the Loss of Aboriginal Life* (Regina: University of Regina Press, 2013).

38 Telegraph from Fred White, Walsh, NWT, to E. Dewdney, October 19, 1882, submitted in the House of Commons debate, Hansard, *Debates,* June 30, 1891, 1493–94.

39 Daschuk, *Clearing the Plains,* 105.

40 Sproule-Jones, "Crusading for the Forgotten," 212.

41 Neu and Therrien, *Accounting for Genocide,* 94–95.

42 Ronald Haycock, *The Image of the Indian* (Waterloo, ON: Waterloo Lutheran University, 1971), 1.

43 Peter Henderson Bryce, *The Story of a National Crime: Being an Appeal for Justice to the Indians of Canada* (Ottawa: James Hope and Sons, 1922), www.archive.org/stream/storyofnationalcoobrycuoft/storyofnationalcoobrycuoft_djvu.txt.

44 Quoted in Sproule-Jones, "Crusading for the Forgotten," 217.

45 Andrew Jay Bryce, "Proposing New Media Narratives to Create an Ethical Space of Engagement between Indigenous and Non-Indigenous People in Canada" (MA thesis, Royal Roads University, 2014), dspace.royalroads.ca/docs/handle/10170/735.

46 *Saturday Night,* November 23, 1907, LAC, RG 10, Vol. 4037, File 317021.

47 Bryce, *The Story of a National Crime.*

48 Neu and Therrien, *Accounting for Genocide,* 105.

49 Bryce, *The Story of a National Crime.*

50 John Coldwell Adams, "Duncan Campbell Scott," in *Confederation Voices: Seven Canadian Poets,* www.uwo.ca/english/canadianpoetry/confederation/John Coldwell Adams/Confederation Voices/chapter 5.html.

51 Bryce, *The Story of a National Crime.*

52 R. Alex Sim, "The Education of Indians in Ontario: A Report to the Provincial Committee on Aims and Objectives in the Schools of Ontario," 1967, 14–15, files.eric.ed.gov/fulltext/ED062039.pdf.

53 Ibid., 15.

54 See, for instance, Bettina Stangneth, *Eichmann before Jerusalem: The Unexamined Life of a Mass Murderer* (New York: Alfred A. Knopf, 2014).
55 Milloy, *A National Crime*, 109.
56 Quoted in Adams, "Duncan Campbell Scott."

THREE LITTLE BOYS

57 Metatawabin, *Up Ghost River,* 288.
58 "Statement to RCMP by Father Langlois," June 14, 1941, LAC, RG 10, Vol. 6186, File 460-23, part 1.
59 "RCMP Report, Corporal Dexter," June 27, 1941, LAC, RG 10, Vol. 6186, File 460-23, part 1, Moose Factory Detachment.
60 Ibid.
61 "Letter: Henri Belleau, Bishop, to Phillip Phelan," July 26, 1941, LAC, RG 10, Vol. 6186, File 460-23, part 1.
62 "Report: Corporal W. Kerr," June 25, 1942, LAC, RG 10, Vol. 6186, File 460-23, part 1, Moose Factory Detachment.
63 Ibid.
64 Ibid.

THE '60'S SOLUTION

65 National Indian Brotherhood/Assembly of First Nations, "Indian Control of Indian Education," policy paper presented to the Minister of Indian Affairs and Northern Development, 1972.
66 W. C. Bethune, *Canada's Western Northland: Its History, Resources, Population, and Administration* (Ottawa: J. O. Patenaude, 1937), 60.
67 Robert Carney, "The Hawthorn Survey (1966–67): Indians and Oblates and Integrated Schooling," Canadian Catholic Historical Association, *Study Sessions* 50 (1983): 625.
68 H. G. Mingay, Inspector of Schools, "Report on Albany R.C. Mission School," March 17, 1954, DIAND Residential Schools, Records Office, File 44/23-5-460. See also *Up Ghost River*, where Metatawabin describes the efforts of staff at St. Anne's Residential School in the 1950s to prepare for the annual inspection by the Department of Indian Affairs. The building was thoroughly cleaned. Ripped children's clothing was replaced by clean clothing. All evidence of physical abuse—whips, straps, and the electric chair—was hidden.
69 Ibid.
70 "F. X. Fafard Report to Frank Pedley, Deputy Superintendent of Indian Affairs," DIAND Annual Report, Fort Albany, March 31, 1908, DIAND Library.
71 "Davey to Regional Supervisor F. M. Shaw, Re: Curriculum—Fort George, RC and Albany Residential Schools," September 19, 1960, DIAND Residential Schools, Records Office, Vol. 1 R. F., File 426/25-1-006.
72 F. Matters, Regional Supervisor, to Chief of Education Division, "Subject: Curriculum at Fort George RC and Albany Residential Schools," September 2, 1960, DIAND Residential Schools, Records Office, Vol. 1, File 426/25-1-006.
73 Milloy, *A National Crime*, 182.

74 "Davey to Regional Supervisor F.M. Shaw, Re: Curriculum—Fort George, RC and Fort Albany Residential Schools," September 19, 1960, DIAND Residential Schools, Records Office, Vol. 1 R. F., File 426/25-1-006.

75 H. B. Hawthorn, ed., *A Survey of the Contemporary Indians of Canada: Economic, Political, Educational Needs and Policies, Part 2* (Ottawa: Indian Affairs Branch, INAC, 1967), 57.

76 H. B. Hawthorn, ed., *A Survey of the Contemporary Indians of Canada: Economic, Political, Educational Needs and Policies, Part 1* (Ottawa: Indian Affairs Branch, INAC, 1966), 103.

77 Ibid., 106.

78 Ibid.

79 Hawthorn, *A Survey . . . Part 2,* 46–47.

80 Hawthorn, *A Survey . . . Part 1,* 127.

81 Sim, "The Education of Indians in Ontario," 11.

82 "Statement of the Government of Canada on Indian Policy (the White Paper)," Department of Indian Affairs, 1969, www.aadnc-aandc.gc.ca/eng/1100100010189/1100100010191.

83 Harold Cardinal, *The Unjust Society* (Vancouver: Douglas and McIntyre, 1999), 118.

84 National Indian Brotherhood/Assembly of First Nations, "Indian Control of Indian Education."

THE CHRÉTIEN LETTER

85 National Capital Region, Federal Records Centre, File DM 6-2-3, Vol. 5 (Locator #N346-2), "Letter to Mr. Shaw," Fort Albany, December 15, 1968.

86 National Capital Region, Federal Records Centre, File DM 6-2-3, Vol. 5 (Locator #N346-2), "Letter to Jean Chrétien," name redacted, December 28, 1968.

87 Ibid.

88 National Capital Region, Federal Records Centre, File DM 6-2-3, Vol. 5 (Locator #N346-2), "Letter to Mr. Shaw," Fort Albany, December 15, 1968.

89 National Capital Region, Federal Records Centre, File DM 6-2-3, Vol. 5 (Locator #N346-2), "Letter to Jean Chrétien," name redacted, December 28, 1968.

90 Ibid.

91 R. F. Hall, "Memorandum to Regional Supervisor," North Bay, July 10, 1964, DIAND Residential Schools, Records Office, File 44/25-2.

92 Ibid.

93 Daryl Balia and Kim Kirsteen, eds., *Witnessing to Christ Today,* Edinburgh 2010 Series 2 (Oxford: Regnum Books International, 2010), 98.

94 Ibid.

95 Edmund Metatawabin, affidavit, August 26, 2013, for *Larry Philip Fontaine et al. v. Attorney General of Canada et al.,* Ontario Superior Court, Court File No. 00-CV-192059, 4.

96 Fay Brunning, notes of a telephone interview with OPP Officer Greg Delguidice, April 26, 2013, submitted to Ontario Superior Court Hearing, Justice Perell presiding, December 17, 2013.

97 S. J. Bailey, Regional Supervisor of Social Programs, "Memorandum: Review of Children Enrolled in the Albany Residential School," August 22, 1969, LAC, RG 10, Vol. 11110, File 42411/25-2-023, part 2.

98 Milloy, *A National Crime*, 217.

99 Ibid., 218.

100 The term was coined by Patrick Johnson, *Native Children and the Child Welfare System* (Toronto: James Lorimer, 1983).

101 Quoted in Adrian Humphreys, "A Lost Tribe: Child Welfare System Accused of Repeating Residential School History," *National Post,* December 15, 2014, news.nationalpost.com/news/canada/a-lost-tribe-child-welfare-system-accused-of-repeating-residential-school-history-sapping-aboriginal-kids-from-their-homes.

ONE LITTLE BOY

102 Joyce Hunter, interview with the author, July 15, 2014.

103 Ibid.

104 Ibid.

105 Ibid.

106 The village of Weenusk was destroyed by flooding in the 1980s. The villagers rebuilt their community on higher ground and named their new home Peawanuck.

107 Joyce Hunter, interview with the author, July 15, 2014.

THE DARK LEGACY

108 Metatawabin, *Up Ghost River*, 279–80.

109 Brunning, notes of interview with Delguidice.

110 Metatawabin, affidavit for *Fontaine et al.* case.

111 Bruce Carson, *14 Days: Making the Conservative Movement in Canada* (Montreal: McGill-Queen's University Press, 2014), 170.

112 Department of Justice, evidence narrative on St. Anne's Residential School prepared for the IAP.

113 Affidavit of Haniya Sheikh, Lawyer, Department of Justice, for Angela Shisheesh and Her Majesty the Queen, Ontario Superior Court, June 24, 2003, File No. 10883/00.

114 Metatawabin, *Up Ghost River*, 287–88.

115 Bernard Valcourt, Minister of Indian Affairs, to Charlie Angus, MP, July 17, 2013.

116 Affidavit of Haniya Sheikh.

117 Ontario Superior Court, Justice R. G. Trainor, August 1, 2003, Court File No. 19883/00.

118 Ontario Superior Court ruling in *Fontaine et al.*, Justice J. Perell, January 14, 2014, Court File No. 00-CV-192059.

119 Edmund Metatawabin, Peetabeck Keway Keykaywin Association, to Peter MacKay, Minister of Justice, February 10, 2014.

JAMES BAY EDUCATION AFTER ST. ANNE'S

120 Quoted in Long, *Treaty No. 9*, 94–95.
121 Bryan Cummins, *Only God Can Own the Land: The Attawapiskat Cree, the Land, and the State in the 20th Century* (Cobalt, ON: Highway Book Shop, 1999), 15–16.
122 Paquette and Fallon, *First Nations Education Policy in Canada*, xi.
123 John B. Nakogee, interview with the author, June 25, 2014.
124 Attawapiskat First Nation, "Belated Attawapiskat First Nation Toxic Spill Report," submitted to Spills Research Centre, Environment Protection Branch, Ontario Ministry of Environment, April 9, 2009.
125 Quoted in Linda Goyette, "Still Waiting in Attawapiskat," *Canadian Geographic*, December 2010, www.canadiangeographic.ca/magazine/dec10/attawapiskat. asp.
126 John B. Nakogee, interview with the author, June 25, 2014.
127 Brenda Stewart, "The Contaminated Soil of J.R. Nakogee School," report prepared for the Attawapiskat First Nation Band Council, 2009.
128 Bovar Environmental, "Oil Spill Remediation Project for the Attawapiskat First Nation—Final Design Report," submitted to INAC, December 1996.
129 Bill Blake, interview with the author, June 16, 2014.
130 John B. Nakogee, interview with the author, June 25, 2014.
131 The loan was made possible by leveraging a tuition agreement with Indian Affairs, which signed off on a commitment to pay the tuition based on 168 students attending high school for five years. This tuition agreement served as collateral for the loan.
132 Attawapiskat First Nation, "Belated Attawapiskat First Nation Toxic Spill Report."
133 Ibid.
134 "Remediation Site Taking a Toll on Attawapiskat," *Wawatay News*, September 18, 2013.
135 Anebeaaki Environmental, Attawapiskat First Nation, "Environmental Inspection and Sampling Program, J. R. Nakogee Elementary School and Town Hall Teacherage," 2000.
136 Stewart, "The Contaminated Soil of J.R. Nakogee School."
137 Interview conducted by Charlie Angus with Attawapiskat mother, April 6, 2009, www.youtube.com/watch?v=YsOy1Ex3u_E. Lightly edited for readability.
138 The communities of Treaty 9 are under the political representation of NAN, within which are numerous regional tribal councils. The communities of the James Bay Cree in Ontario are represented by the Mushkegowuk Tribal Council, which works with the larger NAN body.
139 John B. Nakogee, interview with the author, June 25, 2014.

PART II: FIRE AND WATER, 2004–06

JAMES BAY JOURNEY

1 Clara Corbiere, interview with the author, May 25, 2014.

THE WATER CRISIS

2 "Residents Have Endured Dangerous Water for Years," *Edmonton Journal*, October 27, 2005, A5.

3 I toured Kashechewan with Allan Teramura during the summer of 2014. Although some of the infrastructure had improved since my first visits ten years earlier, the overall impression of the community remained the same.

4 Allan Teramura, interview with the author, August 28, 2014.

5 Oujé-Bougoumou on the Quebec side of James Bay has often been used as an example of innovative social construction. More recently, the impoverished community of Kitcisakik, Quebec, used local forest products to create cheap but sustainable community housing.

6 Allan Teramura, interview with the author, August 28, 2014.

7 Ibid.

8 Ibid.

9 Office of the Auditor General, "Report of the Commissioner of the Environment and Sustainable Development to the House of Commons," 2005, Chapter 5, "Drinking Water in First Nation Communities," www.oag-bvg.gc.ca/internet/English/parl_cesd_200509_05_e_14952.html.

10 Don Butler, "Points on a Map: The Geography of Water Woes," *Ottawa Citizen*, November 5, 2005, A5.

11 Office of the Auditor General, "Report of the Commissioner," Chapter 5.

12 Quoted in Jessica Leeder and Peter Gorrie, "Bad Water, Wasted Money," *Toronto Star*, November 12, 2005, F1.

13 Ibid.

14 Office of the Auditor General, "Report of the Commissioner," Chapter 5.

15 Quoted in John Ivison, "'Gross Mismanagement' Is in the Water," *National Post*, October 21, 2005, A8.

16 "Health," *Edited Hansard 135*, 38th Parliament, 1st Session, October 17, 2005, www.parl.gc.ca/HousePublications/Publication.aspx?Language=E&Mode=1&Parl=38&Ses=1&DocId=2026965#Int-1412576.

17 Quoted in Scott Paradis, "Evacuation of Ontario First Nation Community Called Off: Bottled Water Sent in after High Levels of E. coli Detected after Treatment Plant Breaks Down," *Sudbury Star*, October 20, 2005, A6.

18 "Aboriginal Affairs," *Edited Hansard 137*, 38th Parliament, 1st Session, October 19, 2005, www.parl.gc.ca/HousePublications/Publication.aspx?Language=E&Mode=1&Parl=38&Ses=1&DocId=2038234#Int-1417149.

19 The baby had been badly scalded by a pot knocked over in the narrow kitchen of an overcrowded house in Kashechewan. In homes that are overcrowded or heated with makeshift stoves, children can be exposed to burns on a more frequent basis than children in the south.

20 Quoted in "Reserve Caught in Bureaucracy: Ottawa, Ontario Spent Years Ignoring Water Concerns at Reserve: Critics," *Sudbury Star*, October 25, 2005, A7.

21 Quoted in "Ontario Will Evacuate Most Residents of Reserve with Bad Water; Minister Says Entire Community Might Have to Be Abandoned," *New Brunswick Telegraph-Journal*, October 26, 2005.

22 "Reserve Caught in Bureaucracy."

23 Quoted in Richard Roik, "Scott Offers to Move Band: Native Leaders Say 10 Year Timeframe for Project Is Reasonable," *New Brunswick Telegraph-Journal*, October 28, 2005.

24 Ivison, "'Gross Mismanagement.'"

25 Quoted in "Ontario Will Evacuate."

26 Quoted in Tayo Adesanya, "Attawapiskat Students Get Their New School after Five-Year Struggle," *Timmins Daily Press*, November 14, 2005.

FIRE AND FLOOD

27 Julius Strauss, "A Hero's Welcome for Kashechewan Chief," *Globe and Mail*, October 29, 2005, A4.

28 This promise never amounted to much. A 2011 report by the auditor general noted the failure of the Conservative government to produce meaningful improvements in water safety. The auditor general reported that, as of March 2010, more than half of the reserves in Canada faced medium or high risk from unsafe water.

29 Jim Prentice, Minister of Indian Affairs, to Mike Carpenter, Chief of Attawapiskat First Nation, December 4, 2006.

30 Brian Holm, Capital Management Officer, to Attawapiskat Chief and Council, "Re: School Capital Planning Study," July 30, 2007.

31 Quoted in "Ontario Reserve Grieves Two Men Killed in Jail Fire," *Whitehorse Daily Star*, January 11, 2006, 12.

32 Quoted in Adrian Humphreys, "Ontario Reserve Hit Hard by Deadly Fire," *National Post*, January 12, 2006, A11.

33 Quoted in Charlie Angus, "First Nation Cops Are Facing 'Combat Level' Stress," *Huffington Post*, February 18, 2013.

34 In addition to the E. coli evacuation of October 2005, there had been a flood evacuation the previous April.

35 Hilda Hoy, "Hard-Luck Reserve Evacuated Again," *Toronto Star*, April 24, 2006, A6.

36 "Floods Force Evacuation: Minister Wants Talks to Find New Homes for 1700 Residents," *Windsor Star*, April 25, 2006, B8.

37 Quoted in Steve Erwin, "Ontario Government Supports Move of Kashechewan Territory 30 Kms up Albany River," Canadian Press, May 2, 2006.

38 Ken Kokanie, Capital Management Officer, Aboriginal Affairs and Northern Development Canada, "Kashechewan First Nation Community Redevelopment Progress Report," 2011.

39 House of Commons Order Paper Question 537, signed by Minister Bernard Valcourt for MP Charlie Angus, June 2, 2014.

40 "Kashechewan Evacuees to Stay in Kapuskasing for Two Years," CBC News, July 31, 2014, www.cbc.ca/news/canada/sudbury/kashechewan-evacuees-to-stay-in-kapuskasing-for-2-years-1.2724184.

41 House of Commons Order Paper Question 537.

42 Hatch Engineering Management, "Assessment of Dam Safety Risks and Dam Safety Management Requirements for the Kashechewan Ring Dyke," prepared for the Kashechewan First Nation, February 19, 2015.

PART III: ATTAWAPISKAT SCHOOL CAMPAIGN, 2007–09

THE THIRD GENERATION

1 Brian Holm, Capital Management Officer, INAC, "Internal Briefing Note: Funding for New School at Attawapiskat," November 13, 2007, obtained April 8, 2009, through Access to Information legislation.

2 Ibid.

3 Ibid., 4.

4 April Wesley, speaking at Shannen's Dream Youth Forum, Elgin Street Public School, Ottawa, November 17, 2010, www.youtube.com/watch?v=ykSWH-s7c7-I.

5 Sky Koostachin, speaking at Education Is a Human Right Conference, Toronto, November 26, 2008. Koostachin is a common Attawapiskat name, as are Wesley, Nakogee, and Hookimaw.

6 Carinna Pellatt, interview with the author, June 15, 2014.

7 Ibid.

8 Clara Corbiere, interview with the author, May 25, 2014.

STUDENTS HELPING STUDENTS

9 Ron Grech, "'Educational Apartheid' Must End, MP Says," *Timmins Daily Press*, January 25, 2008, A2.

10 Media Q, transcription of news conference, January 24, 2008, obtained April 8, 2009, through Access to Information legislation. Lightly edited for readability.

11 Ibid.

12 Department of Indian Affairs, Indian and Northern Affairs Media Lines (for internal use only by spokespersons), approved by Susan Bertrand, Communications and Media Relations, INAC, March 3, 2008, obtained April 8, 2009, through Access to Information legislation.

13 Through Access to Information requests, I received a heavily redacted email exchange among department bureaucrats that included my original email sent from my BlackBerry to an internal group of New Democrats.

14 J. R. Nakogee grade eight class (Attawapiskat) to David (student at St. Patrick School, Cobalt), March 18, 2008, archives of the author. Lightly edited for capitalization conventions only.

15 Carinna Pellatt, interview with the author, June 15, 2014.

16 "School Funding," Global National News, March 6, 2008.

17 Quoted in Richard Brennan, "YouTube Used in Fight for New School: Native Community Says It Has Been Waiting for Almost 30 Years," *Toronto Star*, March 5, 2008, A19.

18 Louise Brown, "School Boards Join Reserve Fight: Ontario Students Encouraged to Write Letters Calling for Funds to Build School for Attawapiskat Children," *Toronto Star*, March 14, 2008, A17.

19 Quoted in ibid.

CONTAINING THE DAMAGE

20 Susan Bertrand, Communications and Media Relations, INAC, email to Tony Prudori, Acting Senior Information Officer, INAC, re CBC Radio on Attawapiskat, February 11, 2008, obtained through Access to Information legislation.

21 Kyle, St. Patrick School (Cobalt, ON), to Minister of Indian Affairs Chuck Strahl, February 19, 2008, archives of the author. Lightly edited for readability.

22 Greg Coleman, Acting Regional Communications Director, INAC, email to Bob Maguire, Associate Regional Director, INAC, re Ontario Issues Management Report for Sr. ADM—Jan 23, January 23, 2008, obtained through Access to Information legislation.

23 Sue Bailey, "Funding Crunch Puts off Badly Needed Native School Repairs," *Cornwall Standard-Freeholder*, January 24, 2008, 5.

24 Chief Victor Michael Lesperance Jr. to Minister Chuck Strahl, February 25, 2008, archives of the author.

25 Quoted in Bailey, "Funding Crunch," 5.

26 Jill Caines, email to Daryl Hargitt, re Attawapiskat Media Lines and *Timmins Daily Press* Article, January 21, 2008, obtained April 8, 2009, through Access to Information legislation.

27 Susan Bertrand, Communications and Media Relations, INAC, to Public Affairs Team, re Media Relations Report–Ontario Region, February 13, 2008, obtained April 9, 2009, through Access to Information legislation.

28 "Aboriginal Affairs," *Edited Hansard 041*, 39th Parliament, 2nd Session, January 31, 2008, www.parl.gc.ca/HousePublications/Publication.aspx?Language-E&Mode=1&Parl=39&Ses=2&DocId=3236293#OOB-2291050.

29 Ibid.

30 Sara Strawczynski, Health Canada, email to Ivy Chan, Director, Environmental Public Health Division, Health Canada, re Disparity of Health Standards between Many Aboriginal Schools and Non-Aboriginal Schools, December 17, 2008, obtained through Access to Information legislation.

31 Deborah Richardson, Regional Director General, INAC, email to Anne Van Dusen, Communications Manager, INAC, re QP-Attawapiskat/Angus, January 31, 2008, and Anne Van Dusen email response, obtained through Access to Information legislation.

32 Gus Foresto, memo to Joseph Young, re School Construction Ask, November 27, 2007, obtained April 8, 2009, through Access to Information legislation.

33 Susan Bertrand, Communications and Media Relations, INAC, email to Public Affairs Team, re Media Relations Report – Ontario Region, February 26, 2008, obtained April 8, 2009, through Access to Information legislation.

34 Greg Coleman, Acting Regional Communications Director, INAC, memo to Leigh Jessen, INAC, March 12, 2008, obtained April 8, 2009, through Access to Information legislation.

35 Susan Bertrand, Communications and Media Relations, INAC, to Anne Van Dusen, Communications Manager, INAC, re QRT Notes—Communications, February 22, 2008, obtained through Access to Information legislation.

36 Chuck Strahl, Minister of Indian Affairs, interview with *Canada AM*, CTV, March 8, 2008.

37 Office of the Chief Coroner, "The Office of the Chief Coroner's Death Review of the Youth Suicides at the Pikangikum First Nation 2006–2008," June 11, 2011, 45, provincialadvocate.on.ca/documents/en/Coroners_Pik_Report.pdf.

38 Martin Patriquin, "Canada, Home to the Suicide Capital of the World," *Maclean's*, March 30, 2012, www.macleans.ca/news/canada/canada-home-to-the-suicide-capital-of-the-world/.

39 Office of the Chief Coroner, "Death Review," 144.

40 The government has announced that a school is scheduled to be open for students in 2016.

41 Anne Van Dusen, Communications Manager, INAC, email to Jill Caines, March 10, 2008, obtained through Access to Information legislation.

42 (Name redacted), email re Attawapiskat School CTV National News – Saturday March 8, 2008, to Minister Chuck Strahl, March 9, 2008, obtained through Access to Information legislation. Lightly edited for capitalization conventions only.

43 "Editorial: Misplaced Priorities," *Toronto Star*, March 11, 2008, AA04.

44 Quoted in Daniel Lanigan, "Weekly Opportunities and Risk Report," Ontario, March 20, 2008, obtained April 8, 2009, through Access to Information legislation.

45 Ibid.

46 Ibid.

THE SPARK

47 Shannen Koostachin (Attawapiskat) to Minister of Indian Affairs Chuck Strahl, March 17, 2008, archives of the author.

48 Attawapiskat School Campaign, "Sacred Fire Lit for Attawapiskat Children," press release, March 11, 2008, archives of the author.

49 Chelsea Edwards, interview with the author, June 17, 2014.

SHANNEN MEETS CHUCK

50 Emma Wesley (Attawapiskat) to Minister of Indian Affairs Chuck Strahl, March 2008, archives of the author.

51 Quoted in Linda Diebel, "Native Students Go Away Disappointed," *Toronto Star*, May 30, 2008, A18.

52 Quoted in "Local Students Lobby for Decent School in Attawapiskat," *Waterloo Record*, May 27, 2008, B1.

53 Chuck Strahl, Minister of Indian Affairs, to Charlie Angus, MP, September 5, 2008, archives of the author.

54 Shannen Koostachin, Chris Kataquapit, and Marvin Kioke to Minister Chuck Strahl, May 9, 2008, archives of the author.
55 Quoted in Chelsey Romain, "Attawapiskat Youth to Meet with Minister," *Northern News,* May 28, 2008, B7.
56 "Attawapiskat Press Conference in Ottawa, May 28, 2008," uploaded May 31, 2008, www.youtube.com/watch?v=dPAfgsKefDg.
57 Ibid.
58 Ibid.
59 John's older brother Michael had been one of the three boys who disappeared from St. Anne's Residential School in 1941.
60 Author's recollection of the event.
61 Shannen Koostachin, "Education Is a Human Right," presentation at the Education Is a Human Right Conference, Ontario Institute for Studies in Education, Toronto, November 26, 2008, www.youtube.com/watch?v=shX-KTTKsZto.
62 Quoted in Janet Wilson, *Shannen and the Dream for a School* (Toronto: Second Story Press, 2011), 105.
63 As told to me by Janet Doherty, my parliamentary assistant. She was sitting in the outer room of the meeting with the minister when Shannen walked out of the office.
64 Koostachin, "Education Is a Human Right."
65 Carinna Pellatt, interview with the author, June 15, 2014.
66 Ibid.
67 Author's recollection of the event.
68 Karihwakeron (Tim Thompson), interview with the author, May 27, 2014.
69 Cindy Blackstock, interview with the author, June 30, 2014.
70 Ibid.

THE DISAPPEARING SCHOOL

71 Email correspondence between Bob Maguire, INAC, and Deborah Richardson, Regional Director General, INAC, March 11, 2008, obtained through Access to Information legislation.
72 Brandon Walker, "School Never Was in Plans," *Timmins Daily Press,* November 25, 2008.
73 Ibid.
74 Parliamentary Research Department, Parliamentary Order Paper Question Q-231, June 2008, office of Charlie Angus, MP.
75 Office of the Parliamentary Budget Officer, "The Funding Requirements for First Nation Schools in Canada," May 25, 2009, www.parl.gc.ca/PBO-DPB/documents/INAC_Final_EN.pdf.
76 Ibid.
77 Aboriginal Affairs and Northern Development Canada and Canadian Polar Commission, 2013–14 Performance Report, 88.
78 Cost Drivers and Pressures – the Case for New Escalators. Internal PowerPoint presentation, Aboriginal Affairs and Northern Development Canada, June 2013, archives of the author.

79 Terry Waboose, speaking at Education Is a Human Right Conference, Ontario Institute for Studies in Education, Toronto, November 26, 2008.

80 First Nations Education Council, "Paper on First Nations Education Funding," February 2009, 17, http://www.cepn-fnec.com/pdf/etudes_documents/education_funding.pdf.

81 Auditor General of Canada, "Chapter 5: Indian and Northern Affairs Canada: Education Program and Post Secondary Student Support," in *Report of the Auditor General of Canada*, November 2004, 6, 11, www.oag-bvg.gc.ca/internet/english/parl_oag_200411_05_e_14909.html.

82 Ibid., 6.

83 Ibid., 15.

84 Ibid., 1.

85 Karihwakeron (Tim Thompson), interview with the author, May 27, 2014.

86 John B. Nakogee, Attawapiskat Education Authority, interview with the author, June 25, 2014.

87 April Wesley, speaking at Shannen's Dream Youth Forum, Elgin Street Public School, Ottawa, November 17, 2010, www.youtube.com/watch?v=ykSWH-s7c7-I.

88 Karihwakeron (Tim Thompson), interview with the author, May 27, 2014.

89 First Nations Education Council, "Paper on First Nations Education Funding," 20.

90 Louise Brown, "Ontario's Forgotten Children: Making the Grade," *Toronto Star*, April 25, 2005.

91 North-South Partnership for Children in Remote First Nations Communities, "Mishkeegogamang Ojibway Nation Assessment Report," 2007, 17.

92 Vince Dumond, Principal, J. R. Nakogee School, Attawapiskat, public letter, November 14, 2005, archives of the author.

93 John B. Nakogee, interview with the author, June 25, 2014.

94 Lawson Bate, "Thank You Kashechewan," July 7, 2014, archives of the author.

95 Ibid.

THE FIGHT GOES INTERNATIONAL

96 Cindy Blackstock, announcing her nomination of Shannen Koostachin for the International Children's Peace Prize, 2008, www.youtube.com/watch?v=ZsWxHm-llVA.

97 Cindy Blackstock, "Jordan's Principle: Editorial Update," *Paediatrics and Child Health* 13, 7 (2008): 589.

98 Cindy Blackstock, interview with the author, June 30, 2014.

99 Notes from Cindy Blackstock provided to the author, August 31, 2014.

100 Quoted in ibid.

101 Shannen Koostachin, Solomon Rae, Chris Kataquapit, and Jonah Sutherland to Marie-Claude Côté-Villeneuve, Human Rights Program, Department of Canadian Heritage, re Attawapiskat Children Seek Input into UN Report on the Rights of the Child, July 11, 2008, archives of the author.

102 Shannen Koostachin to Kids Right Foundation, July 27, 2008, archives of the author.

EDUCATION IS A HUMAN RIGHT

103 Shannen Koostachin, speaking at the Education Is a Human Right Conference, Ontario Institute for Studies in Education, November 26, 2008, unpublished video courtesy of Brenda Stewart, Toronto Catholic School Board, archives of the author.

104 Serena Koostachin, speaking at the Education Is a Human Right Conference, Ontario Institute for Studies in Education, Toronto, November 26, 2008, www.youtube.com/watch?v=w17r5atzNUI.

105 Shannen Koostachin, "Education Is a Human Right." Lightly edited for readability.

106 Jocelyn Formsma, speaking at the Education Is a Human Right Conference, Ontario Institute for Studies in Education, November 26, 2008, unpublished video courtesy of Brenda Stewart, Toronto Catholic School Board, archives of the author.

107 Stan Louttit, speaking at the Education Is a Human Right Conference, Ontario Institute for Studies in Education, November 26, 2008, unpublished video courtesy of Brenda Stewart, Toronto Catholic School Board, archives of the author.

108 Letter from Minister Chuck Strahl, "Minister Questions MP's Motive on School Issue," *Timmins Daily Press*, November 26, 2008, www.timminspress.com/2008/11/26/minister-questions-mps-motives-on-school-issue.

GRADE NINE

109 Shannen Koostachin, "Education Is a Human Right."

110 Quoted in Wilson, *Shannen and the Dream for a School*, 139.

SIX BOYS, ONE GIRL

111 Quoted in Tanya Talaga, "Broad Inquest into Death of Seven Native Teens a Step Closer," *Toronto Star*, May 23, 2012, www.thestar.com/news/ontario/2012/05/23/broad_inquest_into_deaths_of_seven_native_teens_a_step_closer.html.

112 Alvin Fiddler, interview with the author, June 3, 2014.

113 James Murray, interview with the author, June 2, 2014.

114 Quoted in Dave Seglins, "Ontario Calls Joint Inquest in Indigenous Student Deaths," CBC News, May 31 2012, www.cbc.ca/news/canada/thunder-bay/ontario-calls-joint-inquest-in-Indigenous-student-deaths-1.1151765.

115 Quoted in Tanya Talaga, "Seven Native Teens Dead or Missing While Away at School," *Toronto Star*, May 8, 2011, www.thestar.com/news/canada/2011/05/08/seven_native_teens_dead_or_missing_while_away_at_school.html.

116 Quoted in ibid.

117 Alvin Fiddler, interview with the author, June 3, 2014.

118 Ibid.

119 James Murray, interview with the author, June 2, 2014.

120 Quoted in Talaga, "Broad Inquest."

121 Joyce Hunter, interview with the author, July 15, 2014.

122 Ibid.

THE YEAR OF EMERGENCIES

123 Brenda Stewart, Toronto teacher, describing the contamination at J. R. Nakogee School, quoted in Christina Spencer, "Two Toronto Teachers Agree: Fumes Intolerable," *St. Catharine's Standard*, April 6, 2009, www.stcatharinesstandard. ca/2009/04/06/two-toronto-teachers-agree-fumes-intolerable-3.

124 Gilles St. Pierre, Health Canada, to Attawapiskat First Nation, re J. R. Nakogee School—CLOSED SECTION, June 14, 2007, obtained through Access to Information legislation.

125 Brenda Stewart, interview with the author, May 27, 2009.

126 "Attawapiskat School Toxic Contamination," YouTube video posted by Charlie Angus, April 12, 2009, www.youtube.com/watch?v=YsOy1Ex3u_E. Lightly edited for readability.

127 Ibid. Lightly edited for readability.

128 With the temperature at minus thirty degrees, the school windows were already frozen shut.

129 Brenda Stewart, interview with the author, May 27, 2009.

130 "Attawapiskat School Toxic Contamination." Lightly edited for readability.

131 Quoted in Chelsey Romain, "Angus, Bisson Demand Action in Attawapiskat," *Sudbury Star,* April 8, 2009, www.thesudburystar.com/2009/04/08/angus-bisson-demand-action-in-attawapiskat.

132 Quoted in Christina Spencer, "MP Perplexed over Closure of Schools," *North Bay Nugget*, March 26, 2009, www.nugget.ca/2009/03/26/mpperplexed-over-closure-of-schools-2.

133 Quoted in Chelsey Romain, "School Conditions Shock Southern Ontario Teachers," *Timmins Daily Press*, April 1, 2009, www.timminspress. com/2009/04/01/school-conditions-shock-southern-ontario-teachers.

134 "Attawapiskat School Toxic Contamination."

135 Quoted in Rick Garrick, "Diesel Fumes Contaminate Attawapiskat," *Wawatay News*, April 16, 2009, www.wawataynews.ca/archive/all/2009/4/16/Diesel-fumes-contaminate-Attawapiskat_16421.

136 Ron Grech, "If Strahl Leaves Will Attawapiskat Finally Get a New School?," editorial, *Timmins Daily Press*, April 9 2009, www.timminspress. com/2009/04/09/if-strahl-leaves-will-inac-finally-build-new-school.

THE DARKEST PART OF THE NIGHT

137 Margaret Philp, "A Slap in the Face of Every Canadian," *Globe and Mail*, February 3, 2007, www.theglobeandmail.com/news/national/a-slap-in-the-face-of-every-canadian/article1070221/?page=all.

138 Quoted in Tanya Talaga, "Swamped by Teen Suicides," *Toronto Star*, December 28, 2009, www.thestar.com/news/ontario/2009/12/28/swamped_by_teen_suicides.html.

139 Quoted in Charlie Angus, "First Nation Cops Are Facing 'Combat Level' Stress," *Huffington Post,* February 18, 2013, www.huffingtonpost.ca/charlie-angus/first-nation-cops-suicide_b_2712926.html.

140 David Barnes and Vijay Shankar, Barnes Management Group, *Northern Remoteness: Study and Analysis of Child Welfare Funding Model Implications on Two*

First Nation Agencies: Tikinagan Child and Family Services and Payukotayno James Bay and Hudson Bay Family Services, December 2006.

141 Ibid., 4.

142 Ibid., 11.

143 Vandna Sinha et al., Assembly of First Nations, "Kiskisik Awasisak: Remember the Children. Understanding the Overrepresentation of First Nations Children in the Child Welfare System," 2011, 17, cwrp.ca/publications/2280.

144 Cindy Blackstock, interview with the author, June 30, 2014.

145 Barnes and Shankar, *Northern Remoteness*, 72.

146 Rory C. O'Connor, Stephen Platt, and Jacki Gordon, *International Handbook of Suicide Prevention: Research, Policy, and Practice* (Chichester: John Wiley and Sons, 2011).

147 Office of the Chief Coroner, "Death Review of the Youth Suicides at the Pikangikum First Nation," 18.

148 Quoted in Philp, "A Slap in the Face."

149 North-South Partnership for Children in Remote First Nations Communities, "Mishkeegogamang Ojibway Nation Assessment Report," 2007, 12.

150 "Cindy Blackstock Gets Ready to Take on the Government Again: 'I Just Want Them to Stop,'" APTN, July 8, 2013, www.facebook.com/APTNNationalNews/posts/10151572294108772.

151 Quoted in Talaga, "Swamped by Teen Suicides."

152 Ibid.

153 Lenny Carpenter, "Province Slashes Payukotayno Budget," *Wawatay News Online*, August 23, 2012, www.wawataynews.ca/archive/all/2012/8/23/province-slashes-payukotayno-budget_23344.

PEOPLE IN TENTS

154 Wilson, *Shannen and the Dream for a School*, 171–72.

155 Doug Cuthand, "Don't Blame Bands for Reserve Housing Woes," *Times Colonist*, December 6, 2011, www.canada.com/story_print.html?id=1e-3a61c6-615b-4247-99b8-549db6214bd7.

156 Andrew Linklater, email to Kelvin Jamieson, Northern Waterworks First Nation Operations, re Lift Stations—Pumps and Panels—Explanation Additional, September 9, 2009, obtained through Access to Information legislation.

157 Chief Andrew Solomon (Fort Albany) to Minister of Indian Affairs John Duncan, re Fort Albany First Nation, April 7, 2012, archives of the author.

158 Quoted in "Community Crisis Prompts Attawapiskat First Nation to Halt Traffic in Downtown Timmins," *Nation Talk*, August 14, 2009, cnw.ca/gL07.

159 Quoted in "Attawapiskat Demands Respect for First Nation Rights and Entitlements," *Nation Talk*, August 20, 2009, nationtalk.ca/story/attawapiskat-demands-respect-for-first-nation-rights-and-entitlements-2.

160 "Aboriginal Affairs," *Edited Hansard 093*, 40th Parliament, 2nd Session, October 8, 2009, www.parl.gc.ca/HousePublications/Publication.aspx?Language=E&Mode=1&Parl=40&Ses=2&DocId=4137633.

LABOUR JOINS THE FIGHT

161 Wayne Samuelson, speaking at the Ontario Federation of Labour Convention, Toronto, November 27, 2009.

162 Terry Downey, interview with the author, June 7, 2014.

163 Ibid.

164 Katrina Koostachin, speaking at the Shannen's Dream Youth Forum, Elgin Street Public School, Ottawa, November 17, 2010, www.youtube.com/watch?v=-Fy13SYkBYEQ. Lightly edited for readability.

165 Shannen Koostachin, speaking at the Ontario Federation of Labour Convention, Toronto, November 27, 2009, www.youtube.com/watch?v=NQNvOp6sZDg. Lightly edited for readability.

166 Ibid. Lightly edited for readability.

167 Serena Koostachin, speaking at the Ontario Federation of Labour Convention, Toronto, November 27, 2009, www.youtube.com/watch?v=NQNvOp6sZDg. Lightly edited for readability.

168 Terry Downey, interview with the author, June 7, 2014.

169 Ibid.

ATTAWAPISKAT WINS

170 Linda Goyette, "A Report Card No Parent Would Accept," *Canadian Geographic*, December 2010, www.canadiangeographic.ca/magazine/dec10/attawapiskat5.asp.

171 First Nations Education Council, "Supporting a Comprehensive and Equitable Funding Framework: Rationale for Funding Formula for First Nations and Elementary Schools," April 2009, 7, www.cepn-fnec.com/PDF/etudes_documents/Supporting_Equitable_Funding_Framework.pdf.

172 Quoted in "Assembly of First Nations National Chief Welcomes Minister's Commitment on Education Funding Review," CNW, December 14, 2009, cnw.ca/9zenG.

173 In building schools, Indian Affairs routinely refuses to meet the standard formula established in provincial systems for classroom size, storage space, and other basic amenities. The schools are built to a lesser standard.

PART IV: SHANNEN'S DREAM, 2010

TRAGEDY

1 The student was from Pierre Elliott Trudeau School in Gatineau, Quebec. Letter in the archives of the author.

A LITTER OF PUPPIES

2 Quoted in Heather Scoffield, "Tribunal Hears First Nations Child Welfare Case: Does Ottawa Discriminate?," *Whitehorse Daily Star*, February 25, 2013, 12.

3 Linda Diebel, "Meanness Is Just a Way of Life in Ottawa: There's a Daily Atmosphere of Mistrust and Anxiety in Canada's Capital," *Toronto Star*, November 20, 2013, E8.

4   Ibid.
5   Quoted in Tim Harper, "An Unlikely Target for Ottawa's Spying," *Toronto Star,* November 16, 2011, A7.
6   Tim Harper, "Privacy Commissioner Backs Activist's Spy Claims," *Toronto Star,* May 29, 2013, A8.
7   Canadian Human Rights Commission, closing submission in Canadian Human Rights Tribunal hearing between First Nations Child and Family Caring Society and Attorney General of Canada, August 25, 2014, 19.
8   Quoted in Darcy Henton, "Aboriginal Deaths No 'Fluke of Statistics': Children More Likely to Die in Federally Funded On-Reserve Care," *Calgary Herald,* November 26, 2013, A7.
9   Vandna Sinha et al., Assembly of First Nations, "Kiskisik Awasisak: Remember the Children. Understanding the Overrepresentation of First Nations Children in the Child Welfare System," 2011, 18, cwrp.ca/publications/2280.
10   Michael Woods and Sharon Kirkey, "Number of Natives in Foster Care Called 'Tragic,'" *Vancouver Province,* May 9, 2013, A13.
11   John Beaucage, "Children First: The Aboriginal Advisor's Report on the Status of Aboriginal Child Welfare in Ontario," report to Laurel Broten, Minister of Children and Youth Services, July 2011, 2.
12   Bruce MacLaurin et al., "A Comparison of First Nations and Non-Aboriginal Children Investigated for Maltreatment in Canada in 2003," Centre for Excellence for Children's Well Being, 2003, 2, cwrp.ca/infosheets/comparison-first-nations-and-non-aboriginal-2003.
13   Quoted in Jacques Gallant, "First Nations Children's Issues Addressed: Data Indicates that Maltreatment of First Nations Childen Remains High: Long-Term Support Needed," *Moncton Times and Transcript,* July 15, 2011, A10.
14   Henton, "Aboriginal Deaths No 'Fluke of Statistics.'"
15   Ibid.
16   Karen Kleiss, "Alberta Reveals Hundreds More Children Died while Receiving Provincial Care," *Edmonton Journal,* January 9, 2014, www.pa-pa.ca/pdf/20140109 Alberta reveals hundreds more children died while receiving.pdf.
17   The Office of the Alberta Child and Youth Advocate undertook an investigation to provide answers for these numerous deaths. However, the investigation was cancelled in early 2015 by the provincial Progressive Conservative government of Jim Prentice. Despite the pleading of the child advocate for the importance of going ahead with the investigation, the government withdrew funding, stating the need to find savings in public spending.
18   Bart Rosborough, "Report to the Minister of Justice and Attorney General [on the] Public Fatality Inquiry," Wetaskiwin, AB, March 28, 2009, 3.
19   Quoted in Henton, "Indigenous Deaths No 'Fluke of Statistics.'"
20   "Manitoba Child Services Watchdog to Launch Review of Tina Fontaine Case," APTN News, August 19, 2014, aptn.ca/news/2014/08/19/manitobas-child-services-watchdog-launch-review-tina-fontaine-case/.
21   Cindy Blackstock, interview with the author, June 30, 2014.
22   Department of Indian and Northern Affairs Canada, "Fact Sheet: First Nations Child and Family Services," 2006, www.fncaringsociety.com/sites/default/files/docs/Fact-Sheet-FN-Child-Family-Services-Indian-Northern-Affairs.pdf.

23 Office of the Auditor General of Canada, "Chapter 4: Programs for First Nations on Reserves," in *2011 Report of the Auditor General of Canada*, www.oag-bvg.gc.ca/internet/docs/parl_oag_201106_04_e.pdf.

24 Ibid.

25 Cindy Blackstock, "Reconciliation Means Not Having to Say Sorry Twice: Lessons from Child Welfare in Canada," in *From Truth to Reconciliation: Transforming the Legacy of Residential Schools* (Ottawa: Indigenous Healing Foundation, 2008), 172.

26 Quoted in "First Nations Children Still Taken from Parents," Canadian Press, August 2, 2011, www.cbc.ca/m/touch/news/story/1.1065255.

27 Blackstock, "Reconciliation Means Not Having to Say Sorry Twice," 169.

28 "Jordan's Principle—Case Conferencing to Case Resolution—Federal/Provincial Intake Form," November 21, 2012, submitted in factum of evidence for "Memorandum of Fact and Law of the Complainant of the First Nations Child and Family Caring Society," Canadian Human Rights Tribunal CBD, Vol. 15, Tab 420, 1.

29 Ibid., 7.

30 "INAC and Health Canada First Nations Programs: Gaps in Service Delivery to First Nation Children and Families in BC Region, June 2009," CBD, Vol. 6, Tab 78, 2.

31 Ibid., 3.

32 "Terms of Reference Officials Working Group—Canada/Manitoba Joint Committee on Jordan's Principle, Jordan's Principle Dispute Resolution," preliminary report, May 2009, CBD, Vol. 13, Tab 302, 13.

33 Canadian Human Rights Commission, closing submission in Canadian Human Rights Tribunal hearing between First Nations Child and Family Caring Society and Attorney General of Canada, August 25, 2014.

34 "Three Strikes and Hopefully Canada Is Out as It Tries to Escape Accountability for Racial Discrimination against First Nations Children: A Summary of the Hearing of Canada's Motion to Dismiss the Canadian Human Rights Tribunal on First Nations Child Welfare, June 2, 3, 2010," First Nations Child and Family Caring Society, www.fncaringsociety.com/sites/default/files/fnwitness/Motion-to-Dismiss-June2010.pdf.

35 Quoted in Chris Cobb, "Rights Commission Fights for Children on Reserves: Tribunal Ruling Given This Week 'Legalized Racial Discrimination,'" *Ottawa Citizen*, March 17, 2011, A3.

36 Quoted in ibid.

37 Quoted in "Court Victory for First Nations Child Welfare," Canadian Press, April 18, 2012, www.cbc.ca/news/politics court-victory-for-first-nations-child-welfare-1.1249629.

38 Tim Harper, "Tribunal to Rule Whether Ottawa Retaliated against Advocate," *Toronto Star,* October 22, 2012, A6.

39 Quoted in Scoffield, "Tribunal Hears First Nations Child Welfare Case."

40 Doug Cuthand, "Fighting First Nations in Court a Poor Strategy," *StarPhoenix*, November 15, 2013, A13.

41 Ibid.

THE DREAM IS LAUNCHED

42 Cedar Koostachin, speaking at Shannen's Dream Youth Forum, Elgin Street Public School, Ottawa, November 17, 2010, www.youtube.com/watch?v=Fy-13SYkBYEQ. Lightly edited for readability.

43 Parliamentary Motion 571, Notice Paper No. 66, September 20, 2010.

44 Rob Koostachin, speaking at Shannen's Dream Youth Forum, Elgin Street Public School, Ottawa, November 17, 2010, www.youtube.com/watch?v=yk-SWHs7c7-I. Lightly edited for readability.

45 Chelsea Edwards, interview with the author, June 17, 2014.

46 Chelsea Edwards, speaking at Shannen's Dream press conference, Parliament Hill, November 17, 2010, www.youtube.com/watch?v=qnpX3mDTB6A.

47 Clara Corbiere, interview with the author, May 25, 2014.

48 "Helping Keep Shannen's Dream Alive," CBC News, December 13, 2013, www.cbc.ca/islandmorning/2013/12/13/helping-keep-shannens-dream-alive/.

PART V: CANADA'S KATRINA MOMENT, 2011–12

THE 2011 HOUSING CRISIS

1 Doris Grinspun and David McNeil, Registered Nurses' Association of Ontario, to Prime Minister Harper and Premier McGuinty, re crisis in Attawapiskat, November 23, 2011, rnao.ca/sites/rnao-ca/files/RNAO_letter_crisis_in_Attawapiskat.pdf.

2 Meagan Fitzpatrick, "Paperwork for G8 Spending 'Not Perfect' Clement Says," CBC News, November 2, 2011, www.cbc.ca/news/politics/paperwork-for-g8-spending-not-perfect-clement-says-1.1071565.

3 Andy Thomsen, "Resources Belong to All of Us," letter to the editor, *Penticton Western News*, December 7, 2011, 7.

4 Lorne Gunter, "Indian Act Sustains Problems on Reserves," *Times Colonist*, December 7, 2011, A10.

5 Quoted in Wayne K. Spear, "Assimilation Isn't as Easy as It Sounds," *National Post,* December 2, 2011, A17.

6 Peter O'Neil, "Federal Bill Toughens Disclosure Rules for First Nation Leaders Salaries," *Edmonton Journal*, November 23, 2011.

7 Meagan Fitzpatrick, "First Nation Officials' Salaries Target of New Bill," CBC News, November 23, 2011, www.cbc.ca/news/politics/first-nations-officials-salaries-target-of-new-bill-1.1099935.

8 Quoted in Jennifer Graham and Heather Scoffield, "Revived Bill for Native Accountability Won't Fix Basic Problems: AFN," *Whitehorse Star*, November 25, 2011, 17.

9 Christina Blizzard, "Attawapiskat Squalor Is Our Shame," *Lindsay Post*, November 29, 2011, A4.

10 In an isolated, fly-in reserve, the cost of materials and construction for a bargain basement home is about $200,000.

11 Heather Scoffield, "Mouldy Mattresses, Icy Floors in Shacks Where Toddlers Live on Native Reserve," *St. John's Telegram*, November 30, 2011, A12.

12   David Boyd, "No Taps, No Toilets: First Nations and the Constitutional Right to Water in Canada," *McGill Law Journal* 57, 1 (2011): 81–134.

13   Stephanie Levitz, "Auditors Said Native Housing Controls Neglected by Ottawa: Serious Lack of Federal Oversight Cited in 2010 Audit," *Waterloo Region Record*, November 30, 2011, A3.

14   Rita Celli, "Diamond Royalties a Closely Guarded Secret in Ontario," CBC News, May 12, 2015, www.cbc.ca/news/business/diamond-royalties-a-closely-guarded-secret-in-ontario-1.3062006.

15   The Department of Indian Affairs was renamed Aboriginal Affairs and Northern Development Canada in March 2011.

16   Oakland Ross, "'Canada's Version of Third World': But Problem Is Housing Not Money, Say Residents Forced to Live in Tents," *Toronto Star*, December 3, 2011, A6.

17   Charlie Angus, "What If They Declared an Emergency and No One Came?," *Huffington Post*, November 21, 2011, http://www.huffingtonpost.ca/charlie-angus/attawapiskat-emergency_b_1104370.html.

18   Bruce Urquhart, "Editorial: Turning a Blind Eye to the Deplorable Conditions in Attawapiskat," *Sault Star*, November 25, 2011, A10.

19   Quoted in Ryan Lux, "Red Cross Steps In," *Timmins Daily Press*, November 28, 2011, A1.

20   "Editorial: A National Outrage," *Ottawa Citizen*, November 25, 2011.

21   "Editorial: Focus on the Children," *Toronto Star*, November 28, 2011, A14.

22   John Saunders, interview with the author, August 8, 2014.

23   Ibid.

24   "Bruce Power Gives to Attawapiskat," *Kincardine News*, December 6, 2011, 23.

25   John Saunders, interview with the author, August 8, 2014.

26   Ibid.

27   "Harper Vows 'Action' on Attawapiskat," CBC News, November 29, 2011, www.cbc.ca/news/canada/harper-vows-action-on-attawapiskat-1.1028597.

RISE OF THE TROLLS

28   Christie Blatchford, "It's a Disgrace, Not a Surprise," *National Post*, December 3, 2011, A7.

29   Quoted in Charlie Angus, "Attawapiskat's Impact: Canada's Katrina Moment," *Huffington Post*, December 2, 2011, www.huffingtonpost.ca/charlie-angus/attawapiskat-reserve_b_1126595.html.

30   Âpihtawikosisân, "Attawapiskat: Firing Back at the Racist Rants and Ignorant Responses with Facts," Rabble.ca, December 1, 2011, rabble.ca/news/2011/12/attawapiskat-firing-back-racist-rants-and-ignorant-responses-facts.

31   Lorraine Land, "Taking a Second Look at Those Attawapiskat Numbers," December 13, 2011, www.oktlaw.com/blog/taking-a-second-look-at-those-attawapiskat-numbers/.

32   Doug Cuthand, "Conservatives Ignore First Nations Responsibility," *Star-Phoenix*, December 2, 2011, A11.

33   David Krayden, "Treat Native Canadians with Respect, Equality," *Ottawa Citizen*, December 6, 2011, A13.

34 Ezra Levant, QMI Agency, "Crisis of Management: Attawapiskat Reserve Plunged into Despair while $34 Million Is Squandered," *Strathmore Standard*, December 7, 2011, 15.

35 Bronwyn Eyre, "'Banker' Should Get to Bottom of First Nation Finances," *Calgary Herald*, December 13, 2011, A12.

36 Charlie Angus, media scrum on Parliament Hill, December 1, 2011, www. youtube.com/watch?v=6ZQpCGh6hGs.

37 Christian Cotroneo, "Attawapiskat: Charlie Angus and John Duncan Meet in a Stairwell," *Huffington Post*, December 2, 2011, www.huffingtonpost. ca/2011/12/01/attawapiskat-charlie-angus-john-duncan_n_1124521.html.

38 Peter Worthington, "The Problem with Attawapiskat Starts in the Mindset," *Pembroke Observer*, December 9, 2011, A5.

39 Quoted in Barrie McKenna, "Attawapiskat Gets Help with Housing: Chief Denies Government Claims that Reserve Will Accept Third-Party Management of Finances," *Globe and Mail*, December 12, 2011, A7.

40 Quoted in "Emphasize Aid Not Money, Says Attawapiskat Chief," *Windsor Star*, December 7, 2011, A10.

41 Eyre, "Banker."

42 Jack Fountain, "There's Lots of Blame to Go Around in Attawapiskat Debacle," *Orillia Packet and Times*, December 27, 2011, A6.

43 Lorne Gunter, "Political Correctness Caused Attawapiskat," *National Post*, December 2, 2011, A17.

44 Tasha Kheiriddin, "End Native Apartheid," *National Post*, December 1, 2011, A16.

45 Chris Brennan, "One Thing about Attawapiskat: Where Has All the Money Gone?," *Brantford Expositor*, December 16, 2011, A8.

46 Comments posted in response to Angus, "What If They Declared an Emergency?"

47 James Mackay and Niigaanwiwedam James Sinclair, "Canada's First Nations: A Scandal Where Victims Are Blamed," *Guardian*, December 11, 2011, www. theguardian.com/commentisfree/2011/dec/11/canada-third-world-first-nation-attawapiskat.

48 Quoted in Kim Mackrael, "UN Blasts Ottawa over Attawapiskat: Special Rapporteur's Missive an Attention-Grabbing Stunt, Aboriginal Affairs' Spokeswoman Fires Back," *Globe and Mail*, December 21, 2011, A11.

49 Rose Paul Martin to the author, June 30, 2014, archives of the author.

50 During the 2012 hunger strike by Chief Theresa Spence on Victoria Island, the Twitter feed was handled by Craig "Che" Koostachin, a James Bay Cree teenager who had been politicized by the housing crisis. He is now working in photography and journalism.

51 Rose Paul Martin to the author, June 30, 2014, archives of the author.

CHRISTMAS IN ATTAWAPISKAT

52 John Saunders, interview with the author, August 8, 2014.

53 Quoted in Chris Ribau, "Relief Flies North," *Timmins Daily Press*, December 15, 2011, A1.

54 Quoted in ibid.

55 John Saunders, interview with the author, August 8, 2014.

56 Letter written to Prime Minister Stephen Harper, December 6, 2011 (name of author redacted), obtained June 10, 2013, through Access to Information legislation.

57 Email to Prime Minister Stephen Harper, December 7, 2011 (name of author redacted), obtained June 10, 2013, through Access to Information legislation.

58 Email to Prime Minister Stephen Harper, November 15, 2011 (name of author redacted), obtained June 10, 2013, through Access to Information legislation.

59 Kristy Kirkup, "Minister 'Misinformed': Chief," *Welland Tribune*, December 13, 2011, D3.

60 Heather Scoffield, "Third-Party Management Widely Panned: Bureaucratic System Offers No Solution to Complex Problems of First Nations," *Waterloo Region Record*, December 15, 2011, A4.

61 Ibid.

62 Katherine Hensel, barrister, to William Paquin, Atmacinta Hartel Financial Management Corporation, re Algonquins of Barriere Lake—Third-Party Management, September 4, 2013, archives of the author.

63 Email to Prime Minister Stephen Harper, December 9, 2011 (name of author redacted), obtained June 10, 2013, through Access to Information legislation.

64 Quoted in Teresa Smith, "Government Offers to Evacuate Residents from Troubled Northern Ontario Reserve," *Alaska Highway News*, December 9, 2011, C1.

65 Quoted in Joanna Smith, "Band Won't Pay for Manager: Troubled Reserve Can't Afford the Cost of Third-Party Oversight," *Toronto Star*, December 10, 2011, A14.

66 Quoted in "Feds Won't Assure They'll Pay for $1.2M in Emergency Housing for Attawapiskat," *Whitehorse Daily Star*, December 9, 2011, 22.

67 Bob Fife, speaking on CTV News, December 9, 2011, www.youtube.com/watch?v=w1iHT1TaiNI.

68 "Attawapiskat Third-Party Manager 'Sitting on' Funds for New Houses: NDP MP Angus," APTN National News, February 1, 2012, aptn.ca/news/2012/02/01/attawapiskat-third-party-manager-sitting-on-funds-for-new-houses-ndp-mp-angus-2/.

69 Chantal Hébert, "Expanded Parliament, Better Governance? Not Likely," *Toronto Star*, December 9, 2011, www.thestar.com/news/canada/2011/12/09/hbert_expanded_parliament_better_governance_not_likely.html.

FROM HAWAII TO IDLE NO MORE

70 John Saunders, interview with the author, August 8, 2014.

71 Quoted in Bruce Campion-Smith, "AFN Chief Sees 'Tipping Point': Atleo Urges Action on Aboriginal Issues Ahead of Summit with Harper," *Toronto Star*, January 2, 2012, A4.

72 Quoted in Chinta Puxley, "New Relationship Needed with Crown or Risk Widespread Unrest: Chiefs," *Whitehorse Daily Star*, January 13, 2012, 14.

73 Quoted in ibid.

74 Quoted in "Harper Could Face First Nations Uprising, B.C. Chief Threatens," *Prince George Citizen*, January 24, 2012, 8.

75 Bill Curry and Gloria Galloway, "PM Sees Jobs as Key to First Nations' Future: With Skilled Labour in Demand as Resource Sector Grows, Harper Ready to Work on Employment Strategies," *Globe and Mail*, January 25, 2012, A6.

76 Quoted in Tanya Talaga and Bruce Campion-Smith, "PM Vows Indian Act Changes: But Vague Words Won't Bring Clean Water or Indoor Plumbing, Say Frustrated Chiefs," *Toronto Star*, January 25, 2012, A6.

77 "Editorial: The First Nations: A Time for Trust, and for Action," *Montreal Gazette*, January 26, 2012, A16.

78 Brent Wesley, "Depressing Rerun for Anti-Native Stereotypes," *Toronto Star*, December 14, 2011, A23.

79 QMI Agency, "Editorial: First Nations Chiefs' Threats Are Becoming Tiresome," *Kingston Whig-Standard*, February 1, 2012, 4.

80 Bill C-45: Jobs and Growth Act, 2012, passed by the House of Commons, 1st Session, 41st Parliament, December 14, 2012.

81 Second Supplementary Affidavit of Chief Theresa Spence, Federal Court File No. T-2037-11, between Attawapiskat First Nation and Her Majesty the Queen in Right of Canada, April 2012.

82 Written Representations (Canada's Motion to Strike on Grounds of Mootness), Federal Court File No. T-2037-11, between Attawapiskat First Nation and Her Majesty the Queen in Right of Canada, April 19, 2012.

83 Ibid.

84 Charlie Angus, email to Yves Chenier, April 4, 2012.

85 Leigh Jessen, AANDC, email to Joseph Young, AANDC, Subject Fwd: Student Situation, April 4, 2012, obtained through Access to Information legislation.

86 Leigh Jessen, AANDC, email to Yves Chenier, Subject Fwd: Student Situation, April 4, 2012, obtained through Access to Information legislation.

87 "Attawapiskat's Third Party Manager to Be Withdrawn," CBC News, April 5, 2012, www.cbc.ca/news/politics/attawapiskat-s-3rd-party-manager-to-be-withdrawn-1.1174917.

88 Quoted in Meagan Fitzpatrick, "Attawapiskat Handed Victory by Federal Court," CBC News, August 1, 2012, www.cbc.ca/news/politics/attawapiskat-handed-victory-by-federal-court-1.1149282.

89 Les Whittington, "John Duncan Let Financing for Attawapiskat Housing Fall Through, Say Natives," *Toronto Star*, August 10, 2012, www.thestar.com/news/canada/2012/08/10/john_duncan_let_financing_for_attawapiskat_housing_fall_through_say_natives.html.

90 In 2014, a former band manager was charged with fraud, after band officials called in police to investigate.

91 Theresa Spence, speaking at the Economic Club of Canada, Ottawa, January 25, 2012.

PART VI: THE FUTURE IS NOW, 2012–15

THE UNITED NATIONS

1   Letter reproduced in Ontario, Office of the Provincial Advocate for Children and Youth, *Our Dreams Matter Too: First Nations Children's Rights, Lives, and Education: An Alternate Report from the Shannen's Dream Campaign to the United Nations Committee on the Rights of the Child on the Occasion of Canada's 3rd and 4th Periodic Reviews, 2011*, 35.

2   Shannen Koostachin et al. to Marie-Claude Côté-Villeneuve, Human Rights Program, Canadian Heritage, July 11, 2008, archives of the author.

3   Chelsea Edwards, talking on *As It Happens*, CBC Radio, July 28, 2014, www. cbc.ca/radio/asithappens/monday-grassy-narrows-mercury-report-ebola-liberia-lumberjack-camp-and-more-1.2903262/after-14-years-new-school-finally-set-to-open-in-attawapiskat-1.2903267. Lightly edited for readability.

4   Quoted in Lenny Carpenter, "Attawapiskat Youth Takes Shannen's Dream to UN," *Wawatay News*, December 21, 2011, www.wawataynews.ca/archive/all/2011/12/21/attawapiskat-youth-take-shannen-s-dream-un_22180.

5   Chelsea Edwards, interview with the author, June 17, 2014.

6   Convention on the Rights of the Child, September 2, 1990, United Nations General Assembly, www.ohchr.org/en/professionalinterest/pages/crc.aspx.

7   Jean-François Noël, "The Convention on the Rights of the Child," April 30, 2013, justice.gc.ca/eng/rp-pr/fl-lf/divorce/crc-crde/conv2a.html.

8   Jonathan D.N. Tarlton, Civil Litigation and Advisory Services, Department of Justice, to Maryse Choquette, Canadian Human Rights Tribunal, re *FNCFCS et al. v. Attorney General of Canada*, Tribunal File No. T1340/7008, December 17, 2010.

9   Office of the Provincial Advocate, *Our Dreams Matter Too*, 11–12.

10   Ibid., 9.

11   Chelsea Edwards, interview with the author, June 17, 2014.

12   Facebook status update from Chelsea Edwards, United Nations, Switzerland, February 2012.

13   Scott Haldane et al., *Nurturing the Learning Spirit of First Nation Students: The Report of the National Panel on Elementary and Secondary Education for Students on Reserve*, National Panel on First Nation Elementary and Secondary Education for Students on Reserve, 2012, 45, www.aadnc-aandc.gc.ca/DAM/DAM-INTER-HQ-EDU/STAGING/texte-text/nat_panel_final_report_1373997803969_eng.pdf.

14   "Duncan Lukewarm to National Panel's Call for Immediate Fixes to First Nation Education," APTN National News, February 8, 2012.

15   Haldane et al., *Nurturing the Learning Spirit*, 2.

16   TD Economics, "Estimating the Size of the Aboriginal Market in Canada," June 17, 2011, http://www.td.com/document/PDF/economics/special/sg0611_aboriginal.pdf.

17   Shannen's Dream rally on Parliament Hill, 2011, recorded in *Hi-Ho Mistahey!*, dir. Alanis Obomsawin, National Film Board, 2013.

18   "Business of Supply, Opposition Motion—Education for First Nation Children," *Edited Hansard 082*, 41st Parliament, 1st Session, February 16, 2012,

www.parl.gc.ca/HousePublications/Publication.aspx?Language=E&-Mode=1&Parl=41&Ses=1&DocId=5393819.

19 Quoted in Lenny Carpenter, "With *Shannen's Dream* Motion Passed, First Nations Wait for Funding Commitment," *Wawatay News*, March 16, 2012, www.wawataynews.ca/archive/all/2012/3/16/shannen-s-dream-motion-passed-first-nations-wait-funding-commitment_22537.

20 "Business of Supply, Opposition Motion—Education for First Nation Children [Shannen's Dream]," *Edited Hansard 084*, 41st Parliament, 1st Session, February 27, 2012, www.parl.gc.ca/HousePublications/Publication.aspx?Language=E&Mode=1&Parl=41&Ses=1&DocId=5403051.

21 Recorded in Obomsawin, *Hi-Ho Mistahey!* Lightly edited for readability.

THE ROGUE CHIEFS

22 Laura Brown, *Moncton Times and Transcript*, July 14, 2011, A6.

23 Alvin Fiddler, interview with the author, June 3, 2014.

24 Aboriginal Affairs and Northern Development Canada and Canadian Polar Commission, 2013–14 Departmental Performance Report, www.aadnc-aandc.gc.ca/eng/1403268280586/1403268381797.

25 Ibid., 43.

26 Karihwakeron (Tim Thompson), interview with the author, May 28, 2014.

27 Bill Blake, interview with the author, June 16, 2014.

28 John B. Nakogee, interview with the author, June 25, 2014.

29 Gloria Galloway, "First Nations Schools Need a Bigger Boost, Economist to Warn Chiefs," *Globe and Mail*, December 11, 2013, www.theglobeandmail.com/news/politics/first-nations-schools-need-a-bigger-boost-economist-to-warn-chiefs/article15862012/.

30 Ibid.

31 Outlining the Path Forward: Conditions for the Success of First Nation Education, resolution passed by the Assembly of First Nations, December 11, 2013.

32 Bill C-33: First Nations Control of First Nations Education Act, first reading, *Edited Hansard 073*, 41st Parliament, 2nd Session, April 10, 2014, www.parl.gc.ca/HousePublications/Publication.aspx?Language=E Mode=1&Parl=41&Ses=2&DocId=6535642.

33 Jorge Barrera, "Atleo Kept Key Chiefs in Dark about Education Bill Announcement: Court Records," APTN News, September 3, 2014, aptn.ca/news/2014/09/03/atleo-kept-key-chiefs-dark-education-bill-announcement-court-records/.

34 Quoted in "How the First Nations Education Act Fell Apart in a Matter of Months," Canadian Press, May 11, 2014, www.cbc.ca/news/politics/how-the-first-nations-education-act-fell-apart-in-matter-of-months-1.2639378.

35 Judith Sayers, "Understanding Bill C-33: 'First Nations Control over First Nations Education (FNCFNEA)': A Guide," First Nations in British Columbia, April 25, 2014, fnbc.info/blogs/judith-sayers/understanding-bill-c-33-first-nations-control-over-first-nations-education.

36 Jorge Barrera, "Harper, Atleo Signed Secret Agreement on FN Education Bill: Document," APTN News, September 11, 2014, aptn.ca/news/2014/09/11/harper-atleo-signed-secret-agreement-fn-education-bill-document/.

37 Pam Palmater, "Chief Shawn Atleo Should Tear up First Nations Education Act," Rabble.ca, April 30, 2014.

38 Quoted in Gloria Galloway, "Conservatives Put First Nations Education Bill 'On Hold' after Atleo Quits," *Globe and Mail*, May 5, 2014, www.theglobeand-mail.com/news/politics/conservatives-put-first-nations-education-bill-on-hold-after-atleo-quits/article18460523/.

39 Quoted in Susana Mas, "First Nations Relations with Ottawa Tested over 'Economic Shutdown' Threat," CBC News, May 15, 2014, www.cbc.ca/news/politics/first-nations-relations-with-ottawa-tested-over-economic-shut-down-threat-1.2644538.

SHANNEN'S TEAM

40 Cindy Blackstock, interview with the author, June 30, 2014.

41 Ibid.

42 Brenda Stewart, interview with the author, May 27, 2014.

43 Email to author.

44 Cindy Blackstock, interview with the author, June 30, 2014.

45 Terry Downey, interview with the author, June 7, 2014.

46 Chelsea Edwards, interview with the author, June 17, 2014.

CONCLUSION

1 Email to the author.

2 "Markham Students Send School Supplies to Kashechewan Evacuees," CBC News, December 22, 2014, www.cbc.ca/news/canada/sudbury/markham-students-send-school-supplies-to-kashechewan-evacuees-1.2881050.

3 Ken Kohanie, Capital Management Officer, AANDC, "Kashechewan First Nation Community Redevelopment Progress Report," prepared for Kashech-ewan Community Redevelopment Steering Committee, November 2011, 34.

4 Rebecca Bateman, "Talking with the Plow: Agricultural Policy and Indian Farming in the Canadian and U.S. Prairies," *Canadian Journal of Native Studies* 16, 2 (1996): 211–28.

SELECTED BIBLIOGRAPHY

Abley, Mark. *Conversations with a Dead Man: The Legacy of Duncan Campbell Scott*. Vancouver: Douglas and McIntyre, 2013.

Adams, John Coldwell. "Duncan Campbell Scott." In *Confederation Voices: Seven Canadian Poets*. 2007. www.uwo.ca/english/canadianpoetry/confederation/John Coldwell Adams/Confederation Voices/chapter 5.html.

Anebeaaki Environmental. "Environmental Inspection and Sampling Program, J. R. Nakogee Elementary School and Town Hall Teacherage, Attawapiskat First Nation." 2000. Archives of the author.

Arendt, Hannah. *Eichmann in Jerusalem: A Report on the Banality of Evil*. New York: Penguin Books, 1963.

Ash, Michael. *On Being Here to Stay: Treaties and Aboriginal Rights in Canada*. Toronto: University of Toronto Press, 2014.

Attawapiskat First Nation. "Belated Attawapiskat First Nation Toxic Spill Report." Submitted to Spills Research Centre, Environment Protection Branch, Ministry of Environment, April 9, 2009. Archives of the author.

Auditor General of Canada. Reports of the Auditor General, 2000–13.

Balia, Daryl, and Kim Kirsteen, eds. *Edinburgh 2010: Witnessing to Christ Today*. Oxford: Regnum Books International, 2010.

Barnes, David, and Vijay Shankar, Barnes Management Group. *Northern Remoteness: Study and Analysis of Child Welfare Funding Model Implications on Two First Nation Agencies: Tikinagan Child and Family Services and Payukotayno James Bay and Hudson Bay Family Services*. December 2006.

Beaucage, John. "Children First: The Aboriginal Advisor's Report on the Status of Aboriginal Child Welfare in Ontario." Report to the Honourable Laurel Broten, Minister of Children and Youth Services, 2011.

Bethune, W. C. *Canada's Western Northland: Its History, Resources, Population, and Administration.* Ottawa: J. O. Patenaude, 1937.

Blackstock, Cindy. "Reconciliation Means Not Having to Say Sorry Twice: Lessons from Child Welfare in Canada." In *From Truth to Reconciliation: Transforming the Legacy of Residential Schools* (Ottawa: Aboriginal Healing Foundation, 2008), 164–78.

Bovar Environmental. "Oil Spill Remediation Project for the Attawapiskat First Nation: Final Design Report." December 1996.

Boyd, David. "No Taps, No Toilets: First Nations and the Constitutional Right to Water in Canada." *McGill Law Journal* 57, 1 (2011): 81–134.

Brown, Edwin Killorin. "Duncan Campbell Scott: A Memoir." In *Responses and Evaluations: Essays on Canada,* edited by David Staines. Toronto: McClelland and Stewart, 1977.

Bryce, Andrew Jay. "Proposing New Media Narratives to Create an Ethical Space of Engagement between Indigenous and Non-Indigenous People in Canada." MA thesis, Royal Roads University, 2014.

Bryce, Peter Henderson. "On the Indian Schools of Manitoba and the Northwest Territories." Report of the Chief Medical Officer, Department of Indian Affairs, 1907.

———. *The Story of a National Crime: Being an Appeal for Justice to the Indians of Canada.* Ottawa: James Hope and Sons, 1922.

Canada. Department of Indian Affairs. Annual Reports, 1907–36. Library and Archives Canada, RG 10.

Carney, Robert. "The Hawthorn Survey (1966–67): Indians and Oblates and Integrated Schooling." Canadian Catholic Historical Association, *Study Sessions* 50 (1983): 609–30.

Choquette, Robert. *The Oblate Assault on the Northwest.* Ottawa: University of Ottawa Press, 1995.

Cummins, Bryan. *Only God Can Own the Land: The Attawapiskat Cree, the Land, and the State in the 20th Century.* Cobalt, ON: Highway Book Shop, 1999.

Daschuk, James. *Clearing the Plains: Disease, Politics of Starvation, and the Loss of Aboriginal Life.* Regina: University of Regina Press, 2013.

First Nations Education Council. "Supporting a Comprehensive and Equitable Funding Framework: Rationale for Funding Formula for First Nations and Elementary Schools." April 2009. www.cepn-fnec.com/PDF/etudes_documents/Supporting_Equitable_Funding_Framework.pdf.

Goyette, Linda. "Still Waiting in Attawapiskat." *Canadian Geographic,* December 2010. www.canadiangeographic.ca/magazine/dec10/attawapiskat.asp.

Haldane, Scott, et al. *Nurturing the Learning Spirit of First Nation Students: The Report of the National Panel on Elementary and Secondary Education for Students on Reserve.* National Panel on First Nation Elementary and Secondary Education for Students on Reserve, 2012. www.aadnc-aandc.gc.ca/DAM/DAM-INTER-HQ-EDU/STAGING/texte-text/nat_panel_final_report_1373997803969_eng.pdf.

Harding, Robert. "The Demonization of Child Welfare Authorities in the News." *Canadian Journal of Communication* 35 (2010): 85–108.

Harper, Alan. "Canada's Indian Administration: The Treaty Sytem." *America Indigena* 7, 2 (1947): 127.

Hatch Engineering Management. "Assessment of Dam Safety Risks and Dam Safety Management Requirements for the Kashechewan Ring Dyke." Prepared for Kashechewan First Nation. February 19, 2015.

Hawthorn, H. B., ed. *A Survey of the Contemporary Indians of Canada: Economic, Political, Educational Needs and Policies, Part 1.* Ottawa: Indian Affairs Branch, 1966.

——. *A Survey of the Contemporary Indians of Canada: Economic, Political, Educational Needs and Policies, Part 2.* Ottawa: Indian Affairs Branch, 1967.

Haycock, Ronald. *The Image of the Indian.* Waterloo, ON: Waterloo Lutheran University, 1971.

Long, John. *Treaty No. 9: Making the Agreement to Share the Land in Far Northern Ontario.* Montreal: McGill-Queen's University Press, 2010.

MacLaurin, Bruce, Nico Trocmé, Barbara Fallon, Cindy Blackstock, Lisa Pitman, and Megan McCormack. "A Comparison of First Nations and Non-Aboriginal Children Investigated for Maltreatment in Canada in 2003." University of Toronto,

Centre for Excellence for Children's Well Being, 2003. cwrp.ca/infosheets/comparison-first-nations-and-non-aboriginal-2003.

MacLaurin, Bruce, Nico Trocmé, Barbara Fallon, Vandna Sinha, Richard Feehan, Rick Enns, Jordan Gail, Olivia Kitt, Shelley Thomas-Prokop, Carolyn Zelt, Gabrielle Daoust, Emily Hutcheon, and Danielle Budgell. *Alberta Incidence Study of Reported Child Abuse and Neglect (AIS-2008)*. Calgary: University of Calgary, 2013.

McDougall, R. L., ed. *The Poet and the Critic: A Literary Correspondence between D.C. Scott and E.K. Brown*. Ottawa: Carleton University Press, 1983.

Metatawabin, Edmund. *Up Ghost River: A Chief's Journey through the Turbulent Waters of Native History*. Toronto: Alfred A. Knopf, 2014.

Milloy, John S. *A National Crime: The Canadian Government and the Residential School System 1879–1986*. Winnipeg: University of Manitoba Press, 1999.

Morrison, James. "Treaty Research Report: Treaty 9 (1905–06)." Prepared for Treaties and Historical Research Centre, Indian and Northern Affairs Canada, 1986.

National Indian Brotherhood/Assembly of First Nations. "Indian Control of Indian Education." Policy paper presented to the Minister of Indian Affairs and Northern Development, 1972.

Neu, Dean, and Richard Therrien. *Accounting for Genocide: Canada's Bureaucratic Assault on Aboriginal People*. Black Point, NS: Fernwood Publishing, 2003.

Noël, Jean-François. "The Convention on the Rights of the Child." Department of Justice, April 30, 2013. justice.gc.ca/eng/rp-pr/fl-lf/divorce/crc-crde/conv2a.html.

North-South Partnership for Children in Remote First Nations Communities. "Mishkeegogamang Ojibway Nation Assessment Report." January 9–11, 2007.

O'Connor, Rory, Stephen Platt, and Jacki Gordon, eds. *International Handbook of Suicide Prevention: Research, Policy, and Practice*. Chichester, UK: John Wiley and Sons, 2011.

Office of the Auditor General. "Report of the Commissioner of the Environment and Sustainable Development to the House of Commons." Chapter 5, "Drinking Water in First Nation

Communities." 2005. www.oag-bvg.gc.ca/internet/English/
parl_cesd_200509_05_e_14952.html.

Office of the Chief Coroner. "Death Review of the Youth Suicides
at the Pikangikum First Nation 2006–2008."

Office of the Parliamentary Budget Officer. "The Funding Requirements for First Nation Schools in Canada." May 25, 2009. www.
parl.gc.ca/PBO-DPB/documents/INAC_Final_EN.pdf.

Office of the Provincial Advocate for Children and Youth. "Our
Dreams Matter Too: First Nations Children's Rights, Lives, and
Education: An Alternative Report from the Shannen's Dream
Campaign to the United Nations Committee on the Rights of
the Child on the Occasion of Canada's 3rd and 4th Periodic
Reviews." 2011.

Ontario Public School Boards Association. "Good Governance:
A Guide for Trustees, School Boards, Directors of Education
and Communities." 2014. cge.ontarioschooltrustees.org/files/
en_good-governance.pdf.

Paquette, Jerry, and Gérald Fallon. *First Nations Education Policy
in Canada: Progress or Gridlock?* Toronto: University of Toronto
Press, 2010.

Rosborough, Bart. "Report to the Minister of Justice and Attorney
General [re] Public Fatality Inquiry." Wetaskiwin, AB, March
28, 2009.

Scott, Duncan Campbell. "The Last of the Indian Treaties." *Scribners,* November 1906, 573–82. www.unz.org/Pub
Scribners-1906nov-00573.

Scott, Duncan Campbell, Samuel Stewart, and Daniel McMartin.
"The James Bay Treaty—Treaty No. 9. Report to Superintendent of Indian Affairs." November 6, 1905. www.aadnc-aandc.
gc.ca/eng/1100100028863/1100100028864.

Sim, R. Alex. "The Education of Indians in Ontario: A Report
to the Provincial Committee on Aims and Objectives in the
Schools of Ontario." April 1967. files.eric.ed.gov/fulltext/
ED062039.pdf.

Sinha, Vandna, et al. "Kiskisik Awasisak: Remember the Children.
Understanding the Overrepresentation of First Nations Children in the Child Welfare System." Assembly of First Nations,
2011. cwrp.ca/publications/2280.

Spears, Ellen Griffith. *Baptized in PCBs: Race, Pollution, and Justice in an All-American Town.* Chapel Hill: University of North Carolina Press, 2014.

Sproule-Jones, Megan. "Crusading for the Forgotten: Dr. Peter Bryce, Public Health, and Prairie Native Residential Schools." *Canadian Bulletin of Medical History* 13 (1996): 199–224.

Stangneth, Bettina. *Eichmann before Jerusalem: The Unexamined Life of a Mass Murderer.* New York: Random House, 2014.

Stewart, Brenda. "The Contaminated Soil of J. R. Nakogee School." Report prepared for Attawapiskat Band Council, 2009.

TD Economics. "Estimating the Size of the Aboriginal Market in Canada." June 17, 2011. www.td.com/document/PDF/economics/special/sg0611_aboriginal.pdf.

Tootoosis, Darcy (Joey) Joseph. "Canadian First Nations Child Welfare Care Policy: Managing Money in 'Ottawapiskat.'" *University of Saskatchewan Undergraduate Research Journal* 1, 1 (2014): 65–69.

Wilson, Janet. *Shannen and the Dream for a School.* Toronto: Second Story Press, 2011.